IN THE
NICK
OF TIME

IN THE NICK OF TIME

The autobiography of John Altman,
EastEnders' Nick Cotton

JOHN
ALTMAN

JOHN BLAKE

Published by John Blake Publishing Limited,
3 Bramber Court, 2 Bramber Road,
London W14 9PB, England

www.johnblakebooks.com

www.facebook.com/johnblakebooks **f**
twitter.com/jblakebooks **t**

First published in hardback in 2016

ISBN: 978-1-78418-995-2

British Library Cataloguing-in-Publication Data:
A catalogue record for this book is available from the British Library.

Design by www.envydesign.co.uk

Printed in Great Britain by CPI Group (UK) Ltd

1 3 5 7 9 10 8 6 4 2

Papers used by John Blake Publishing are natural, recyclable products made from
wood grown in sustainable forests. The manufacturing processes conform to the
environmental regulations of the country of origin.

Every attempt has been made to contact the relevant copyright-holders, but some
were unobtainable. We would be grateful if the appropriate people could contact us.

To the memory of Tina Florence Schofield (1920–2016), the best mother anyone could ever hope to wish for.

Grateful thanks to: Rosanna Altman, Bridget O'Halloran, Louise Green, Maxine James, Colin James, William Stewart, Tina Stewart, Paul Fitchie, Dave Rodgers, Tommy 'Manchester', Richard Flatau, Jeff 'the Jumper', Kenny Edge, Pete Townshend, Paul Bennett, Peter K., BBC Chris, Sheila Burnett, Nim Arnold, Neil and Suzy Aspinall, Haylie Oliver, Mamie Schofield, Rachel Doyle, Scottish Joe, Diana Marchment and Mr Monty, Mark Wingett, Brian Larkman, Paul Pearson, Toby Buchan, Lucian Randall.

CONTENTS

Look to this day,
For it is life,
The very life of life.
In its brief course lie all
The realities and verities of existence,
The bliss of growth,
The splendour of action,
The glory of power –

For yesterday is but a dream,
And tomorrow is only a vision,
But today, well lived,
Makes every yesterday a dream of happiness
And every tomorrow is a vision of hope.

Look well, therefore, to this day.

Sanskrit proverb by Kālidāsa, Indian poet and playwright,
fifth century AD

PROLOGUE

Nicholas Charles Cotton made his final appearance onscreen on 19 February 2015 – although by then he was only shown as a corpse, having already breathed his last. As an actor it felt like I might breathe my last too while shooting those scenes, having spent long periods during takes without daring to take in any air!

It's not easy playing dead when the camera has you in close-up. Often I look for telltale movement when I'm watching a similar scene in the movies. I had to debate whether to hold my breath entirely or to breathe shallowly while portraying the dead Nick. In the end I opted to hold my breath. It was something I did regularly at my local swimming pool – I'd keep going for an entire length without taking in any air and that was how I began my half-mile, 32-length swim. I'd always known one day it would come in useful. Ironically, Nick died in the same room in which he had murdered a minor character called Reg Cox 30 years previously in the first ever episode of *EastEnders*.

Watching my final scene for the first time was not an emotional experience – I viewed it technically. On the second viewing I did feel more, because of June Brown's incredible performance as Nick's mother Dot and the tragic years that encompassed their relationship.

As an actor, you have to love a character and I'd grown to love Nick despite the darkness of his soul, and after working for thirty years together he and I had bonded with one another. I had nurtured hopes that Nick might be a part of Albert Square well into his old age, nursing a pint in the corner of The Queen Vic and quietly cursing everyone. But it wasn't meant to be.

Nick murmured his final words, 'Ma, come closer. I'm sorry, Ma, everything I've ever put you through, forgive me.' And, with a kiss from Dot to his forehead, that was the end of Nick Cotton.

CHAPTER 1

BERKSHIRE POPPIES

I have often said, 'If it wasn't for Adolf Hitler, I probably wouldn't be here.'

On 2 October 1944, 25-year-old Jack Whittington was flying a Spitfire south of Wuestwezel in Belgium. It was his second mission in two days and although he had now become an instructor – having survived so far in World War II – he stood in for someone who couldn't make the operation.

Tragically while strafing German railway lines he was shot down and left my mother, Tina Florence Schofield, a war widow. At the time they had a daughter, my half-sister Maxine, who was just five years old.

The son of Lewis, a butcher and builder, and Georgina Whittington, Jack and my mother were teenage sweethearts from Lake and Shanklin on the Isle of Wight. They had married in a chapel and went through most of the war together, travelling all over the UK. My mother recalled surviving a run through the blazing streets of Portsmouth, a sailor carrying Maxine in his arms. She and Jack had met at a local dance (mother sang popular tunes of the time in a jazz band). Jack was great fun and a good footballer too.

His death was a second great sadness for my mother as she had lost her own mother, Florence, to cancer two years after her birth. My mother is a strong woman though and despite what she went through, she has always had a bright and kindly, friendly and loving nature.

My sister, Maxine, finally visited Jack's grave with her husband, Colin, 60 years later, on 20 April 2004 at Schoonselhof Military Cemetery, Antwerp, Belgium. The inscription on his headstone read: 'Just a thought, true and tender, of one we loved and will always remember'.

Maxine was a war baby, travelling the length and breadth of the country while my mother kept the family unit together as best as she could. But she was now a war widow with a small child to support, as were so many, with the added sadness of having no mother of her own to turn to, but Aunty Mora (Florence's sister) gave her all the love and comfort that she could.

My mother and her sister, Mamie, had been brought up on the Isle of Wight by their Aunt Mora and Uncle Charlie Baker, at 195 Sandown Road, Shanklin. Their father was Johnny Schofield junior. When I was born, he was delighted as I was the first grandson. He'd had three daughters himself: Mamie, Tina and Yvonne. Johnny was part of the theatrical side of the family. A character actor, he played pantomime dames and had bit parts in Noël Coward's play *Blithe Spirit* and old war films such as *The Cruel Sea* and *Went the Day Well?* In the latter he died a hammy death in a churchyard. I like to think that I took after him in catching the acting bug.

After my mother was widowed, the only choice she had was to go back home to her Aunt Mora – whom I also knew as 'Aunty Mora'. Mora was like a second mother to Mother and was much loved by my sister Maxine and they always remained close. A star of pantomime and music hall all over the UK, in her day she had been a petite beauty, who sang like a nightingale. Later she saved up threepenny bits for my brother William and me. In the evenings she would sit at her dressing table, combing her long silver hair, before she handed us coins when we said goodnight.

For my mother, being back in the Isle of Wight where she and Jack had first met must have been a sad experience but also ultimately healing in the care of her aunt. Seeing all the places they had been together, even going to the local butcher, must have brought it all back as that was where Jack had worked before he was called up. My mother passed some time during the late 1940's working as a hairdresser, being a single mother and in need of money, but her main role, as she saw it, was to be a good mother – and she was. She and Maxine were enveloped back into Mora's household. She buried her sadness and got on with life. That's the way it was then. It wouldn't have occurred to her to be any other way. It seems to me that the generation who lived through the war nurtured great strength and spirituality, more so than many people do today.

My mother first met my father, Cecil Clarkson Stewart, in 1949 at the Green Man pub, in a little village called Hurst, near Reading, in the Berkshire countryside. She had made the trip from the Isle of Wight to visit her sister Yvonne Green and her husband Frank as my cousin Louise had just been born. Later, during that same trip, when my mother needed a bath, Aunty Yvonne (who didn't have one) asked Cecil if they could use his. He lived nearby in a house called Little Hinton with his widowed mother, Frances – known as 'Fanny'. Cecil and my mother stayed in touch after she returned, and before he eventually visited the Isle of Wight to be introduced to Mora.

For a year they courted before getting married in a registry office and honeymooning in a caravan in Seaford, Sussex, and then settling down to a life in the Berkshire countryside. It wasn't always easy – a forty-something bachelor who lived with his mother and a young war widow with a child, but somehow it worked. My father accepted Maxine into the family but they were never close. She never called him Dad, he was always 'Uncle Cecil' to her and she moved out of the family home at the age of seventeen, going on eighteen, when she became a nurse at The Rowley Bristow Hospital in Woking.

In later years Maxine and I became close although when I was young she referred to me as a 'little beast' – I once painted her bedroom window ledge with her nail varnish. Despite the hardships of her early days she went on to marry her childhood sweetheart, Colin, and made a great success of her life. He used to take her out on his motorbike when she still lived at home and I remember the scent of his leather jacket on a cold winter's night in the kitchen. Although they broke up they still kept in touch. Years later in 1961 they met up again and realised how much they still loved one another, married in 1962 and now they've been together for something like fifty years. They have two sons, Andrew and Sean, and four grandchildren, Alexander, Sebastian, Christian and Genevieve.

Grandmother Frances (Fanny) was pretty easy-going and the domestic scene was fairly harmonious given that it could have been potential minefield.

I suppose my father was a bit of an enigma to me in many ways. Very much the old-fashioned gentleman, he would raise his hat if he stopped to say hello to a lady on the village high street and firmly believed in the old saying 'Ladies first'. My brother and I were taught to hold doors open, pull out chairs and always treat a lady with respect, such as walking on the roadside of the pavement. As I've said, my father came to marriage and children late in life, his early-forties, but he adapted fairly well even though there were many rigid habits for my mother to break. One in particular always amused me. Every Sunday, he would gently touch the side of his dinner plate with his thumb and forefinger to check that it had been heated in the oven. He didn't say a word but my mother would see him and say, 'Yes, Cecil, I *did* heat the plates.'

***

The firstborn, I was named John Clarkson Stewart. Mine was a dramatic entry into the world on Sunday, 2 March 1952 as I was whisked away from my mother in Battle Hospital in Reading and placed in an incubator due to breathing problems. The difficulties were quickly resolved. That particular hospital has since been demolished and my birthplace is now inside a Tesco store. In the year of my birth the *New Music Express* (*NME*) was founded and created the first pop music charts. Britain's first hydrogen bomb was detonated in October of that year too.

During my early days the business of looking after me was very much left to my mother. She used to take me with her to the shops. When we visited the village post office I remember the manager pointing out a sack and telling me it had an elephant inside it. I became quite frightened. I was also upset when the greengrocer, Mr Freeman, picked me up and told me he was going to put me on the bacon slicer.

I didn't see a lot of my father as he commuted to the city and back every day from Hurst. He had to cross London, from Paddington to the City, and so he would leave the house at 6.30am and would do his best to be back in time to read me my bedtime story. I remember that clearly as he had a very deep voice that would often send me straight off to sleep.

I definitely grew up closer to my mother. As a child I used to talk to her about movies, music, books and art. She was also the one who told me the facts of life – we were always very open. Father could best be described as an Edwardian gentleman. He worked in the Bank of England as a first-class clerk and his shoes were always perfectly polished and so shiny you could see your face in them. He wasn't, as some newspaper once wrote in an article about me, the Governor of the Bank of England – far from it. He was very tall – six foot three inches – I remember being fearful of him at first. I always wanted to be as tall as him but I never quite made it past five foot ten. From Day One I respected him. He captained the Bank of England rugby team and spurred them on to many victories but strangely never spoke to me about rugby or even went to a match although he did once dream he was performing a flying tackle and leapt out of bed, hit the wardrobe and cut his head open, waking my mother in the process.

It was the time of the male provider and the female homemaker and it worked well in my house. He worked hard, and he had his routine – he drank his blue mountain coffee and ate his bacon and eggs every morning and then he would ride his bike, to the station at Twyford for the commute. As a keen young cyclist I would sometimes accompany my mother on my tricycle the long distance to Twyford, where I would see steam trains on the Great Western line hurtling under the red-brick bridge on their way to Paddington.

My parents were happy and I remember a childhood full of order, security and calm, with traditional Christmases and exciting bonfire nights and bluebells in the springtime woods. For Christmas I would be given an *Eagle* annual, a satsuma, some nuts and a toy in my stocking. I found out about Father Christmas at quite a young age when our cleaner, Mrs Pibworth, handed two presents to my mother and said, 'You can put these in the boys' stockings.' Then I knew.

We never had a lot of money in the family but my parents, bless them, always tried to give us anything they thought we really needed. Over the years I got a bike and a small Pye radio (which my mother paid for on the hire purchase – the old fashioned 'Credit scheme'). But I wasn't spoilt and I appreciated what I was given.

Later, when it came to making my own marriage and family life, the one thing I wanted more than anything for my wife and daughter was a steady home full of fun and routine – sadly, in the long run this wasn't to be.

The one time when I really did bond with my father was on Saturday mornings when, to give Mother a break, he would drive my little brother William and I – and sometimes Granny Frances ('Fanny') – in the vintage Delage to go shopping in Twyford. I remember the joy of buying *Walt Disney's Weekly* comic, particularly when it had a free gift. Memories of a couple of childhood misdemeanours during those trips come flooding back. Once I took the handbrake off the car when we were parked on a hill in order to wind up my grandmother and as the vehicle began to coast down the hill with my grandmother and brother inside it, Father ran out of the shop, jumped on the running board and at the last minute leaned inside the car to apply the brake.

The other incident took place in a local scrap merchant and car dealer's whose owner, Mr Goody, lived in a railway carriage. He and Dad were having a couple of whiskys when I found a pot of green paint and decided to decorate one of his wooden caravans with it. A few hours later, a very irate Mr Goody stormed down our garden path and demanded to know why I'd done it. No doubt I was sent to bed early that night.

When my cousin, Stephen Chrulew, came to visit from London we would have great fun standing in the back garden and hurling rotten apples over the house. My Auntie Joan would often say, 'Go and find your cousin Stephen and whatever he's doing, tell him to stop it.' My other cousin, Guy Green, didn't much enjoy the bonfire nights we had because apparently I had threatened to put a banger down his wellington boots and he never forgot it.

I grew much closer to my father in later life, when we would drink together, he with his Johnnie Walker Black Label and me with my Captain Morgan's Spiced Rum. It was hard to get him to open up but once we'd had a few drinks he would become more relaxed, express his feelings and reel off some bawdy limericks – which he'd learned at the Bank of England sports ground – out of Mother's earshot.

It is definitely safe to say he didn't know much about the acting world. He would have liked me to follow in his footsteps and work at the Bank of England. I remember he once tried hard to sell it to me based on the fact that they had their own drama society! On reflection, he was so right in many ways: for me it would have been a much more secure and steady way of life. But I know myself and I would have died of boredom and besides I was shockingly bad at maths. Although my life has been hand-to-mouth for more years than I care to remember, I can't imagine doing anything else – there's nothing like the buzz of being onstage in front of two thousand people or filming in front of a camera.

When I think about it now, my parents were pretty easy going and very accomodating. When it became clear that I was geared towards the Arts they were supportive. As I've already mentioned, I know that my father would have dearly loved me to have a job that was steady and secure. Being a dad myself now, I can see there is nothing you want more than the knowledge that your child is safe and secure – emotionally and financially – and happy. As a parent it is your greatest wish and I can't imagine how my own parents squared that with my desire to pursue a deeply unsteady and insecure job like acting. But they let me go and let me do what I wanted. As it wasn't against the law, they took it all in their stride.

Their easy-going natures didn't mean I wasn't disciplined as a youngster when I needed it. I remember vividly once swearing at my mother and getting a backhander from my dad that sent me flying across the kitchen floor. That slap was memorable coming from my father – Mother usually dealt out the corporal punishment. 'Don't you ever swear at your mother again,' he told me. I was quite a naughty boy and I did need a firm hand.

Unlike Nick I was lucky – I came from the definition of a happy home. I don't recall any drama, they stuck it out and seemed to love each other.

My brother William ('Willy') was two years younger than me. I wasn't a great elder brother when we were small; I used to bully him and encourage him to be naughty. I'm reliably informed that I welcomed him into the world by weeing in his cot! We had fun digging holes in the bedroom wall in order to put some plaster in our Matchbox toy cement mixers; we also created World War I trenches in the back garden while wearing Civil Defence helmets. I remember asking William to throw a rock at my head when I was wearing my helmet to see if they deflected shrapnel and heavy objects as they were supposed to – it *did* deflect but it bloody well hurt too!

I think my father enjoyed having two sons but we were quite different. I always loved my music, films and books whereas Willy was practical and enjoyed using his hands. When we lived in Herne Bay, north Kent, for example, while I was at the local Odeon Willy could be found searching the beach when the tide was out, looking for the remains of World War II bombs. Some of these were remnants of the Dam Busters' bombs, tested by Barnes Neville Wallis and his team off the coast near Reculver. We also used to search the bushes on the Downs at Herne Bay for live .22 calibre bullets dumped by the army during World War II. We would take them back to the garage at home, 19 Beltinge Road, put them in a vice, carefully take the nose out of the bullet and use the explosives inside and set them off in the garden.

Dad loved his films and his music, particularly the silent comedy actor Harold Lloyd and American jazz pianist Fats Waller. Together with William we would occasionally go into the woods to cut wood with a machete to make poles, which Dad would use to grow runner beans. He had a great love of the outdoors, having been partly brought up in Halifax, Nova Scotia, Canada.

When it came to hugs, Dad was often slightly reticent to go in for the full Russian-style embrace, perhaps due to his Edwardian upbringing. But as the years went by, he seemed to warm to it. By contrast I have always found it very easy to give affection and I find that life is all the better because of it. I guess we are all different and I have my mother to thank for my physical ease.

Sunday lunchtimes were a happy time for Dad given that he spent his whole week going back and forth on a train; it was the one day when he could relax in the home he hardly saw all week. To me the atmosphere always felt special. Dad would drink whisky and ginger ale while my mother and Grandma Frances cooked the lunch – always roast lamb on Sundays. He would have his music drifting through the house. The sound of Fats Waller, Russ Conway, Mrs Mills and Eddie Calvert in the background.

If I had to sum up my father's parenting skills in one word, I suppose it would be 'practical'. A patient man, he helped me to learn to read and we shared a love of books. I clearly remember sitting on his knee as his deep voice instructed and encouraged me to repeat the sound of the letter on the page in front of me. He had a really old Victorian spelling book, which I still have, called *Grandpa's Spelling Book*, and we used to go through the alphabet meticulously and methodically until it was all drummed into me. 'Reading is the key to all knowledge,' he always said. I think that dedicated skill of reciting and learning things off by heart definitely stood me in good stead, for my eventual career. If I have ever dried onstage or during a T.V. scene for the most part it has only ever been due to lack of rehearsal, never because I was under-prepared. Whatever else has been going on in my life, I have always known my lines off by heart. Anyway Dad was a cultured man: he read three books a week on his commute to London and my mother loved books too – I was lucky enough to grow up in a household where books and music really mattered and it was something, along with a love of film, that I have passed on to my daughter, Rosanna.

Many years later, when I got older I would enjoy a few drinks with Dad and I remember thinking, 'Now he is quite at ease with me and I'm more mature perhaps he might reveal some of the secrets of his past, especially about his time in India during the war.' But he was always very evasive about that. Often he would gloss over it but I was always keen to know more. When he married my mother, in 1950 he had a picture of a beautiful Indian lady on the wall of his bedroom. It could have been a movie star for all I know, but what I do know is that he wouldn't talk about it and Mother insisted it was taken down.

After a few rums I would pluck up the courage and say, with a raised eyebrow: 'How was the war in India, Dad?', thinking he might reveal some of his dalliances with the local ladies in Kerala. But his answer was always the same: 'I had a lovely war!'

He was a bit disappointed that he couldn't go to sea, as his eyesight was no good for spotting enemy submarines, etc. Instead he was seconded to be part of a team that repaired the planes for the Fleet Air Arm in Cochin, Kerala. He was a loving and caring father until he died at the age of eighty-four in 1995.

As a child, I was definitely the naughty one and I would lead my brother, William, astray. I remember how we would watch Westerns on my Aunty Bunty's TV in Winersh and the Red Indians would do something exciting, like launch a flaming arrow into the cowboys' log cabin. It looked like great fun, so I turned a toy bow and arrow we had been given into our very own Western prop. I went into the garage to get a rag, doused it in some petrol and wrapped it round the arrow. Then I set light to the rag and fired the arrow square into the neighbour's fence. I remember my mother spotting my brother and I through the kitchen window and then running out with a huge bowl of water to extinguish the blaze. I got into a lot of trouble in situations like that and Mother would deal out the appropriate punishment.

It's funny when I think about how vigilant parents are now. Back then there was nothing more fun than a box of matches and they were left lying all over the place for whenever we wanted to use them. Dad was a smoker and one of my overriding memories is the scent of tobacco as he washed up – he would always have a Senior Service cigarette between his lips as he rinsed the dishes. Health & Safety wasn't top of the list back then but a good thrashing was, if I got my hands on something I shouldn't have.

I was often a show-off in front of my poor little brother. One early memory is boasting to him that I could throw a rock like a shot-putter. So I picked up a large stone to impress him and said to him: 'Watch me throw this rock *over* that car coming towards us.' I was full of bravado in the way only young boys can be, never mind that I was small and could barely see over the car – it was higher than me! Predictably, the rock didn't in any way actually clear the car instead it made a great big dent in the side of this shiny, seemingly brand-new vehicle. My God, I got in trouble for that – it was probably an occasion that warranted the wooden spoon or the riding crop! In fact, that riding crop was the bane of my life. So well acquainted with it was I that once I was tall enough, I decided to climb up on a chair in the kitchen, pull it down from its hiding place on top of a cupboard and spirit it away to the end of the garden, where I threw it in a ditch. It was never seen or mentioned again.

A smoker in the house meant there were lots of incidents with matches and we (or should I say 'I') had hours of fun misbehaving, including setting fire to Granny's sofa. Another riding-crop moment, I'm sure.

Later, I became a dedicated smoker. It's hard to say whether it was the influence of those early days. I did steal a couple of Dad's Senior Service. Will and I smoked them under an old Oak Tree, but I didn't like the taste.I gave them up in 2004. It was one of the hardest things I ever did. A strict Russian nurse at my local doctor's surgery got me through it using patches and weekly consultations. For me one of life's great pleasures used to be a coffee and a cigarette in the sunshine outside a café reading the morning paper and I really missed it. When I finally kicked the habit I didn't get much sympathy from my onscreen mother, June Brown. Her only comment was: 'John, have you noticed you are so tense since you've given up the cigarettes. I think you should start again. Giving up like that is bad for you!'

Bless her heart, she meant well.

CHAPTER 2

HOOKED TO THE SILVER SCREEN

For as long as I can remember I have loved film. We didn't have a TV so I used to go to the cinema twice a week and also the 'Saturday morning pictures', a habit that put me firmly on the path to acting even if I wasn't aware of it at the time.

I was lucky enough to be born in the 1950s when the golden age of cinema was very much in evidence: one large screen, uniformed doormen and usherettes, Pathé newsreels and the searchlight beam of the projector cutting its way through the smoky atmosphere. For me, all manner of emotions, magic and far-off worlds shone from that tiny room above the circle.

My father didn't allow television in our house when I was a boy but I have him to thank for my love and appreciation of the cinema. In the summer of 1958 he took me to see my first film. We travelled by steam train from our village in Berkshire to Paddington and from there took a grimy old tube train to the West End, where we saw *Wind Jammer*, an epic documentary about huge sailing ships. From that day on the wonders of the silver screen had me hooked.

During the school holidays my mother would treat my brother

and me to a visit to the Regal in Wokingham or the Reading Odeon. During the latter days of the 1950s we saw mostly Walt Disney films such as *Old Yeller, Bambi, Treasure Island, Swiss Family Robinson* and *Sleeping Beauty*. I also remember sitting on red velvet seats and seeing Kenneth More in *North West Frontier*, Peter Sellers and Sophia Loren in *The Millionairess* and Jerry Lewis in *The Bellboy* in Reading.

When we moved from the village of Hurst in Berkshire to Herne Bay in Kent, on 6 January, 1961, I discovered that I was now in a town with its own Odeon! I soon joined its Saturday Morning Picture Club. Having seen the cartoons, serial and main feature, my friends and I would re-enact the plot and play the characters of the film we had just seen as we made our way home along the beach. Damsels tied with seaweed to a breakwater would be rescued from the incoming tide by knights carrying driftwood swords; young cowboys trotted across the pebbles, slapping their thighs to recreate the sound of a galloping horse. Looking back, those film games probably gave me my first taste of acting.

In 1962, at the age of eight, I took my first journey to the cinema alone. It was a matinee showing of *The Magnificent Seven* at the Odeon. My mother had given me two shillings and sixpence (equivalent to sixteen pence today). It was enough for a stalls' seat (one shilling and eleven pence) and the rest went on strawberry Fruitella sticks. For me it was a big day and I felt that I'd grown up at last. From then on I went to the Odeon as often as I could, sometimes visiting three times in a week.

I befriended one of the usherettes, Betty, who eventually let me in to see films given an 'A' certificate, even when I was not accompanied by an adult as I should have been. Thanks to her, I was able to see early Bond films such as *Dr. No* and *From Russia with Love*, as well as Stanley Kubrick's *Spartacus, Ben Hur* and the Samuel Bronston epics *El Cid* and *The Fall of the Roman Empire*, to name but a few.

***

Locking my bike at the back of the cinema one day I noticed that the staff had thrown some of the film posters into the steel wheelie bins. I was thrilled to retrieve these to take home. Some weeks later it dawned on me that I should ask the Edgar doorman for the poster of that week's film after he had taken it down at the end of the week. For me it became a regular trip. Every Saturday night, at nine o'clock, I would cycle across town and pick it up. Soon my bedroom began to look like the foyer of the Odeon. I built up quite a collection and I still have some of those posters to this day – for example, *Blow-Up* and *You Only Live Twice* decorate the hallway of my London flat. They are now worth a great deal of money. I was always a bit of a hoarder and luckily my parents let me keep film posters, records and pop memorabilia in my old bedroom at home.

A high point of my early love for film was in the summer of 1963, when Ken Russell invaded the town with his film crew to make his first feature film, *French Dressing*. It was possibly a cinematic debut he'd rather forget as the movie was slated by the critics, although it was later shown at the British Film Institute as a bit of a curio. Starring James Booth and Roy Kinnear, it was set in a faded seaside town, Gormleigh-on-Sea. The movie depicted Herne Bay as the great resort it once was, with the town pier, rows of deckchairs and a lord mayor that it now no longer has.

And the making of the film itself filled me with great excitement. As soon as primary school finished for the day I would be on my bike, searching for the location of that day's filming. I befriended some of the crew, who gave me scalding hot tea in polystyrene cups and sandwiches, and for me it was a sad day when they packed up and left town: the circus of film-makers had moved on.

My uncle, Frank Sherwin Green, also gave me a greater insight into the art of making movies when he took my cousin Guy and me on a grand tour of the MGM studios at Borehamwood on 11 January 1965. I watched Patrick McGoohan as 'Dangerman' fighting in a wine cellar and saw the V2 rockets used in *Operation Crossbow*, a film about the German flying bombs. MGM had once been one of the best equipped studios in Europe. Tragically, it was shut down in the late 1960s and turned into a storage facility. Little did I dream then that many years later I would be working at EMI studios, just down the road and less than a mile away, on *The Return of the Jedi* and *Birth of The Beatles*.

I experienced one of my first X certificate film three years early when I was thirteen. The management of the Odeon knew my age so I had to take a train 12 miles down the coast to Margate. In the almost total darkness of the vast Dreamland cinema I watched Anthony Perkins in a re-release of Hitchcock's 1960 shocker, *Psycho*. The only other patron was an old lady sat three or four rows away. As the lights went up at the end of the matinee it seemed to me that she looked remarkably like Mrs Bates' corpse… I was very glad to see daylight and be out amid the jolly surroundings of Margate seafront.

Throughout the 1960s I saw a vast cross-section of films, from *Carry On* to Kubrick and Disney to *Dollars* Westerns. *A Fistful of Dollars* was a revelation after the dull plodding films of Audie Murphy and John Wayne. I was there to see the passing of the epics as a genre and to witness the fall in attendance as people watched more TV.

Four favourite movies of this time were *Cool Hand Luke, Lawrence of Arabia, Bonnie and Clyde* and *2001: A Space Odyssey* (which I saw nine times). My heroes were Sean Connery, Paul Newman and Clint Eastwood. I would feel their influence for hours after leaving the cinema. Feeling as cool as Paul Newman or as rugged as Clint Eastwood made me believe one day I might perform equally as well on the big screen.

I had an unbridled passion for the Swiss actress Ursula Andress and kept a huge scrapbook dedicated to her. Much to my excitement I actually got to see her in the flesh when I won two tickets for the premiere of *The Blue Max* at the Odeon in Leicester Square, London, on 30th June in 1966. Arriving by taxi with my mother, dressed in a tuxedo and walking down the red carpet into the foyer as flashbulbs popped around us was quite an experience.

When *The Blue Max* reached north Kent I organised a raid on the stills cases at the front of the Oxford cinema in Whitstable with a friend of my mine from school called Donald (the cinema cases featured pictures of the wonderful Ursula). I forged a key in metalwork class at school and the raid took place late one Sunday evening. The key opened the cabinet with ease and I took out all the colour stills with the help of Donald. We ran off down some back alleyways towards Whitstable station, where I gave him a ten-shilling note for his assistance with the operation. We were lucky not to get caught and to this day I have those stills – I wouldn't have done it for anyone else but Ursula!

In the 1970s the Cannon chain bought my local Odeon from Classic Cinemas and cut the art-deco 'O' above the entrance into a 'C'. This was a foretaste of their eventual decision to demolish the cinema in 1989, despite protests from hundreds of local people, myself included.

***

My brother Willy and my father used to spend a lot of time together in the garage tinkering with cars and all things mechanical and electrical. Meanwhile Mother and I would be in the kitchen talking about art or a book we had read and loved. A lovely lady, she was a wonderful wife to my father and was a loving and supportive mother.

One of Father's guilty pleasures was to buy the *Sun* newspaper every day but he always made sure he hid it, and page 3 from my mother in his office – an indicator of the fact he was an Edwardian gentlemen. Eventually, we did have the *Sun* delivered to our front door, though not in the early days of the tabloid.

Our summer and Easter holidays were taken on the Isle of Wight and we would take the steam train and then ferry at Easter and drive down in the summer, picnicking along the way. Those Isle-of-Wight days with Aunty Mora in Shanklin were idyllic times. We would read Enid Blyton's *The Famous Five* adventure novels and then head down to the beach to recreate the stories and explore the caves. Summer was one of the rare occasions when I spent father-and-son time with Dad and I remember vividly going up on the Downs with him. I watched in awe as he decided we were going to set fire to a gorse bush and then burned it to the ground. I was really impressed and so was my brother.

'Don't tell your mother,' Dad said at the time.

***

At school I was an average student who worked hard but never really excelled across the board, though I was always good at the more artistic subjects like English and Art. From a young age I got involved in the end-of-year plays and nativity productions.

My first school was in Hurst, near Reading in Berkshire. It was a small Church of England primary called St Nicholas. When I first started, I didn't take to school at all, I hated it in fact. As a child I was incredibly shy. I'm told that when my sister Maxine and her boyfriend Colin used to walk me round the village in my pram, and when people pushed their faces in to coo over me, I would cry my eyes out – particularly at people with glasses. I believe that was because my doctor wore glasses and he gave me some very painful inoculations at a very young age. Also, because my sister was much older than me, people thought that I was her baby.

To me the whole concept of school seemed interminable. I remember so clearly sitting in my classroom and watching the clock ticking away on the wall, its hands seemingly frozen in time. I used to will it to go round faster. One day in particular, I remember standing in the playground and seeing my dad drive past. Horrified by the idea of having to stay in that playground while my parents were elsewhere, I bawled my eyes out.

Once at school I was forced to finish eating the fat and veins in some liver served up for lunch. I was the last to leave the canteen, the liver still lodged in my throat, and I ran over to a drain where I was sick. It didn't put me off liver and bacon however and to this day I enjoy a slice of decent liver and bacon with mashed potato.

Miss Pounds was my first teacher – all these years later and I still know her address in Reading, Berkshire, backwards, thanks to her technique for teaching us how to count. I remember her telling us to repeat: '1, 2, 3 Peppard Road,' she would say, 'that's the name and number of my house.'

Many years later I actually went to see it. I was doing a radio interview in Reading and I was in a cab chatting to the driver about my local knowledge and I told him about the address. Very kindly he decided to make a detour and took me to see the house. It brought back memories, not least as she was also the first person to wash my mouth out with white soap and water for saying, 'Bloody hell!' There were a few occasions like that – for example, the time I got the slipper in front of the whole school for calling a girl with the surname Fleming 'Flannel Face' and making her cry. I was the opposite of my brother William in that way – he was the quiet and steady one, with no desire to be a showman.

***

We moved to Herne Bay on 6 January 1961. The move was designed to make life easier for my father by cutting down the number of hours spent commuting. If we moved to Kent then he could get the train to Cannon Street or Victoria. The move would mean a new school, which was a big deal, but I was growing in confidence. William and I were pleased to be moving. I recall pelting some of the local yobs with rotten apples just before we set off, knowing they couldn't catch us. My sister Maxine was working away from home near London. I recall she visited us a few times and once drove a 'bubble car'. Granny Frances stayed with my Aunty Joan in Finchley and joined us once we moved to 19 Beltinge Road.

Our house in Herne Bay was being decorated so we stayed with my Aunty Mamie and Uncle Jim Cope, at 83 Central Parade, Herne Bay. I used to go swimming in the sea just across the road. On the way back one day I went into the public toilets. I fell down the stone steps and the first thing that hit the ground was my mouth. One of my top front teeth came flying out and there was blood everywhere.

The dentist took a look at my injury and said, 'If we're lucky, as Johnny's still growing, the gap between his teeth will close up.' I was then aged about eleven and as I grew older, the teeth did grow together but it was a rare thing to have just one tooth in the front and many dentists have remarked upon it along the way.

In the playground at Kings Road primary school you had to have a favourite football team (alongside a Beatle – mine was George). I spent most of my spare time swimming so I read a *Roy of the Rovers* annual that included the history of Tottenham Hotspur. When they started they had a wooden hut as a changing room, wore baggy shorts and didn't have nets behind the goalposts. I took Tottenham on the basis of their name although I suppose I should have chosen Reading because that was where I was born. At the time Spurs were doing very well, with star players such as Jimmy Greaves. I'm pleased to say they're still doing well today (at least, they are at the time of me writing this) and Harry Kane is the Jimmy Greaves of this generation.

I've played football myself, in the Showbiz XI team run by Jess Conrad, OBE, sixties pop star, actor and a very dear friend. Jess is a modest man, who is celebrating 100 years in show business this year. Jess was always in goal, so he could wear a different colour 'costume' to everyone else! He's never been known to pass a mirror without having a mirror check. It was all good fun and Jess raised £15 million for charity over the year. I remember at one match in Gillingham I mocked up a fight with Paul Hendy, presenter and pantomime producer. As we rolled about, pretending to hit one another, a huge chorus of boos and hisses rose up from the small stadium. It was just the way that the punters expected me to behave, thanks to years of playing N. Cotton Esq.

***

I've always thought my childhood was idyllic in many ways. I spent half of it in the countryside and the other half beside the sea in north Kent. I remember endless summer days on the beach at Herne Bay and when the winter came, heavy snowfalls were brought on as the ice-cold north wind came in across the bay. Often the snow began to fall on a Sunday and I loved walking out, wrapped up warm and secure, as a great silence fell on the town. I would be the first to experience the fresh, white carpet. Those were special moments. In the winter of 1963, the sea actually froze over, a very rare occurrence in the UK.

There were some dangerous cliffs near Herne Bay but undeterred I used to organise expeditions across them with my friends. My mother let us go out on adventures but emphasised that we should always be careful. I'm happy to report that neither my brother William nor I broke any bones.

Beneath the cliffs was some quicksand-like mud. Children had on occasion sunk into it and needed to be rescued by the Fire Brigade. The expedition would make its way to a local beauty spot called Bishopstone Glen, a small valley with steep, sandy cliffs on either side and a stream running through the centre into the sea. To this day you can find prehistoric sharks' teeth buried in the sand. I used to pretend that the sandy cliffs and the river were the Grand Canyon.

We would dig into the cliffs to make a cave. One time we went so far that a tree came crashing down and there was a small avalanche of sand and dirt. My good friend Robert Opie lost his glasses in the landslide and was in big trouble with his mum. This was also a good spot to take a girl.

Two doors down from us lived a pretty Irish girl called Martina Reed when I was about nine years old. She and I used to walk our dogs – mine was Jarvie the mongrel, named after a dog in a Disney film. At the top of Beltinge Hill there was a field, where I had made a camp out of grass and branches with my brother. I would go there with Martina and our dogs but I couldn't work out a way of getting round to kissing her so I invented a game. 'I tell you what,' I said. 'Let's play "Letting the dogs run free". But when they come back, we have to kiss each other.' She agreed and this game went on at regular intervals for something like a week until she unfortunately told her strict Catholic mother that she had been kissing John from No. 19! She was promptly banned from ever seeing me again and I was rather upset. Some weeks later I did see her again and her beautiful blonde hair was cut short.

I wonder where she is now.

***

In the first half of the 1960s in the summer holidays I went by train to London on my own with my little suitcase to stay with my Auntie Elsie and her daughter Nina in Marylebone. I was about twelve and it was my first trip alone. Elsie had been married to my grandfather, Johnny Schofield junior – she was his third wife.

Auntie Elsie would on occasion be charged with taking me across London and putting me on the Great Western Line steam train at Paddington. Changing at Twyford, I would take what was called the 'Marlow Donkey'. I stayed in Marlow on Thames with my favourite aunt and uncle, Yvonne and Frank Green, and my cousins, Guy and Louise. They had two beagles – the 'Beagle Boys' – and there was a swimming pool next door.

Louise was gorgeous, she wore a miniskirt, had long brunette hair with a fringe, a perfect figure and a beautiful speaking voice and loved The Beatles too, whom she had met. When she was fourteen she came to visit I had a huge crush on her. Guy and I shared a similar sense of humour. We loved Peter Cook, Dudley Moore and the Goons – we used to do all the Goon voices together. I always thought Guy should have been an actor but he ended up in the technical side of the business, working for Samuelsons and then Panavision. Together we romped around the Thames Valley on bicycles on glorious summer days, seeing films such as *The Great Escape* and sailing in his dinghy on the river at Marlow and swimming in the pool at High Wycombe.

Auntie Yvonne was a would-be *cordon bleu* chef and compared to my dear mother, her dishes were quite exotic. I once made the mistake of complaining to Mother that her cooking wasn't so exciting. 'If you carry on like that,' she told me, 'you won't be going there again.' From then on I kept quiet. Having said that, my mother was a very good cook and besides Father preferred standard English fare.

***

My other cousin was Stephen Chrulew of the apple hurling days (see earlier). He was the son of my Auntie Joan – my father's sister – and Serge. Uncle Serge escaped Stalin's Georgian purge in which many of his family were killed. I spent many happy days staying at their house at the top of the Finchley Road, near Golders Green, northwest London. The family were always very kind to me. Auntie Joan had a heart of gold and would bring me delicious sausages from a butcher in Belsize village when I was unemployed at 111 Sutherland Avenue in Maida Vale. This was in the late 70's when I was in between jobs.

Sadly Joan and Serge have since both passed away but I still see

Stephen and, as with my other cousin Guy, we share a similar sense of humour and outlook on the world. We hope to visit Halifax, Nova Scotia, the childhood home of my father and Stephen's mother.

Cecil, my father, told me the story of how he and his sister Joan bought market eggs when they were in Halifax and had great fun hurling them from their garden at passing carriages. Grandmother Fanny – Frances Stewart – wasn't the greatest of disciplinarians and my grandfather, William, was often away at sea. When a woman banged on the door to complain about the children's behaviour, Fanny was quite relaxed.

'Oh dear,' she murmured. 'I wonder where they got the eggs?'

Furious, the woman left. So that's where I got my childhood naughtiness from!

***

Like so many people, I remember where I was when I learned of President John F. Kennedy's death. Young, but still deeply shocked at the 1963 assassination, I read the story in the *News of the World*, sitting on the stairs at home. This was the first world event to make an impression on me. That same year I was given *Please Please Me*, The Beatles' first LP record. Unfortunately, I left it on my record player where it was warped by the hot valve inside. I tried to straighten it out by ironing it. Despite covering it first with a damp tea towel for protection the results were pretty much what you might expect! The 1960s was also a time of listening to the Pirate Radio stations such as Caroline and Radio London. John Peel's shows were particularly memorable. A great D.J.

***

The best way to describe my attitude to school was that it was something to be endured. I was placed in a private school called Mickleburgh in Herne Bay for a year or so as I didn't pass the 11 Plus.

It was here that I learned French, flooded the headmaster's vegetable garden and took lead off the roof, (to melt down at home). You can still see the gaps in the roof to this day. But things got a bit tight and Father couldn't afford to have two children in the private system so William went on to another private school and I first attended a secondary modern in Whitstable called Sir William Nottidge on 8 September 1966. I remember being really annoyed to have failed my 11 Plus, not through a sense of pride but mainly because all my close friends had passed and were going on to the Simon Langton Grammar School in Canterbury.

In the end I quite enjoyed the last two years of secondary school, where I found myself getting more and more into acting. At school my first leading role was in *Pygmalion* in which, aged fifteen, I played Professor Henry Higgins. I was also a member of Theatrecraft, an amateur dramatics society in Herne Bay. With them, I performed in *My Fair Lady*, *Calamity Jane* and *Oliver!* to name but a few productions.

At fourteen I played the baddie for the first time. I was Noah Claypole, the undertaker's assistant, in the Herne Bay Theatrecraft production of *Oliver!* It was the first of a number of villainous parts I played. Someone once said it was the way I look, dark and a bit dangerous, but I think we all have an element of wickedness in us – I certainly couldn't have played Nick Cotton convincingly if I hadn't.

Despite failing the 11 Plus I ended up doing OK at school and picked up a few accolades along the way, like the English Prize for Language and Literature, along with Geography and History O Levels and CSE Maths. My dream had been to go to art school so naturally I was upset when I failed my Art O Level and was left not really knowing what to do next.

A couple of friends, Roger Jarrett and Paul Fitchie, were doing a Business Studies course at the local college in Canterbury, so

I applied. In truth, we all signed up simply to pass the time and socialise. So we sat in the back row, lazing about, making jokes and reading the *New Musical Express*. I hung out amidst the late-sixties Canterbury scene, smoking hash, watching bands and generally not achieving much at all. Meanwhile my mother, who understood my love of acting, sent off for some prospectuses and encouraged me to apply to drama school although it soon transpired that we didn't have enough money for me to go.

***

Lots of bands came to Herne Bay in the 1960s, including The Big Three, The Merseybeats, The Rolling Stones, and Screaming Lord Sutch and the Savages. I got the autographs of The Searchers as they got out of the back of a Dormobile van next to the stage door of the King's Hall. Another time while waiting for Georgie Fame's autograph one cold winter's night at the back of the Starlight ballroom I embarrassed myself. A gentleman approached in a big parka with a fur hood. I asked him when Georgie Fame would be arriving. He dropped the hood and said, 'I am Georgie Fame.' I apologised and he kindly gave me his signature.

***

When I got into my teens I started to experiment with alcohol and the odd bit of dope, which was all was fine until I was busted in Canterbury. I woke up in a squat with a police torch shining in my face. I remember exactly what I said: 'OK, yeah, I have got some dope, a tiny bit. Whatever you do, please don't ring my house and wake up my father, he has to get up early for work in the morning.'

Then what did they do? My response had fallen on deaf ears, it seemed. They drove round to the house in Herne Bay and rang the doorbell in the middle of the night and woke up my poor father, demanding he come and pick me up from the station. Let's just say, it wasn't a very happy drive home from Canterbury police station. He had to bail me out too. Once he got me home I thought he was going to slap me, but he didn't. For a long time he was silent and eventually, very quietly, said: 'How long will it take you to get off this, my boy?'

Bless him, he had no idea what dope was and didn't know that it wasn't addictive in the sense that you needed the next fix to keep going. I tried to explain to him it wasn't like heroin. It was the time that people read a lot in the papers about dope and the scaremongering was rife, especially to upstanding people like my father.

Like most people in my situation, I felt the arrest was deeply unfair. They arrested a few others and myself just because they had the power to do so and because they knew where all the squats were and which bars we liked. But we weren't doing anyone any harm: it was all peace, love and Pink Floyd. Inspector Brian Darnell of Canterbury drugs squad was to be the bane of our lives.

My parents took it well, considering – Mother didn't say a lot but I think she was quite upset about it. I suppose at just sixteen I was quite young but they didn't sit me down and give me the big drugs and drink lecture, although one thing Dad didn't appreciate was my shoulder-length hair. A visit to the hairdresser was practically a weekly request, uttered every Sunday once we had sat down to a family roast. Dad would say: 'Right, my boy, when are you going to get your hair cut?'

As an upright Conservative from the Edwardian era, he had no understanding of the current fashion among young people of the late 1960s. By contrast Dad was always immaculately turned out with a short back-and-sides and neatly pressed trousers and well ironed shirts, courtesy of my mother. She had exacting standards despite the fact that we didn't have a washing machine – just a mangle and an airer. Long hair wasn't appreciated but no offence was greater than being late as far as Father was concerned. My childhood was characterised by three-minute warnings being called out from the hallway. When Father said, 'It's high tide, we're going for a swim at eleven,' he meant it, and if you weren't there you simply got left behind.

***

I'd always been a water baby. Even before I could walk, my mother would have to stop me crawling fearlessly towards the sea when we were on the beach at Shanklin on the Isle of Wight. She always told me that I would have gone in if she hadn't scooped me up. When I got a little older I went on to be a great swimmer. I learned to swim using a pair of flippers (bought by my mother) in the River Loddon near Hurst. Later, I won the annual two-mile coastal swim two years running, an event organised by the Herne Bay Swimming Club. I also played water polo, for which you had to be a very strong swimmer. It was a contact sport a bit like rugby in water and you would constantly get your head pushed under by the opposition.

Given my love of the water I've no idea why, at the end of a blissful summer spent swimming in the North Sea, I decided to continue doing it once a day, every day, for the next year, from 1965 to 1966. There was a regular Boxing Day swim in Herne Bay and maybe that prompted me. Dozens of people would go down to immerse themselves in the icy winter waters. That was my challenge – to get myself used to the temperature of the sea.

The experience toughened me up. I set my own rules, the main two being that I had to fully immerse myself and swim the length of two breakwaters – the wooden poles positioned about half the length of a swimming pool apart on the beach to stop the sand and stones being washed away. Believe you me, when it was freezing cold and I could hardly feel my toes, even that distance was far enough!

As the winter drew on the challenge became harder and harder. At one point I became ill and I knew it would be foolish to enter the freezing waters with the flu, but I made up for the days I missed once I'd recovered by doing some extra breakwaters.

I remember one day when the temperature was way below zero and the ground was frozen solid with frost and the only time I could swim was in the morning. As the tide was out I made my way across the freezing sand. By the time I got out, I think I was close to having frostbite – I couldn't feel my extremities at all! I got back to the kitchen at Beltinge Road and almost passed out due to the pain of the cold. My mother managed to revive me with a warm towel and hot Bovril.

Even though it was cold at times I must have become acclimatised and the greatest joy was when the late spring came and I could feel the water slowly warming up on my skin. It was like a reward for all the suffering I had endured over the past winter months.

During the last part of that year-long endurance test a local hard boy called Paul took it upon himself to pick up some of the larger pebbles on the beach and hurl them at me while shouting abuse. Luckily, my dear brother William, who had often accompanied me to the beach and held my towel for me, witnessed this and ran back to the house to get Father. Although Dad was quite reserved, he could be roused to anger when someone parked in front of his garage or upset a member of his family. (The police were once called when he verbally threatened someone who had blocked the garage entrance. Fortunately the officer was someone Dad knew and he was apologetic as he gave an official warning.) Anyway, when William came back with him, Dad leapt into action and pushed Paul to the ground, while brandishing a gnarled old wooden walking stick.

Paul in turn hightailed it back to his own home and his father soon appeared to complain about the punishment. But Dad told him what Paul had been up to and he seemed satisfied – I think he knew his son was no angel.

IN THE NICK OF TIME

On Thursday May 19th, 1966, I completed my 365 days of swimming in the cold North Sea, the day before a partial eclipse of the sun. I wasn't given any award or certificate but I had a feeling of satisfaction with my achievement. This experience made me a stronger person, as did a later trip to India, and it helped me to toughen up to face challenges that occurred much later on in my life.

CHAPTER 3

A KISS IS JUST A KISS

From a young age I was quite receptive to the ladies, something I have cultivated well over the years (and a tendency that has got me into a fair amount of trouble).

It has always been about pretty girls and some of my first crushes are still imprinted on my memory. There was a girl called Marilyn Small, who lived in a house with a white wooden five-bar gate – the house had a gravel drive and a big tree right at the entrance. I remember so clearly the one time my mother gave her a lift home after school as it was raining. She was sat in the back of the car. The next day I sat in the same seat she had been in – I was six or seven – and I remember feeling so happy that I was close to where she had been.

Then there was Sally Gale, the baker's daughter, and the time I kissed Maureen Neville in a haystack on a hot summer's day. I remember playing in a field in Berkshire with her and her brother, Paul. He went off to get us some sweets and I remember his parting words were, 'Don't kiss my sister while I'm gone.' So of course I did. The crushes didn't stop at girls my own age either. There was an American teacher called Miss Parks at Kings Road primary school.

I cried real tears when she left to go back to America. I was very sad and remember clearly the contrasting elation when she sent me a postcard of a baby bear sitting in a North American pine tree.

***

The jobs I took from a young age marked a determination to support myself and be able to make my own decisions and whilst at school, I washed up in a seaside restaurant, during the holidays and was a caddie on a local golf course. There was no lying in bed all day, it was all about building up the cash in my post office savings account, and unlike some of my friends I didn't have my parents putting any pressure on me to find my vocation. There was the odd chat about what I was going to do with my life and my dad was pleased when I signed up for the Business Studies course. I enrolled after being given a grant but was then asked to leave after the second term owing to my lack of attendance and asking deliberately stupid questions when I was there.

Unbeknownst to my parents I was off being a part-time roadie for a band called Turnstyle with my friend, Paul Bennett. With Paul I tried to get a band like Cream going. We rehearsed in his lounge with me on drums.

CHAPTER 4

PURPLE HAZE ALL IN MY BRAIN . . .
JIMI HENDRIX

My head was definitely turned by the whole Canterbury scene; it felt fresh and cool and very much where it was at. It was the end of the sixties and anything was possible. A lot of our social scene centred around the Olive Branch pub, the Foundry and the Seven Stars pub in Canterbury. Dreamland Ballroom in Margate had also featured largely. When I was still at school, my friend Paul Fitchie and I went there, when we decided to go and see The Who in August 1966 – we had worked out a way of getting into the ballroom for free.

We attended Saturday morning pictures in a cinema that was part of the same complex as the ballroom and watched *Hopalong Cassidy* and the cartoons. When the film ended, we left the cinema and hid in the ballroom itself all day. We scrawled messages on the dressing room wall like, 'Smash your kit up, Keith!'

Our plan was to wait until the crowd started to arrive. We stayed in the dark – apart from when Paul went out through a fire exit to get ice creams. And at one other point we had to slip into the ladies' toilets because we thought someone was going to catch us. We stayed in there until the fans arrived – the girls were rather shocked to see us emerge from the cubicles. But we'd done it: we were in! Paul recalled that the hall manager assumed we were roadies and asked us to make sure the speakers were secure.

The gig was, of course, amazing. We were right down the front being blasted by some of the most powerful rock'n'roll imaginable. In those days security was virtually non-existent and we managed to get into The Who's dressing room afterwards, where they willingly gave us their autographs. Paul remembered Keith Moon swinging from a light fitting. Roger Daltrey was not amused.

We spent so long in the dressing room that we missed the last train home and as many young people did in those days we decided to hitchhike back home along the coast. A big American 1963 Lincoln Continental pulled up, down went the electric window and inside was Pete Townshend and his wife Karen. We couldn't believe it.

'Alright, lads? Do you need a lift? We're heading back to London. Jump in!' said Pete.

So we got in and off we went. He pulled in a bit further up and bought us some lemonade and chips and then he dropped me at my house in Herne Bay and Paul at his home in Chestfield before driving off into the night, up to London. It made me realise that superstars were human. When we went to school on the Monday morning and told our classmates what had happened, they didn't believe a word of this and said, 'Sure you did.' We didn't need to prove ourselves. We knew it was true.

***

The sixties were truly the most exciting times, but for me 1 December 1967 will always be a major milestone as it was the day I met Jimi Hendrix. With my best friends, Paul Fitchie and Roger Jarrett, we took they day off school. Despite other antics it was the only time I actually played truant – but who wouldn't to see

Hendrix? He was touring with Keith Emerson's band, the Nice, Pink Floyd, PP Arnold and Aire Apparent. It was like the ultimate package tour. Sometimes those tours in the sixties produced the most extraordinary line-ups, like The Ronettes and The Beatles and Roy Orbison on the same tour.

That day with Hendrix was something else. We took the train from north Kent to Chatham. When we got to the Central Hall they were unloading all the gear – in those days it wasn't a lot, about three trucks. We helped them in with their amps and speakers and the next thing we knew we were locked in the back stage area with all these rock stars.

I had a Philips reel-to-reel tape recorder that I used to carry around with me and so I interviewed them all individually. From star to star I went and eventually got to Hendrix's dressing room. It was an extraordinary thing. I tapped on the door and he invited us in. I could have been a journalist or anyone really – imagine what the security around him would have been like now. We would have been lucky to be in the same building! I said I'd love to ask him a few questions, which I did after he agreed to this. Then we had a debate about the cover image on the new album, *Axis Bold As Love* and he told me that he wanted to put Red Indians on it but the record company had refused. I decided to be cheeky and ask for a copy, not realising it was the day of the actual release. So he pulled a copy out of his bag and looked me straight in the eye. He was a very gentle guy, Jimi, and he said: 'No, I tell you what, guys, you all head to Oxford Street and when you get there, it's very easy. You will see a sign. HMV. You go in there and you buy one.' I loved Jimi's dry sense of humour.

Jimi also showed us some of the cine film he had taken. The sun setting like a big red ball behind silhouetted trees. A man drilling up the road. Dust and stones flying everywhere. His visual eye was as colourful as his musical ear.

The last thing he said to us all was: 'Take it easy, be good as bunnies. And we all know what they do all day!'

Then he went on stage and put on the most spectacular show, getting sounds out of his guitar that should have been impossible and producing incredible affects out of very little equipment; a 'wah wah paddle', 'fuzz box' and feedback. He played 'Sergeant Pepper's Lonely Hearts Club Band', 'Hey Joe', 'Purple Haze' and 'Wild Thing'. We saw both shows as they were doing two sets. Back then I wasn't playing guitar myself but I often think gigs like that spurred me on to learn. It was such a special day . I got my final sighting of him in September 1970, at Marble Arch, not far from where he ended up dying. He was dressed in the gypsy gear he loved so much and he was hailing a taxi. I never got to see The Beatles but seeing Jimi up close like that and hearing his amazing music was a memory I will cherish forever. When he got up to play in London clubs people like Pete Townshend and Eric Clapton must genuinely have thought: 'Oh my God, he is fucking amazing! Where has *he* come from?' (I got to see Paul McCartney at the O2 in 2015, thanks to my good friend Rachel Doyle. This made up for missing The Beatles in Margate back in 1963.)

Hendrix was simply doing things they thought impossible. On the day of its release he heard *Sgt. Pepper* and that night went down to the Speakeasy, got up and did a bit of a jam, then launched into his own version and blew everyone away. I always think his death was suspicious and a truly great loss, though of course it was almost certainly drink- and drugs-related and unintentional: he had so much to live for. Another tragic loss in the crazy world of rock 'n' roll.

***

Looking back, it still amazes me that I didn't get found out when I smoked joints in my bedroom. There was a lot of that happening back then but I didn't think my parents knew what was going on. I would have my friends back to 19 Beltinge Road, we would get stoned and listen to music. Traffic. The Stones. The Beatles. Pink Floyd. The Who. Burning incense sticks to cover up the smell. We would buy a deal of hash for £1, in Canterbury, or drive to friendly street in New Cross, southeast London, and buy it from the Jamaican boys. We were acutely aware that the police had it in for us. I remember well the feeling that I really had to watch myself and not get into trouble before the trip to India that I was determined to take.

My first experience of LSD was in June 1969. I prepared for it by washing my hair, having a bath and recording some music. I had the nearest thing to an iPod of the time – a Philips reel-to-reel tape recorder (the machine I'd used to interview Pink Floyd, Jimi Hendrix and Pete Townshend). I put on my choice of what I thought was appropriate music, including the Floyd's *More*, the Incredible String Band and *Led Zeppelin I*.

My friend Andy and I spent the early part of the afternoon looking for someone to buy the LSD from. I took half a tab in a house in Canterbury along with a very hot chilli con carne for lunch. From there I went to Pat and Roger's flat on Ethelbert Road. As I sat in their bedsitting room, a strange feeling came over me. When I looked at the pictures on the wall I saw people's hair begin to move. The wallpaper constantly shifted and swirled and the white ceiling formed patterns. In the diary entry made soon afterwards I wrote: 'Beautiful music. I fell in love with a flower. Roger Rees said that observing that moment looked nice.'

I closed my eyes and long tunnels of harlequin patterns formed. Everything was dreamlike but the room and being in it soon grew boring to me. Dave, another friend, and I picked up the 'sounds' – that was the way that we then described our music– and off we tripped. We skipped and ran down the road outside the flat, observing the trees and the road form beautiful patterns, as if we were in a film. The birds seemed to come close to us. We reached Canterbury College and it was as if the grounds had become the Garden of Eden. At this point in my diary entry I wrote, 'Really tripping now' – the page itself decorated with curving multi-coloured pencil lines.

Philip Glass came on the tape machine just as an ice cream van rolled up and it seemed it had been sent there for us alone. I burst into laughter although the van driver's face looked like that of the devil. We bought orange lollies for nine pence, old money, and ran along the pavement, both barefoot, past the law courts. People looked as if they were characters in a book.

We scored 'straights' (in other words, we bought cigarettes) in a shop that was colourful and the owner had no XL fruit gum. At this point I wrote in my diary, 'really hallucinating now as Dave hid his pound.' I don't know why that was important at the time. Outside, the pavements slid away and it felt like a hot day in the US. 'People didn't seem to matter,' I wrote, 'and we asked for a light quite freely.'

I felt so good as we went into Canterbury Cathedral but we were shushed at by staff and more than once they threw us out. I threw my cigarettes at some people we met and pulled Dave away. We found another garden – as beautiful to us as those we'd seen before – and we were laughed at by French day-trippers. It wasn't quite as nice in there – 'we found horrors,' I wrote – and so we went on. Elsewhere we saw what I thought was a 'live dead bird' and other 'horrors'.

Back at the cathedral we found Roger, John, Pat, Jan and Andy – all of them tripping too. I ran off with Jan and we met up with another John. The cathedral glass looked amazing with its webbed faces and the steps of the building seemed to move. The day was a succession of images. Inside I tried to move a charity box meant for Biafra and we were again asked to leave the premises. Jan found Dave and I in a garden. Some more people we knew turned up, Molush and Mick, and they took Jan's flowers. Another man popped out of nowhere and told us to go away. We met some lovely Indian people, including an old woman and a little girl who shouted at us. Molush was dressed in orange and this colour seemed to dominate my vision. 'You're filling this garden with orange!' I yelled at him. When you're tripping, bright colours seem to have an effect on everything. Molush beat a retreat.

In my diary I recorded that I didn't want to swap cigarettes with Barry and also that, 'The rat moved in the chemist's window.' I shouted out, 'Evil fuzz! Fuzz are evil!' three times, loudly, in the high street. Dave ran off to the library.

Hot and dirty, I wrote about looking into shops: 'The honeycomb looked like a pie. The sugar teeth were vile. We couldn't take the modern shop male model, "No, Jan."' I met poor Molush in the gardens by the West Gate. He was still wearing his orange jumper and we ended up taking it off him.

'I really sussed him out,' I wrote. 'He wasn't one of us.'

We took a taxi back to Pat's – 'The scene there was terrible.' The trees outside looked like a painting, 'orange mucked the feelings up.' I left with Jan and Chris and Bob gave us a lift back to Herne Bay. We met with Roger and Pat and others. Mick had gone and Jan and I tripped off over the beach as the stars came out, 'and car lamps like whipping eyes and forks in raw meat'. We went back to find only a suitcase with a blanket on the clifftop then we made our way back to my house. It was nice to see colours again after the dark of the cliffs. We dined on baked beans and sausages on toast, followed by iced orange and apple pie with cream. I had a View-Master, which you could use to see 3D pictures, and I got visuals of lava eruptions.

We took my bike and my mother's too and cycled to Jan's house, wearing fur coats. The colour orange kept recurring in my mind's eye and the reflections off the basket on my mother's bike seemed too much to me. Jan and I kissed back at her place and didn't want to part. We wanted to go on all night – 'until dawn and beyond'.

I cycled home, coasting half the way to the bus garage. I washed, went to bed about 3.30am and realised I was still tripping. 'My nose nearly blew my head off at one point during the day,' I wrote, which probably had something to do with the hayfever I suffered. 'A drag, but all feelings are multiplied. Jan was good.'

This was my first big psychedelic experience. I felt tired for a couple of days afterwards. My view on the world had changed in a way that was hard for me to put into words. I knew this feeling was said to wear off after a while. Also watched The Beatles' *Yellow Submarine* tripping, but had to sit through a dreadful war film called *Danger UXB* before we saw *2001 – A Space Odyssey* on acid too. In 1969.

***

Not long after there was a music festival in Bishopsbourne – the whole place went into meltdown when Rod Stewart and The Faces came on. Caravan were also playing, so I celebrated by taking a tab of acid just as I left my house. That would have been fine if my dad hadn't been driving me to the gig – we were in his Triumph Spitfire Convertible on a hot, beautiful summer's day, just as it took hold. Swirling colours and muted sound effects were wrapping themselves around me and Father's face was a myriad of psychedelic patterns. I got out of the car just before the full trip came on. It was just an experiment, really, with my friend John. There was some very pure LSD around in those days and my philosophy for the next two decades was, 'Don't say you don't like it until you've tried it.'

Some of my best times back then were on acid. It opened up a part of my brain that wasn't usually available to me and I soon realised that my favourite time to take it was on a sunny day in the open space of a park or garden, during the summertime. The only thing I didn't like about it was that you couldn't turn it off.

Acid isn't like cocaine, where you can take it, have fun and then it wears off and you just go to bed: acid goes on for hours. One particular time I was on the 137 bus ride to Battersea from Hyde Park and everyone on it looked like an animal from the zoo. I remember a white guy with a really long neck who looked like a giraffe, and a little dumpy black lady who resembled a hippopotamus.

When I reached 66 Albert Palace Mansions, in Battersea, I put on some Emerson Lake and Palmer through headphones and thought I was hurtling through outer space. It was all too much! So I took the headphones off.

CHAPTER 5

HERE COMES THE SUN

During the summer of 1969, having failed to get into art school, I changed direction completely and decided to accompany my good friends from Canterbury, Dave Rodgers, Roger Rees and another Dave, known as 'Gaskets', on an overland trip to India. The Beatles having already been there to meditate with the Maharishi, people of my generation followed in their footsteps. I was only seventeen and my father wasn't keen on me going at such a young age but he eventually relented and signed a special stipulation form from the passport office that allowed me to go.

That summer, in order to save up enough money I got a job as a dustman (before they were known as 'waste disposal operatives') working for the Herne Bay Urban District Council. The money was good and it kept me fit, although the work could be grim when we had to dispose of dead animals from the local vet. We had our fun times too, when someone threw out old army uniforms and we spent the day collecting rubbish dressed as soldiers. While I was busy being a binman, The Stones played their legendary Hyde Park gig (I was there at that one), then there was the Woodstock Festival, Bob Dylan played the Isle of Wight with The Who (I was also there), the US began to withdraw from Vietnam, Neil Armstrong was the first man to walk on the moon (I *wasn't* there) and the 50p coin was issued.

In the late summer of 1969, my friends and I were called by my father to a meeting in the dining room at 19 Beltings Road. He had spent some time in India during World War II and wanted to give us a few tips on how to deal with life in the Asian continent. Being of the old school, he conducted the discussion as if it was a military operation, with a map of India spread out on the table. In particular, he warned us about the prickly heat. That became something of a running joke when we were away – 'Watch out for that prickly heat!'

On Sunday, 21 September, I left home – bound for India. My parents dropped Gaskets and I off at the Dover ferry terminal and we took the boat to Ostend. Our group travelled in pairs as we were hitchhiking and we thought it would be quicker – we were to rendezvous at The Pudding Shop in Istanbul. My mother had given us one of her very popular fruitcakes for the journey; it was heavy but nourishing and we lived off it for two days. I didn't know Gaskets that well although he seemed a straightforward and solid companion. We spent our first night in a field somewhere in Belgium and I remember we lay on our backs, gazing up at the stars stretched out above us.

'Have you ever thought,' I began, 'there might be other worlds out there?'

'Not really,' said Gaskets.

My idea of Germany was influenced by the *War Picture Library* comics and films like *The Great Escape* and *The Dam Busters* so I was pleasantly surprised by the wonderful hospitality and kindness that Gaskets and I experienced as we crossed the country. In Karlsruhe a family put us up for the night, provided us with a shower and breakfast and took us back to the Autobahn. Virtually the same thing happened in Munich, where we stayed in a flat owned by a young man. He also took us to a particular spot on the road, which he said was good for hitchhiking. That day our luck was in because we were picked up by a truck driven by some Jordanians heading through Istanbul, at 1,200 miles (and three days) the longest single journey I had while hitchhiking. We were likely to reach our destination long before Dave and Roger.

The drivers didn't speak any English – and seemed to be constantly arguing from what we could make out – but we managed to communicate. We would sleep in the back of one of the trucks in our sleeping bags; there was a convoy of four in all. One morning one of them threw a large lump of metal over the back and narrowly missed my head.

We sped on through Austria, Yugoslavia and Bulgaria. In Belgrade we were approached by two gentlemen who looked very much as though they were part of the Secret Police of the Communist bloc country. With our long hair we must have stood out from the local population as we had to show our papers. I remember thinking how much evidence of poverty there was around us, as well as noticing the many posters celebrating communism that lined the road. As we travelled I had a recurring dream, that I got out of my bed, in my bedroom at Herne Bay, and gazed out of the window to look at the North Sea. This went on each night for a few weeks.

We had to wait a few days in Istanbul. We'd been warned not to smoke any Turkish dope because the dealers were known to sell the gear to the 'hippies from the West' and then inform the police (they would bust the buyers and give some of the dope back to the dealers). Istanbul was like nothing I'd ever seen before in my life: vibrant, dirty, noisy and colourful, it was wondrous to behold. Formerly known as Constantinople, it was the gateway to the East.

Our next stop was the capital, Ankara, which we reached by train. We shared our carriage with a Swedish couple and their blonde hair fascinated the Turkish men, who wanted to come in and touch it. Roger kept his foot on the door to keep them out until we got too tired and then a few people came in to stare at the Scandinavians.

It was another 2,000 miles or so by gruelling bus journey to Tehran. Halfway across the desert, at Mount Ararat (near where Noah's ark was said to have settled), the driver stopped the bus and demanded more money from every passenger. Our group protested and he immediately started to unload our bags and threatened to leave us stranded. We backed down. He lined his wallet with some more Turkish lira and then we were allowed on board again.

Westerners weren't popular in Iran at the time as we discovered when we were spat on in the bazaar, so we didn't stay long in Tehran. Another coach took us to Herat in Afghanistan, passing many incredible sights on the way. We spent a week or so in Kandahar, where we heard that the hash was particularly good. The bus stopped in the desert mid-journey, but this time it was so that the Muslim passengers could get out with their mats to offer up prayers to the setting sun.

We met Ali at the Pamir hotel, where we proceeded to get stoned for several days. It was some of the best hash in the world although no matter how much Gaskets smoked, he never seemed to get stoned. When he ate two lumps, we gave him an hour and then asked how he felt.

'Well,' he told us, 'my toes feel a bit funny.'

For me there was never the same difficulty feeling the effects. I smoked a hookah pipe with a Scandinavian guy in a basement somewhere in town and he seemed to have taken on the appearance of a cat. The next day I mentioned it to him and he said, 'Strange you should say that, because back home I have a very great affinity with cats.'

Back at the hotel I became very ill with a stomach problem. I ended up having to make a dash for the toilet. As we penetrated ever further East I had noticed that toilets were less likely to be sit-down rather the squatting type, set into the floor with space for feet either side. There was no paper, just a tap and a tin bucket for the water. It took a bit of getting used to, but it was perhaps even a bit more sanitary than the Western system. In any case at that moment my need was too urgent to worry about design issues.

To my horror I discovered the first toilet was occupied and locked. So too was the second... *and* the third. I was left stranded and all I will say is it's a good job my jeans were tucked into my boots! It was a very unpleasant experience.

***

We decided to leave Afghanistan at the southern border, heading for Quetta in Pakistan. The border post was just a hut with a pole across the road, but the guard said there was a vital stamp missing from my passport (he was being particularly difficult as the others were waved through). I had to go back to Kandahar alone for the first time and it was upsetting finding myself in the desert without my friends. Back at the Pamir hotel, it turned out that Ali had designs on me and I ended up being chased around the premises to escape his advances – he'd shown no sign of being that way inclined when the others were around. I needed to leave quickly.

The next day I went to the police station, where the dishevelled police chief brushed a chicken off the desk, rummaged for the stamp in the drawer and added the appropriate stamp to my passport. To me this was two days travelling wasted. It was highly irritating but now I realise that it was quite strange to be just seventeen and adrift in Afghanistan with only the address of a hotel in Quetta to give me any sense of where I was going.

The journey in Pakistan through the Toba and Kakar mountain ranges was hair-raising – the overloaded bus had people inside and out and on top while the roads had hairpin bends and frequently hundred-foot drops off to the side with no barriers on the edge. I remember thinking, if my number's up, this is it – so be it.

Somehow we made it to Quetta and I miraculously met up with my friends again. I didn't like Pakistan so much. Observing a man beating a donkey's face with a stick, to me it seemed to be much more of an uptight society as opposed to the proud and dignified people and culture of Afghanistan (with the possible exception of Ali). At least these were the considered opinions of a 17-year-old on his first trip to the Continent.

Together again, the four of us travelled by bus and train via Lahore to Delhi. Very hot – my father was right about that prickly heat – dusty and noisy, but full of character. Our hotel was called The Crown, situated in Old Delhi which sounded very grand, but it was in a rundown area of town. You could have a bed on the roof for one rupee or rent a room for a few rupees more. The 'Delhi Belly' soon struck my sensitive tummy and once more I spent some time positioned, legs astride, over a hole in the floor with the tin at the ready, one of the least pleasant experiences of the trip.

***

I could fill a whole book with the experiences of this journey. By now we realised that we were interested in different destinations: Gaskets and I wanted to go down to the west coast and Goa, while Roger Rees and Dave Rodgers decided to go to Kashmir and elsewhere. Roger would eventually go on to Australia to link up with his girlfriend Pat, while Dave and I agreed to meet back in Delhi at a later date.

Gaskets and I left Delhi at dawn. It took ages to buy a ticket to Bombay (which would later change its name to Mumbai) via Agra. When we got to our platform and the sun rose I was amazed to see in the distance dozens of gentlemen squatting at the side of the railway tracks. As is often the case in India the train had been delayed and I remember asking the stationmaster in Delhi when it would arrive.

'The train is coming soon, sir,' he replied.

It usually turned out that 'soon' could mean any time from now to some hours in the future. Amid the hustle and bustle of the railways I was taken aback to see how the women would fight with the best of them to get on board, digging their elbows into other would-be passengers' chests.

Once in third class, if you were very lucky you might secure a luggage rack on which to stretch out. Occasionally the train would stop in the middle of the countryside and people would appear from nowhere, selling lychees and mangoes. At every station the platforms would echo with the chai wallahs singing out 'Coffee, coffee, chai, chai!' I was given a lesson in how to eat a mango without a spoon or a knife, by biting off the top and squeezing the contents out of the hole.

Foolishly, I had decided to avoid the Taj Mahal as I thought it would be a commercialised tourist trap. I mentioned this to a man in Delhi. He implored me to stop off at Agra to see it on my way because 'It is one of the most beautiful buildings you will ever see in your life – if not *the* most beautiful.' So I changed my mind. Sure enough, the Taj Mahal, built by a Mughal emperor as a tomb for his favourite wife, defied all expectations. Words cannot convey how that building made me feel – I was dazzled by its beauty in the mid-morning sun.

***

'We were very pleased to receive your letter from Agra,' my father wrote later on, in December 1969. 'You are certainly getting about and seeing more of India than I did. If you ever get to Cochin, I knew a timber merchant there named Luiz in 1946 but I don't remember his address. The naval air station was on reclaimed land near the harbour. There was a fine beach a few miles away.' Knowing my plan to get to Ceylon – later Sri Lanka – he added, 'Regarding Colombo, the capital, several British servicemen were drowned at the local bathing place which is called Mount Lavinia, so you have been warned.'

**

Bombay in November of that year was even noisier and dustier than Delhi. According to the 1966 map that I used for the journey the population was then 1.2 million (according to Wikipedia it is now an extraordinary 12.4 million). We left as soon as possible and took a passenger ship along the west coast to Panjim, the capital of Goa, a former Portuguese colony. The sun was coming up over the jungle with the dawn and we boarded a bus to Calangute Beach, north of Panjim. I'll never forget the thrill of getting off that bus and seeing the blue Arabian Sea just over the top of a golden sand dune flanked by coconut palms. I'd loved the sea ever since I first saw it as a child on the Isle of Wight but this was my first taste of a tropical paradise. Dropping my bags, I disrobed and ran into the warm, crystal-clear waters. What a joy!

Back then there were no hotels on the beach as there are now, just wooden houses and small bungalows without glass in the windows, rented out to Western hippies. We stayed for a few weeks and it was there that I had some of my happiest times of the entire trip. I made lots of friends and heard The Beatles' *Abbey Road* for the first time from some speakers placed in the sand next to a wealthier traveller's house. The lyrics to 'Golden Slumbers', about finding a way to get back home again, made me feel a little homesick.

Most nights there were parties on the beach and I remember drumming as the moon came up over the jungle and I was still going as it went down over the sea. The Goan people were particularly beautiful, being a perfect mix of Portuguese and Indian. I also remember taking a bus into town that was stopped by a giant snake slithering from one side of the road into the paddy fields on the other.

Hippies shared the beach with local fishermen, wild dogs (who never harmed anyone) and wild pigs. Unbelievably, the pigs performed the function of cleaning the outside toilets. These facilities consisted of a small bamboo hut, open to the sky, with a rickety door and a wooden latch. Once inside, the occupant – as elsewhere – had to squat. But the difference here was that you had to take a stick with you to prevent one of the local pigs from thrusting his nose into the base of the toilet. You would give the creature a gentle poke in the nose before continuing with your business.

Christmas soon arrived and the local Catholic priest generously hosted a barbecue. Unfortunately, the main meat on offer was pork and so most of us immediately decided to stick with the fish! Despite the hospitality the priest and others in the local community were unimpressed by some of the hippies going naked on the beach. I thought it was a little disrespectful in a culture that is very conservative about nudity and so I always wore a thong.

One morning I heard some yells further down the beach. I stood up to see what was going on and spotted a woman, accompanied by the priest and a few others, giving nude, sunbathing hippies a lashing on their bare buttocks with a branch from a tree.

More seriously, Gaskets contracted hepatitis and was told by a doctor that he needed complete rest. The two of us moved to the much quieter Colva Beach, further south down the coast, where we constructed a shack out of palm branches. This was a wild beach and the only other people there were fishermen. Each day they rowed out early in the morning into the bay and we could see them there all day, almost on the horizon, wearing their big hats. What a chilled lifestyle! Slowly they rowed back towards the shore, dragging a net between them. By sunset it was full of fish. People appeared from nowhere and gathered up as much of the catch as they wanted. One of the fishermen taught us how to cook the fish by wrapping it in a palm leaf, burying it under a light covering of sand and building a fire over it that burned for an hour or so – delicious!

Despite his illness – that did worry me – Gaskets managed to shin up the palm trees and kept us supplied with coconuts, he was a better climber than me, and stronger. It was a time of my life when I felt most free. No one said no to anything – it was OK to light fires, pick coconuts and camp on the beach for as long as we liked.

***

My father wrote a letter to me at the end of December 1969: 'You haven't mentioned anything about swimming yet so I hope you have been able to make use of the sea.' Moving on to Ceylon, he added, 'I don't know how many English people are left in Ceylon now. Several fellows at school with me had parents who were tea planters in Ceylon and I gather that it was a pleasant life. When I was in Columbo in 1943 we were billeted in the stand of the racecourse.'

Gaskets eventually recovered in January 1970 and decided that he wanted to become a smuggler. It was a mark of how much we'd changed on our trip – previously he'd worked in the Luggage Department at Gatwick Airport. For my part I wanted to visit Kerala, where my father had been stationed during the war so we parted company and for the first time in my life I would be travelling alone. (Gaskets did indeed end up transporting various kinds of goods along the coast from Bombay to Goa. Apparently he did quite well! He was never caught and eventually returned home safely.)

It was easy to make new friends along the way. One of the highlights of my journey south was the palace at Mysore, home to the eighteenth-century ruler of Mysore, Tipu Sultan – known as 'Tipu the Tiger' – scourge of the British colonial powers. I visited the hill station of Ootacamund, more than 7,000 feet above sea level and a cooling escape from the tropical heat of southern India (Father had recommended it as a favourite of the British because it had a climate very much like ours in the UK). It was a long climb up from the plains, but well worth it for the refreshing air that awaited me at the top. The British named it Ooty.

Cochin is the capital of Kerala and it was there I saw the remains of the barracks in which my father had lived, just some old Nissen huts. I recall writing a long letter home dated 8 February 1970, saying how much I appreciated my parents for all they'd done for me. This extended period away made me see them in a different light and appreciate what good souls they were, as you can see below:

Hello

Well, I've made it as far as Cochin and I guess here is as good a place as any to write to you from. India has certainly grown up since you were here, Father. Bus services nearly everywhere and new buildings, factories and railroads opening up in many areas. I'm in the best of health and find I can even now eat in native restaurants and not contract any stomach troubles. The people themselves are often cleaner than most of us and always wash their hands before eating.

The part of Cochin I'm staying in is the Fort area. It's a fairly modern residential area of green lawns and quaint little factories and laughing locals. There's even a place you can hire bicycles. Is that the same place you used, Father, I wonder?

I hope you had a happy and restful birthday, Mother. I'm sorry I couldn't send you a card but there don't seem to be any places you can buy them. It was just by chance I found a card shop in Goa.

It's strange to walk the same streets you once walked on, Father. Pity you're not here to show me around and to see how things have changed.

I hitched down here from Mysore, after leaving Dave in

Goa on his way to Bombay and Africa. I came down through Ooty, a beautiful little mountain town that sold incredible fruit cake for 1.5 rupees (about 1/6). After sleeping on a truck, as the driver sped on into the night, I awoke at dawn. I was looking out over the green paddy fields of Kerala, a beautiful sight in the cool, early morning. Everything was so green and women gathered bunches of rice, standing ankle-deep in the shallow water.

Cochin is a busy port and as I crossed the first bridge I could see some derelict huts on some flat land to my left. Was this your base in the war, Father?

I'll be leaving here for Ceylon in a few days and then on to Kashmir, where I'll write to you all again.

I'm spending some of the happiest times of my life here in India and once again, thanks to you for letting me come. It's an exciting and grand feeling to be travelling, not knowing what story is around the next corner. After all, travelling abroad and across the seven seas is in our family blood. Think of the talks we can have when I eventually return home.

Remember that boy in the *Boys' Own Annual* eating a huge red watermelon in full colour? I saw him the other day, sitting outside a native hut, ready to take a bite. That's just one of the things I've seen. In those few seconds, as the bus sped past him, it brought that picture straight back to me. It must be years since I've seen that book, too.

Has Jan been round to see you? She's written some incredible letters to me.

I had a very simple but happy Christmas in Goa. No gifts and Christmas pudding but a warm and happy feeling inside. Besides, I was on a palm-fringed silver, sand beach and that was a good enough gift for me. I missed Christmas cake at home – no one equals your cakes, Mother. You couldn't make me a Sunday lunch, could you? Yes, as you once said, I now realise your cooking is quite something. When I return I should be able to equal Father in my taste for hot curry. How's that, Dad? The palate grows stronger out here as I usually eat rice and curry at least once every two days. The flavours out here seem to go on forever. Every state seems to put something different in spices, in its cooking – makes eating fairly interesting.

Yes, do open Blanche and Bill's gift and if it is useful for any of you, please accept it from me, as there's no use in having it sit around in my room.

Thank you, Doris, for your gift of £1. That's worth about 40 good meals out here in India. I hope Maxine [my sister] is well and the winter hasn't been too unkind to her. She really doesn't deserve all the ill health she's been having so far in her life. Love to her and the kids and Colin.

Up to you to teach Andrew a little geography. Perhaps Grandpa could show him where I am on *The Sunday Times World Atlas*. (I remember he taught me to read at a fairly early age.) Sorry to hear about the film industry in England. The Indian one is stronger than ever. Even small villages have at least one cinema and I saw *2001* for the seventh time when it was on in Goa. Thanks for stashing my records away from the harm of the outside air and dust.

Jarvie would have been in his element in Goa. On the beaches there are dozens of wild puppies, all quite tame, clean and playful (surprisingly enough). I don't know where they all come from.

Re: Michael Hull card. I met him again in the last few weeks when I was in England. That's why he wrote, probably.

You and Father come over very well in your letters and it seems I know you better than I did before. When you're set apart from a person or persons, after knowing them a long time, one seems to be able to see them in a different view against others and not only as Mother and Father but as human beings and I must admit you stand very high as human beings. That's the way I see you, anyway. Hope you can understand this blurb but it's difficult to put over, really. When you write, say if you understand me or not.

Tell Will to write a few lines as well. It doesn't matter what as long as he puts something.

Must end now as it's time to take a shower, then sleep.

Love and happiness to all of you,

From John (nearly 18) XXX. February 1970.

***

I was close to the southern tip of India and being tidy-minded, I thought I should visit. Cape Comorin. It was the wildest place I saw in India, with trees bent by the powerful sea breeze and the ears of the fisherwomen elongated by the heavy metal jewellery they wore.

Moving further north, I gazed in wonderment at the love temples of Madurai. Many of them portrayed erotic carvings with positions as various as any you would find in the Karma Sutra. Crossing the sea, I visited Ceylon (now Sri Lanka) and saw hundreds of butterflies in the temples of Ammadhapura. From Columbo, the capital, I took a picturesque train ride along the coast to Galle, then backtracked up into the mountains and the tea plantations of Kandy – more than 8,000 feet above sea level. Sri Lanka was so peaceful and beautiful back then. Sadly, this was to change in recent times when thousands of Tamils were murdered under the former President Mahinda Rajapaksa.

Back in India, I moved up the east coast to Pondicherry, once a French colony. I'd been told I could find a wise guru there called 'The Mother'. One of my reasons for visiting India was to possibly attain the high spiritual state of nirvana and become all-wise. Perhaps this woman could lead me along that path, I thought.

Upon entering the town, I discovered a strange thing: that the hippies and disciples of the Mother seemed reluctant to talk to me. The east coast was unfriendly and cold compared to the people of the west coast and it was where I felt most lonely. Also, it wasn't as pretty as the other side, which can often be the case between east–west coasts around the world. Even though I was still very young, I decided if this was the way the Mother's disciples turned out, her ashram wasn't for me.

I left town the very next day with a French travelling companion, Jean-Claude, whom I had got to know previously. He had no money and had to hide under the seat and I covered him with a blanket before the ticket inspector came.

Jean-Claude and I went on to Madras (now Chennai), where I spent my eighteenth birthday night asleep on the floor of the main railway station. While there I saw *The Greatest Story Ever Told* with Max von Sydow playing Jesus Christ and ate the hottest curry ever cooked.

***

Puri was worth visiting, on the way to Calcutta (now Kolkata), with its temples built along the beach. I was amused by the sight of women bathing in the sea while dressed in full-length saris. Calcutta was the site of many adventures, including getting caught up in a small riot, where I took one of the participants' sunglasses off and got thumped for it. I visited a Chinese opium den – which was more like an opium pub. Two guys from Norway took me in a rickshaw to a rundown tower block, where we ended up in a room full of elderly Chinese men reading newspapers. I'd expected something a bit more dramatic or colourful, like something out of a Fu Manchu film.

The procedure for taking opium was as follows: I handed some rupees to the manager, who gestured for me to lie down on my side on a mat on the floor. He then placed my head on a block of soft wood and prepared for me a small ball of black, sticky opium, which he presented to me to smell: it was indeed very fresh. The ball went into the bowl of a highly decorated, long pipe. All this time he didn't say a word, but looked me in the eye to check I was ready to smoke. I nodded and he put a flame to the opium, which bubbled. After ingesting the smoke very quickly I felt most relaxed, calm and content. I had possibly two or three of these pipes and then left with the boys. As we got outside, I threw up – not as if drunk, but a short, sharp vomit. On reaching the hostel, I lay down again and had the most beautiful visions and hallucinations of tropical birds, blue skies and all manner of exotic sights, amidst the quite shabby surroundings.

***

Less happy times arrived when I ran out of money, after it wasn't cabled to the bank, as arranged. Threatened with eviction from the hostel, I had no alternative but to beg on the streets of Calcutta. I also gave blood in Calcutta and was given 5 rupees, a boiled egg and a banana, (more than I get in Teddington today). Finally, in a park square I found a gentleman who believed me when I told him I would have the money but not for a week or so. He lent me about thirty rupees, enabling me to survive. When the money finally arrived, I found him where he worked, in a Dickensian office filled with rows of desks with fans whirring above them. He was pleased to see me and using some of the money I'd given back to him insisted on buying me lunch. With that I left Calcutta and headed to the hill station of Darjeeling, world-famous for its tea.

The train journey, thousands of feet into the foothills of the Himalayas, takes a whole day. It was a bit like a toy train and children lined the tracks waving, with wondrous sights around every bend.

At one point I could see the Himalayas to the north and behind me the plains of India stretching out into infinity in the golden sunlight far below.

Darjeeling was absolutely charming and one of my greatest memories was a pre-dawn horse ride up Tiger Hill – and I'd never ridden a horse before. I watched the sun rise over the mountains. The horses galloped back at top speed, knowing the path very well, but I only just managed to hold on, with terrifying drops into the valleys far below on the edge of the road.

Tibetan refugees lived nearby in a camp that I visited. They had escaped the Chinese purges of the 1950s and theirs were the happiest faces I would encounter on my journey, despite all they'd been through. From that day on I always felt great sympathy for the Tibetan cause.

I headed back to Delhi to meet Dave Rodgers with the idea of going to Kashmir. Back at the Crown hotel I saw his name in the guestbook – sadly, I'd missed him by about two days. To make matters worse I had probably the worst LSD trip of my life in that hotel. While tripping, I went to see a friend in his room. He'd left a glass morphine cap on the floor, which I trod on with bare feet. Blood started to ooze from my foot. In my hallucinogenic state it looked much worse than it was and I thought I was bleeding to death. Someone calmed me down and the blood stopped flowing from what was actually a minor cut. Just as LSD can make beautiful things more so, it makes the bad stuff much darker. And because you can't turn it off, you're locked into your trip for a good eight hours. At one point I truly believed that I was trapped in the night-time... *for ever* (it was no joke at the time).

To top off this sorry episode, at the bus station at the edge of Delhi the next day someone stole all the camera film I had in my bag – my entire trip, all used but undeveloped. Film was worth a fortune on the black market but the thief had no way of knowing this was worthless because I'd used it. It was the big regret of my trip. I've still got it all in my head, though and on the remaining film that was in my camera. At least that was the only crime that affected me on the journey – a guardian angel must have been watching over me for I was not once harmed in any other way.

I went on to places such as Kathmandu and Nepal and Banares (also known as Varanasi), the holy city on the River Ganges. Here I lived on a houseboat with some Danish friends, saw the burning ghats where the cremations take place and sat beneath the Bodhi Tree where the Buddha is first said to have preached his message of peace and wisdom. To this day I still have a leaf from that tree, printed with the image of the Buddha in the lotus position.

It's fair to say the trip made an indelible impression on me and I'm leaving out a lot of the ten-month journey when I say that in June 1970 I finally began to make my way home. I headed out of India with my French friend Hibiscus and an American chick who freaked out in Goa and spent some time in a Bombay mental hospital.

I travelled swiftly, via the Khyber Pass and then on to Kabul, where I met up with a local dealer. The quality of the hash was incredibly good and I would have loved to take some home. This was something my mother might have predicted. A couple of months earlier she had written in one of her letters, complete with judicious underlining for effect, 'I have something on my mind and feel I must say it, although I expect you think I'm being silly – anyway, here goes.

'Please don't be talked or tempted into bringing any packages back for other people. There has been so much of that in the papers lately and of course it's the person who goes through the customs who gets the trouble!

'Forgive me if you had already decided along those lines yourself but it was worrying me. XXX I'm rather fond of you!'

Instead of taking anything myself, I packaged a couple of thin slabs of 'best Afghani' between a couple of books and sent it back home, rather than carrying it myself. I addressed it to the name of 'Bilbo Baggins', c/o Poste Restante at Canterbury Post Office before moving on again to Tehran and Istanbul.

∗∗∗

My diary from this period doesn't record much – I was keen to get back home and made as short work of the travelling as possible. As it turned out, it would be far longer than I could ever have imagined. Just outside Cologne, having said goodbye to my friend Wolfgang, I was standing on the Autobahn when the police drew up and demanded a fine – I wasn't permitted to be standing by the motorway while hitchhiking. I refused to pay and they threw me into a nearby field. My next lift came from a man who began to run his hand up and down my leg. I forced him to stop the car and we stopped on the Autobahn. Lo and behold, the police arrived and it was his turn to be fined.

I hitched on to Aachen, where I met an English lad called John I'd previously run into. We decided to head to Ostend together. Near the end of the day we went off to a small village called Henstel, where we had a delicious mushroom omelette and Belgian fries with mayonnaise. We were alone in a back room and John decided to skin up a joint for the road. I didn't have any hash so he used his own dope. At the end of the meal, two Belgian gendarmes came in and sat near us. They kept glancing over and I had an uneasy feeling, even before they got up, came over and arrested us. John passed me the joint and in the car I had the presence of mind to stuff it down the seat. No one noticed. At the police station John and I were separated and I never saw him again. It was 29 June 1970.

Next morning I was taken to the prison in Liège. Up to that point I'd assumed I'd be given a slap on the wrist and sent on my way but now I realised that things were more serious than I'd imagined. It wasn't until a week or so later, when I was piecing together one of the newspapers that they would tear up for us to use as toilet paper, that I found out how we'd been shopped. The child of the restaurant owner had peeked through the door and watched John rolling the joint – and had presumably seen on TV that what we were doing was wrong. His parents had called the police.

CHAPTER 6

**THERE AIN'T NO BARS CAN KEEP BACK A
HERNE BAY HEAD, MAYBE IN BODY BUT NOT IN SOUL**
ALAN HUGHES (1951–2008)

From England to India and back again – almost. I was so close to completing my life-changing trip and now I found myself in a Belgian prison on account of a small lump of hash that hadn't even belonged to me.

Even here, locked up with a very uncertain immediate future, I kept up writing the diary that has been a part of my life for forty years or more. It wasn't easy to do. I used anything that came to hand, scraps of paper, the backs of cigarette packets, and I was only allowed a pencil to work with. It was the diary that kept me optimistic, along with other writings that came in the form of cherished letters from home. Even now I don't think I can describe that terrible period any better than I did as it happened, writing it down every single day as a fearful young man locked up not that far from home, but feeling much further from safety than when he had been in the deepest parts of India and the Afghan deserts.

IN THE NICK OF TIME

TUESDAY, 30 JUNE 1970

I was nearly home, nearly home, when this nightmare came along and it seems as though there's going to be no way out. Looked at the window: barred twice over. Nearly home, to home across the sea: to girls, music, friends and films. And I was only 90 miles away. Now I'm here, I feel so sad and I've cried many tears of sorrow, for I had no shit and they're going to bust me for it. My head hangs heavy as I pace up and down and I feel so sad as I cry into the light. God help me and I mean that because I know how stupid the Blue Meanies can be. And now they got hold of little me. Johnny in the dark, dungeons of Mordor, thinking about his little hobbit hole and all his friends so far away and yet quite near if I think hard enough.

WEDNESDAY, 1 JULY 1970

Three other boys *à la prière* – that's prayers. One here for two years for one ounce of marijuana, which didn't exactly raise my hopes. Gave me some cigarettes; strong and good at this time of problems.

THURSDAY, 2 JULY 1970

New friend at *prio* – prayer session – today, called Ferdinand (and also Smeets) from Holland. Yet one more also here for no shit. No sign of the others. I go to the director.

'Vagabond, eh? Hippy! What a generation!' he says. Can he but know of my happiness and the corresponding misery he and his type cause? They can't see beyond their shiny desktops and their pieces of nothing-white paper. A packet of tobacco and Zig-Zag papers was brought me. I haven't had such a good gift for ages and it meant a lot. Thank you, Ferdinand. I'm glad you speak English.

There's always someone worse off than you, though. I
think my mother once said that and every word of it's true.
For no matter how bad you feel or where you are, it helps
just to say those few words, just to ease the mind in times of
pain hanging down heavy. I love the world and all things in
it and I long to return.

As you know, I've always been free and 'doing', all the
time, all my life. During the last year even more so. So to
suddenly find myself in a nine-by-fourteen-foot cell with no
sunshine or friends and nothing is a nightmare in real life.
When I awoke this morning I kept my eyes closed, hoping
I'd only dreamt the black madness of the past few days. How
I long to be free! Bring the helicopters to the yard at exercise
time, lower the ladder and I'll climb on and fly away in the
sky, over the sea to home. Take me away, before my smile
goes and my mind dies. No, man, no! I'm going to keep on
fighting until I'm out of here. I'm not doing time for no
reason. Why let the Meanies win, anyway?

FRIDAY, 3 JULY 1970

[For some reason, I'd written 'Taurus, Capricorn, Aries,
Aquarius and Pisces' down at this point.] What a time to be
inside, when the fields of England are sunny and green and
all the flowers are scattered afar. The open-air music festivals
are going on into the night and I know life outside this cold,
stone room is going on in this way and I long to be there.
How I'll appreciate it when I am, because I know I will be –
one day.

SATURDAY, 4 JULY 1970

Remember the smile of Buddha and keep it there, always.

IN THE NICK OF TIME

SUNDAY, 5 JULY 1970

In this little cell, even the company of a fly is happiness and the birds playing in outside hills helps me on. For a butterfly to enter would be a moment of glory, perhaps these little creatures are freer than any human on this planet.

Church on Sundays is a strange thing indeed in itself and that's the way I feel about it, anyway. Perhaps it's the East in my mind.

MONDAY, 6 JULY 1970

Pity the Belgian law for its idiocy. A man is here waiting for what will be, in September, six months for stealing a soap and towel. Changes are needed somewhere!

TUESDAY, 7 JULY 1970

A beautiful sunny day, with blue sky above and the roses shedding their scent. One square foot of blue sky inside. What a waste of sunshine and happiness to keep so many people inside. A peach in the evening – what a beautiful fruit to see, feel, smell and eat! Then sad music plays on the radio and sadness comes in waves of lost days in the sunshine beside the sea in the green country lanes with the trees even greener in the wind and again I wish I was free with my friends. And when will sadness end? I don't know yet.

Sometimes I wonder why we're here, on Earth. Sometimes I don't see things so clear and I wonder why. And I wonder why. Sitting by the still, deep pool, rustling in the trees and then a voice came floating on the breeze and telling me not to wonder why I'm here. We're here to love, here, here, here… Here to live and here to die and still I wonder, why? Wonder why we're here, because we'll never know. Never ever know, until we die.

IN THE NICK OF TIME

WEDNESDAY, 8 JULY 1970

Heard today that the boy who was taken with me in the restaurant – and had the shit – was taken by the police and put on the frontier[the Belgian border]. So he's free and I'm here and it could be a good or bad sign for me that he's gone. Him being the guilty party just leaves me to take the kick. But who knows what'll happen? He was only 17 and I'm 18 so perhaps they'll be easy. Even if I get a month it's OK and I won't have to write to my parents – because soon they're going to start pacing up and down and wondering where I am.

Ferdinand, the Dutch boy here, could be free soon and I hope he is for his sake. Good luck to him! His lawyer said that judging by my age I'll either be here for a month or be put on the frontier. So the time drags on with St Michel cigarettes and Mick Jagger on the wall with some friends in the '69 summer below. The sunshine comes and goes.

THURSDAY, 9 JULY 1970

Moved to the next cell. I'm here with a deserter who's quite OK. Talking aloud all day from the other cat with the scar below his eye, who's here for stealing. His talking is incessant and we can't even hear the radio. He comes with things like this. [Here, I drew two huge explosions on the page.] But ten times the size of the paper and the sun went behind a cloud. I've come to the conclusion I'd either like to be alone or with someone who I know well enough to understand where his mind is.

Thunder and heavy rain, dripping down the outside walls.

Out of the prison door in the morning and off to the Palais for further judgement. Whatever will be, will be, so let it be because we cannot change it.

IN THE NICK OF TIME

FRIDAY, 10 JULY 1970

Up early through the streets that never looked that way
before, into the black gates which cut out the hairdresser's
shop from view. And then chains and padlocks around
my hands and a brisk walk to the iron-barred three-by-
three-foot box to wait for crude judgements, with the final
judgement still to come. I returned to the prison with
Ferdinand and his Chinese friend, among others.

Later in the day I met my lawyer, who looks like a public
schoolboy and seemed nervous. On him my hopes rest.

SATURDAY, 11 JULY 1970

The good moments come in sparks, like *More* by the Pink
Floyd [movie soundtrack album released in June 1969]
for five minutes on the radio. And good feelings, colourful
reflections in a spoon. The older guy in our cell, I'm sure,
is slightly over the edge. He talks to me for ages and I never
understand him. I listen to most people, but not when
they're babbling away at full volume in a crude form of
French. Every night he talks for a full hour again at full
volume and I can't sleep because of it. The other cat feels the
same. I'm not sure he can understand it all, so there it is. I
had to complain to someone! And you, piece of paper, heard
it.

News is that Pink Floyd are playing less than 35K from
here tonight! C'est la vie… once again.

For sure, the best part of the day here is those precious
hours of sleep, when I slide between the white sheets, clean
and tired, and smoke on cigarettes a bit and then fly away
into the world of dreams. Books, old as they are, are a great
help too and during these times the mind is in the right
place, far away from this ugly, concrete block. Thank you.

SUNDAY, 12 JULY 1970

It was only today when I walked with bucket in hand into the sunlight that I realised how little colour there is inside, apart from the French comics. And it's a crime in itself to keep human beings inside for 23 hours a day. The blue skies and roses proved all that. Donovan sang about rarely using the word 'freedom' without thinking. It means so much more now.

Just finished a book by Rafael Sabatini.

Apparently, it's known that the older guy with me is a bit mad and his conviction is something to do with an old lady – not so nice an affair.

When you're free to look into a bowl of greasy, clear water, under a light, and there will be the universe, before you.

MONDAY, 13 JULY 1970

The sun shone for *prio* but today's date was a fitting number for the news that I had two and a half weeks to go before my final trial. The same went for Ferdinand and his lawyer told him he could get two years – black news, indeed. The law here is not a law; it is a bastard idiot.

Wrote a letter to Dave, etc. in Kent. The day grinds on into the colourless night while Charlie dances around the floor. I have to be alone – or with Ferdinand.

TUESDAY, 14 JULY 1970

The time ticks by slowly. Turkish music on *The Late Late Show*. Charlie talks on. The sun shone through the rain clouds briefly and the day was cold around my head and hands.

The clouds rolled by, the cold, grey walls looked even

colder, but with that came my advocate and the good news that I would probably be free at the end of this month. If not, another month here at most. God knows, I hope so. The boy who was with me was true to his heart and told them all the right things he could and I thank him for it, even though he's gone. So there it is, two weeks to go and the time is moving on to freedom.

Thank you, Buddha.

As I lay in the dark, the voice said, 'Freedom,' as I walked in everlasting circles. The boy beside me said, 'It will be.'

WEDNESDAY, 15 JULY 1970

[At this point my writing became rather strange for a few sentences – it was hard for me to decipher.] I go to collect my three books. The director said, 'Yes,' the iron gate buzzed all the way to the roof – no one there. One round the body, one round the head – warm and walked back very slowly. I'll see the director tomorrow.

Pink Floyd, for 20 seconds on the radio. Too much for my mind. I was hit by the guard when I went to collect my books, but resisted retaliation. [This would explain why my writing was disjointed when I described going for the books.]

THURSDAY, 16 JULY 1970

So in the evening, Charlie starts a bit too hard on Robert and in comes *chef* [a prison guard]. Rob shaves so violently that his face is blood-covered. After the scene my friend is tearful and I feel sorry for him. I thank God that I'm not so pitiful as he is. It's sad to see the human race in such a state. Then that feeling I hate begins, when I'm going to start laughing and I don't know why. Crazy.

Getting in dinner and a long-haired guy I hadn't seen before walked past and waved, calling out, 'How are you, then?' And just before he disappeared I had time to shout back, 'All right.' Too many young people here and I guess it's all for shit. Half a key [kilogram] equals four years, apparently.

FRIDAY, 17 JULY 1970

Went to the director and asked him about my books and he replied by putting me in another block. Strange but I'd grown used to the old block and I won't be seeing Ferdinand again unless I can get a note through. But better solitude than Charlie's ravings and the new cell's quite bright.

SATURDAY, 18 JULY 1970

Wouldn't accept my note to Ferdinand. I'll try again with a card tomorrow. No one stands together at *prio* and so far away is a hill covered in green trees and birds flying by; a girl walking.

My face has cleared up greatly since the doctor gave me that cream. What a good thing if all my face clears up. It's scarred enough after India and the sun.

Wrote another letter to Dave, etc. in Canterbury. When I see the spires of that cathedral again I can't say how happy I'll be.

SUNDAY, 19 JULY 1970

Gloomy, rainy, Belgium Sunday! Glimpses of Ferdinand and hairy people in chapel this morning – they're quite a tough lot at *prio*.

Rolling Stones on the radio and that's brighter – for what else is there to say today? Canterbury sunsets?

Time is slowly ticking by to the day when I'll be free. Time is slowly floating till the day when I'm on the sea. And I don't want to be here again and I never want to see here again.

A bird went whirling by my head and told me not to cry for the day is drawing nearer, the day when I'll be free.

Bonzo Dog Doo-Dah Band special in the evening and a ripping version of that old favourite 'Ali Baba's Camel'.

MONDAY, 20 JULY 1970

Ferdinand's sign of Aquarius.

They are certainly a tough-looking lot at *prio*: banging of fists and all that.

Rainy day as usual. Canteen early on this side, hence milk in my coffee. Coffee again. Cheese and apples.

In the early evening, when the good music comes on there's always some guy who always changes it over to a Belgian version of Jimmy Young. It's a pity, but he always does.

Sent my letters off to Ferdinand and Dave.

WEDNESDAY, 22 JULY 1970

Sunny day again and pigeons flying fast through the faraway trees. All the rest of the day reading a book called *Freedom Road* [Howard Fast, New York: Duell, Sloan & Pearce, 1944]. I don't know if it's a classic or not, but it should be. Will the world ever realise there's a minority in evil and finish it forever? A strange way the world goes on.

The music on the radio is terrible all day now. That guy keeps it on the wrong station forever.

Strange world: ups and downs, ins and outs, rounds and rounds.

IN THE NICK OF TIME

THURSDAY, 23 JULY 1970

I don't know what's in the director's mind but he said he'd moved me here so that I could have those few things from my bags. When I write and ask for them, he sends the paper back with all the items crossed out and 'Prohibited'. The man must be off his head! I can't understand these idiots.

The world to me is a sea of faces, all moving and wondering what they've just done and what they haven't done and what they're going to do next. All moving round and round and round over all the places in the world, high and low. Nothing in human nature has really changed in a thousand years. Is it changing now? If it's not, when will it? And how will it? Back to the Earth.

FRIDAY, 24 JULY 1970

Six days until judgement. My face is scarred, my hair is all split, my stomach's blown, my feet are cut, but life must go on. On this dark blue day, which today is, it'll end. So will every day here. But it all sure takes time in doing so.

With my drawings I've come to the conclusion that I'm better off drawing things rather than people. I've just about reached the end of smoking. Every time I light one up it's an effort to finish. I'm going to try and stop or just smoke four a day. Maybe I'll appreciate four more than the 16 I get through nowadays.

Well, the thunder rolls around the building, the radio changes and it's time to close.

SATURDAY, 25 JULY 1970

Fine rain and a wind at *prio*. Some of *More* by the Pink Floyd on the radio, which was heaven while it lasted. Reading a book called *Tarka the Otter* [Henry Williamson,

GP Putnam's Sons, 1927], which is a very life-like wild animal story. In fact, all the books I was given by the guards, from the library this week were worth reading.

Every night I have a dream and it's all very clear. Last night I had a piece of paper that could get my freedom and I found myself wallowing in this room of white, oozy mud. And there was another man there, dressed in renaissance fashion. I climbed out as he was being thrown in and up the stone steps I went, leaving my piece of paper in the mud. Then had to buy a more elaborate piece of paper for more money and I was free, wandering on a dark, stone parapet in the night. I suddenly realised my friends had gone and realised that the piece of metal on a chair with white cloth on it was not my friend.

I started to walk back to that part of Herne Bay I'd never seen before and came to a beautiful garden. The sun shone as I gave a flower to a girl and for the second time she refused it. We looked out of a window and said it was like Nepal, pictures of girls or magazine covers, all floating in the water. Sean Connery with short legs outside the Herne Bay cinema, telling me that the *Secret Service* Bond film [*On Her Majesty's Secret Service*, UK: 1969] was terrible and proceeded to imitate [George] Lazenby's acting.

A few nights ago I dreamt I was home and climbing up some stairs to a room with earthen floors. Jarvie my dog, came through to me, greeting, all happy, and he shone in silver light and then vanished. I then had an argument with my parents, who said they had put him down.

In the newspaper-lavatory paper [newspaper torn up by the authorities to act as toilet paper, which I would piece together to stay in touch with the news] I discovered a report from two weeks ago of John and I being busted. It made the child out as the hero, her 'arrest' of the 'two bad hippies'.

Good sunny day, blue sky and fluffy white clouds racing by overhead. The wind was still not so warm.

Books came today and that makes it a good time. While I've got books, I'm happy.

SUNDAY, 26 JULY 1970

It may seem crazy but I'm almost sure I saw Boris in the chapel. And even if it wasn't him, it looked very much like him – hair the same, dark glasses, very large. Even a Levi jacket; also like him. But how could he have got here? I'm sure he saw me but he gave me no recognition. I must know. Ferdinand saw me and knew the sign of three days. All I seem to think about is that day and if I'll be free or not.

I wonder if Dave got my letters? I think of that Bonzo Dog Doo Dah Band song about us all being normal and wanting our freedom.

Sixteen cigarettes or more, three days ago, now down to nine and it'll get low if I can make it.

It can't have been Boris. Occasionally friends in the '69 summer came out of the picture and talked to my mind. Only now and then, though. 'For You Blue' is OK – The Beatles. *East of Eden* is fine.

The light is fading in the window. The night is drawing near.

MONDAY, 27 JULY 1970

If the radio is in the right place some good sounds can be heard and things very much appreciated, I'm sure, by all who hear, who know.

Thank you for the nice banana sandwich in the evening.

Took me back to the place of Goa where I often am in this little room.

Dreams last night: Uncle Frank said, 'How would you like to sleep?' Stanley Mann (the film director) turning around and seeing the poster of his latest film. The next moment I was inside it and in the First World War. A plane soared overheard, raining bullets on me and the ruined town. Bullets pounded into me, hot jabs, and I fell. The man stood over me as I was still breathing and shot again, all in full colour. The sky turned to white, clouds to blue, and I was running down a green hill with a friend who was showing me how to run over the humps. I couldn't stop. I ran over a stream and my friend got wet feet. Uncle Frank said, 'We'd better go now, but you'd better come along because I can't see in the dark – which is bad enough, with all these dogs barking around me.' Try and analyse that one!

I finished *Tarka the Otter* today.

TUESDAY, 28 JULY 1970

For the first time I was back in Europe. The air was warm, friendly and the sun was so good. I even forgot the birds. The boy on my right, No. 27, was Italian. They certainly have a variety of nationalities here – Dutch, French, English, Italian, Chinese, Turkish and German. Even a few Belgians, for good measure.

Waiting outside the doctor's – my feet still haven't healed – I saw the guy I first met here. He signed that he would be free in five days. Good to see someone happy and light in their eyes at last. He wished me good luck on my day of judgement.

I have been worrying too much about my parents and not wanting them to worry. But why should I worry about them worrying? It only makes it worse for me and they needn't ever know anyway – if I'm lucky. [Years later I told my Mother. They had suspected something was up, after a delay in my return and my passport being impounded. It's number was 2001 by the way – my favourite film of all time.

I don't know if it's being completely worn out over the long, nothing days here or what, but just as I ended my meal this evening, a strange, natural stonedness came over me. A very relaxed feeling, all over. Is it stoned? I suppose it must be.

Milk in my coffee canteen today.

WEDNESDAY, 29 JULY 1970

The good young *chef* – or prison guard – entered and he brought with him an envelope. It was from England. Three little pieces of paper floated and blew my mind, sending light cold streaks into me. All my friends had come together and written the most beautiful letter I've ever received: Paul, John, Alan Hughes. So happy was I, I immediately sat beneath the crack of daylight and thanked Buddha and all the gods for their goodness to me, for bringing such good, kind words on the wind that swirled in my soul. All those good people were there in this same room with me, bringing light and happiness to my whole being.

After that letter, books and tipped cigarettes, today floated by on a gentle wave.

LETTER FROM PAUL BENNETT

Dear John

How the hell can you come so far and then get busted? The weather here is fine and did you bring me back an elephant?

Back here the latest craze is polka-dot shorts and we all dig Glenn Miller.

I hope you watched your bowels while you were away. You know how these stomach troubles develop. We've prepared a special snuggly room where we will sit, huddled, and listen to your fireside tales of rajas and so on and such forth.

We will be smuggling in a file in a slab of Mr Kipling Fruit Cake so watch out for it some time next week. Keep your hair on and you can't go wrong. See you very soon.

Paul Bennett, on behalf of Paul Fitchie and John Rodgers

LETTER FROM DAVE RODGERS

Dear John

It's good to hear from you. I think we will have a little celebration in a few weeks. Sometimes one feels there are too many French. I am sitting in the Branch – the Olive Branch pub. You will find life good here when you come back. One mustn't want to go abroad again otherwise it is very frustrating. I still have no job and I'm rather bored with nothing much to do. I have the printing and the photographs I took abroad at the university.

Andy and Dan are somewhere in India. I haven't heard from them in a long time. Roger and Pat are living it up in Melbourne. Roger is moving books. They hope to come back to Europe, Roger and Pat.

Pink Floyd and Led Zeppelin are playing here in the summer. Floyd played in Hyde Park.

My brother John is going to Morocco later in the summer.

The people here are all much younger than I but I don't really mix with them.

Gaskets is coming down with a girl this weekend and is

going to Spain. She wants to go but she has no money. He also wants me to go to India in the winter.

The parents are away this week in Dorset.

Soon,

Dave

PS: sorry, no shampoo.

LETTER FROM ALAN HUGHES

John

So what's the motherfuck of a thing I hear you've got yourself into? But maybe you're feeling a little down and things are all done and there is no more that anyone can say. Maybe it's a gas and maybe it's luck and that must depend on how long you're in for. So what can a guy say, except to hope that it's not long before you're here.

In the gathering dusk, if you look hard enough and long enough, you will see the straining ears of a thousand heads, stretched to the horizon, listening for a pearl of the wisdom and experience which by now must be yours.

Get it on right here and right now. There ain't no bars can keep back a Herne Bay head, maybe in body but not in soul. Looking forward to seeing you pretty soon.

Alan H

LETTER FROM JOHN RODGERS,
AKA 'SHAGGY'

Dear John

It's all been a very long time and I most probably am going to Morocco on 13 August with friends and I hope you will be home again.

Gaskets has been working at Gatwick Airport again. He's coming to Canters this Saturday for the first time. At the moment I am working in London and staying with Paul F and friends. I'm in the office cleaning industry.

Palmer's in Africa, while Dave is printing his films. Just get home soon. Look after yourself. We'll think of you on the 30th.

John R

PS: they can't getcha!

THURSDAY, 30 JULY 1970

Awakening from my dreams of being back in the East, I saw the sun was shining and I could hear the birds singing in their envied freedom.

The door opened and I was with Ferdinand again in the van, driving up to The Palace. Paul had written that he and his friends would be with me today and I know now that they really were.

Out of the cage and along the ancient wooden corridors, past old paintings on the wall and a garden with green lawn and fountain. The crosses in the coloured glass were circles high on a windy, misty mountain and the clear glass cauldron boiled silently.

All my friends were sitting around in lotus position and not a word was spoken as they put all the good forces in their minds to me in the shimmering haze above the cauldron. Must have come on gently and in drops of clear white light as the sun rays, smiling, became a huge cathedral organ and played gently while the world still moved and the drums were… [My writing tailed off here.]

There were no further entries from my prison days but there didn't need to be as it all came to an end within hours. I was elated to hear the case immediately dismissed in court. Lacking prompting from my diary, that incredible feeling is mainly what I remember all these years later – the details of what happened afterwards aren't so clear. But how could they be? I was just floating on air and I didn't need to try and make more sense of it. Going home at last!

I gathered up my things and was released out of the front door of the prison. An official from the British Embassy met me with my passport and a ticket to get back to the UK. He directed me to head for the port of Ostende.

On the journey home I stayed awake all night, far too excited and overjoyed to rest. I took a train (after the boat) to Canterbury from Dover that arrived in the early hours just as the cathedral bells were ringing. I was the only one on the bus on the way home to Herne Bay, sitting on the top. I couldn't believe it – on my own, it felt like a beautiful dream.

I arrived just before breakfast at 19 Beltinge Road almost a year after I'd left for Europe. My brother had grown taller; my parents were delighted to see me. I did think of the package of hash that I'd sent from Afghanistan to the Post Office in the name of Bilbo Baggins but in view of recent events I decided to let it be. Perhaps the parcel is still there to this day, although I think with a name like that on it someone surely would have opened it up by now.

Relieved as I was to be home, I wouldn't stay very long and the next couple of years were to be spent in London, doing odd jobs and trying to work out what I was going to do with the rest of my life.

I didn't go back to my diary for quite a while after my release but I do have one more piece of writing from that time in prison, a poem:

Summer day, gentle faces
Facing the wind
Running water time never ends

IN THE NICK OF TIME

Warm wind blows through golden hair
Sending messages of sunshine to faraway friends
Lovely girl sits by the stream
Eyes of sadness set the scene
As she remembers always being
White horses beside the lake in the rain
Shake their manes and sigh
For winter is coming again.

CHAPTER 7

TO TRAVEL HOPEFULLY IS A BETTER THING THAN TO ARRIVE
ROBERT LOUIS STEVENSON

Having travelled the world for almost a year, I found it hard to settle down in my old bedroom in Herne Bay, despite the warm welcome I'd received from my family.

I came across the prose poem 'Desiderata' ('desired things') and it has been of great benefit to me throughout the trials and tribulations of life – I still have a framed copy of it on the wall of my living room. I now pass it on to you and hope you can benefit from it as well.

Desiderata
Go placidly amid the noise and haste, and remember what peace there may be in silence. As far as possible, without surrender, be on good terms with all persons.
Speak your truth quietly and clearly; and listen to others, even the dull and ignorant; they too have their story.
Avoid loud and aggressive persons; they are vexatious to the spirit. If you compare yourself with others, you may become

vain or bitter, for always there will be greater and lesser persons than yourself.

Enjoy your achievements as well as your plans. Keep interested in your own career, however humble; it is a real possession in the changing fortunes of time.

Exercise caution in your business affairs, for the world is full of trickery. But let this not blind you to what virtue there is; many persons strive for high ideals, and everywhere life is full of heroism.

Be yourself. Especially, do not feign affection. Neither be cynical about love; for in the face of all aridity and disenchantment it is as perennial as the grass.

Take kindly the counsel of the years, gracefully surrendering the things of youth.

Nurture strength of spirit to shield you in sudden misfortune. But do not distress yourself with imaginings. Many fears are born of fatigue and loneliness.

Beyond a wholesome discipline, be gentle with yourself. You are a child of the universe, no less than the trees and the stars; you have a right to be here.

And whether or not it is clear to you, no doubt the universe is unfolding as it should. Therefore be at peace with God, whatever you conceive Him to be.

And whatever your labours and aspirations, in the noisy confusion of life, keep peace with your soul. With all its sham, drudgery and broken dreams, it is still a beautiful world. Be cheerful. Strive to be happy.

Max Ehrmann 1927

It wasn't long before I made my way to London, where Paul Bennett and I stayed with my old school friend, Paul Fitchie, in a flat owned by his mother Irene and her boyfriend Dennis , in Battersea. They let us, a small group of long-haired, dope-smoking hippies, stay on the floor of their front room.

My contemporaries and I were definitely drifting at this time. Over the next few months I spent time getting stoned in London and Canterbury, where I was reunited with my travelling companions, Roger, Dave and Gaskets, and we used to hang out at the Foundry. By the time I was back on the scene, Inspector Brian Darnell of the drugs squad had busted – or tried to bust – just about every young person in Canterbury, it would seem.

I took on part-time jobs, cleaning, working on building sites, but I knew I couldn't stay at the flat forever and so I ended up renting a room in another flat off the Uxbridge Road, Shepherd's Bush. My friends Nick and Carol were renting it and I took one of their rooms.

I was still a virgin at this time. I'd befriended a couple in Whitstable called George and Alex, who had a young child. Alex was a model and she and I were attracted to each other but I resisted the temptation to do anything about it as we were all part of the Canterbury scene. I stayed with them in Whitstable and I remember feeling quite aroused when she brought me a cup of tea in the morning.

Lo and behold, one cold winter's night in 1970, who should turn up on my doorstep off Uxbridge Road but Alex? She asked if she could stay the night. I was very surprised to see her and invited her in. We had a meal and some drinks and she stayed. We fell into each other's arms and that night I lost my virginity. I had wanted it to be good – I never wanted to have to visit a prostitute, fumble around in the back of a car or down an alleyway – and with Alex it was beautiful. Years later I mentioned to my brother William that I lost my virginity in Shepherd's Bush. He has a very dry sense of humour and asked, 'Have you found it yet?'

The second time around I lived in Albert Palace Mansions was for a year or two until Paul and Kate had their baby, Ollie, and they needed the space. In that time I took various jobs, including chipping the plaster off a squash court in Dolphin Square with a hammer and chisel (probably the worst job I ever had). Paul and Kate used to work at Mr Freedom on Kensington Church Street, where stars such as Elton John, Led Zeppelin's Jimmy Page and David Bowie bought camp, colourful stage outfits. It was the time of velvet flares, loon pants and sparkling high heels.

***

During my years in London with my friends Paul Bennett and Brian Larkman I worked on a building site for Taylor Woodrow, contributing to the construction of Kensington Town Hall. The money was always better than in a shop or factory.

At one time I worked for an upmarket cleaning company in Kensington. Sometimes I didn't even have to clean and would end up peeling potatoes or polishing the silver, something I did in Mike Margolis and Anita Harris's home. Many years later, after *EastEnders* had made me well known, I met the couple at a charity event and we laughed about the fact that I'd once put a shine on their cutlery and photo frames.

There were various girlfriends too. Alex and I had parted company and special mention should go to Lydia Tasker, who looked like a princess from a Pre-Raphaelite painting. I adored her but she slipped through my fingertips.

Sadly, as I'd feared, George found out about our passionate affair and it caused a rift with my friends in Canterbury. About a year later, I moved back to Albert Palace Mansions because Paul Fitchie and his girlfriend Kate Martin were now the occupants and I rented a room with them, along with another guy from Canterbury, Andy Bearden.

Paul, Kate, Andy and I had some wild times. Neil Young, Van Morrison, Pink Floyd, The Who, The Rolling Stones, The Beatles and David Bowie were the soundtrack to nights of getting stoned and discovering Southern Comfort (which Paul purchased from an American army base). I remember drinking some of it, piling into a taxi and calling at my friend Annie Marchant's flat off the Finchley Road. Paul Bennett climbed into a bed fully clothed (with his boots on) and a shocked young lady pushed him onto the floor. Such was the power of Southern Comfort!

Paul and Kate bought a Great Dane. His ancestry included dogs with names like Prince of the Desert and King of the Mountains. On the pedigree form they called him Harry 'Snapper' Organs, after the policeman in the *Monty Python* 'Piranha Brothers' sketch. We were all great fans of the Pythons, who had only recently become popular. I remember watching the show, stoned and laughing so much that I ended up rolling around on the floor, clutching my stomach. It was revolutionary in the comedy world.

Another Southern Comfort and dope-fuelled night involved the removal of a wardrobe, filled with paint pots, on the landing of the mansion block. An unsightly addition to the elegant Victorian building, it had irritated us for a long time and despite numerous requests no one seemed bothered to remove it. We lifted up the sash-cord window, slid the wardrobe onto the window ledge – making sure there was no one down below – and pushed the whole thing out of the window. It hit the pavement with an almighty crash, pieces of wood flying everywhere. Unfortunately, some of the paint pots burst open too, spraying the pavement and the walls in various colours of emulsion and gloss. The neighbours were none too pleased. We set to and cleaned up. Years later I visited the flats and could still make out traces of paint on the walls.

Battersea Funfair was still operating and some nights we would take a ride on John Collins' Big Dipper and have a spin on the Waltzer. I remember a booth in which you could make your own record, which was great fun. Sadly, the whole thing was shut down after a major incident on the big dipper in 1972. It was one of the world's worst roller-coaster accidents, taking the lives of five children and injuring 13 adults.

***

Occasionally, we would trip out on LSD and mescaline on the weekends – despite my bad experience in India. If you're interested in my viewpoint on LSD, I recommend Aldous Huxley's *The Doors of Perception*. He took it under supervision and so I was aware of how tricky it could be. I preferred to take it during the day in a beautiful location with someone I felt close to. We travelled out to Virginia Water, Surrey, or tripped out in Hyde Park.

One final Battersea tale: I'll always have fond memories of my time with Paul, Kate, baby Ollie and Harry the dog. Kate came back one day, having walked Harry in Battersea Park.

'You'll never guess what happened, John,' she told me, 'Harry just ate John Wayne's lunch!'

The screen legend was filming *Brannigan* in London in the summer of 1974. He'd put his lunch down on his chair beside the catering truck on location in the park just as Kate and Harry were passing and the dog wolfed the lot.

***

I finally left the flat when I moved in with my girlfriend, Penny, a beautiful, blue-eyed blonde from Taunton, Somerset, in the spring of 1974. We'd met in Harrods at Christmas 1973. Over the festive season I had a packing job in the vast basement of the store and she worked in the tartan department. I managed to fall out with my foreman and got the sack just a week before Christmas Day, which was a bit upsetting, but at least I'd met Penny.

She was a bright soul, we both liked to get stoned and we had shared tastes in music, films and books. We settled into a luxurious bedsit on Prince's Gate near Kensington Gardens. It was a lovely area to live in but we soon ran out of money and so we moved to my parents' house in Herne Bay. Penny made a living by making rag dolls for children; we picked apples in the Kentish orchards for extra cash. We used the money to fund a hitch-hiking trip to the Yugoslavian coast and spent an idyllic time on the island of Korčula (now part of Croatia), reputedly the birthplace of Marco Polo. We built a makeshift shelter by the sea, swam naked and drank the local wine.

Back home I found a full-time job in a factory called Passmore's. The work was pretty awful, but it paid well. We made panels for cold storage units. One day on the production line, 'big' John, a former miner, thrust his thumb towards my face.

'Look at that,' he said.

Hairs grew out of the top of his thumb. I asked him what had happened. He told me that he'd had an accident as a miner and lost the top of his thumb. They grafted skin from his bum to replace it!

I wanted to go on to art college when I left school and although I failed Art O Level, I still wanted to make it. So I took Art A Level at night school in Canterbury and passed. This was to be a time of change. Sadly Penny and I parted company. I had some money in the bank and a student grant enabled me to do an art foundation course at High Wycombe College of Art and Technology.

Prior to leaving Kent I had become quite tired of smoking dope. The people imbibing too much of it didn't seem to get much done and I was glad to be moving on. I remember the cottage of my old friends Roger and Pat, near Canterbury. Everyone was too stoned even to brew up a hot drink so I did it. It seemed like a major effort and when I appeared with the refreshments someone said – sounding like Neil from *The Young Ones* – 'Wow, that's *amazing*! You got it together to make the tea.' It was a turning point. From that day on, except for the odd social joint, I virtually cut dope out of my life altogether.

At art college I had the most fantastic time and started hanging around with a new group of friends including Brian Larkman and Guy Mallin. Brian was four years older than me, so a mature student but in age only. I threw myself into it all and studied glass blowing (very difficult), fine art and painting. It felt good to be using my brain and learning new skills. I settled into the student life well and I would say that there was moderate drinking and drug experimentation, and a good social life.

When my grant failed to arrive at art school, I ended up working in a huge bakery in Bourne End, Buckinghamshire. What a job that was, working the night shift! We had oven gloves to lift up the hot trays, but they were ripped to shreds and for months afterwards I had burn marks up my arms. Damaged bread was dumped in a skip outside but if you took so much as one roll, you were sacked on the spot.

***

It was 1975 and I felt quite steady and settled. I would end up falling in love with a girl called Karen Murphy, was doing well in my course and actually ended up specialising in photography, which I had always had a passion for. That year I had a lot of fun and a few surprises too. Before Karen and I went out there was one girl on the secretarial course who was very attractive. We all used to watch her from afar, not least as she was really snooty and very picky about whom she 'associated' with – she looked like she really thought she was something. One day I decided to be brave so I went up to her and said: 'Do you fancy sex one lunchtime next week?' It was a dare, really. I expected a slap round the face and for her to turn up her nose, so imagine my surprise when she said: 'Sure, sounds fun. When?'

Once I'd picked myself up off the floor we made plans for the following week and I borrowed my friend Brian's Morris 1000 van to get us there and back. I learned to drive in that van, and passed my test first time in Slough, thanks to Brian, and a patient instructor. The famous Nag's Head was the local rock venue, where I was blown away by Dr Feelgood.

***

I completed my year at art college and got my diploma. I had got into Guildford School of Photography with my portfolio, but then I faltered – I'd got the art school thing out of my system and I wasn't sure about committing long term to photography. Over the summer holiday in Buckinghamshire I had worked for an Arab ambassador from Abu Dabi, Mohammed Mahdi Al Tajir. Charlie, one of my friends on the course, had a job there and helped me and another student get some part time work. I did gold leafing on the ceilings, picked up antiques and other bits of labouring and security work. It ended up being full time and I lived in the gatehouse, rent-free, on this beautiful estate, Dropmore. Across the road was Cliveden, the country house notorious for its links to the Profumo affair. Those were idyllic days. I was still seeing Karen, I taught myself guitar and had no electricity or gas so I cooked my food over a camp stove – all I had was running water. To keep the place warm, I had a log fire that I kept going almost twenty-four hours a day. I got my wood supplies from a huge barn right in the middle of the estate, which had been filled with logs during the Second World War. They had been there for thirty-odd years and were the driest logs imaginable.

I struck up a friendship with a mad Scotsman called Pat Whelan. We used to 'duck and skive' as often as possible and we still share a good sense of humour and are friends to this day. Recently I attended his eightieth birthday party.

***

Around this time the acting bug resurfaced and I decided it was definitely the way I wanted to go, so I made a list of all the theatres

I could approach about getting some experience. One of the best ways into the acting world was to become an assistant stage manager (ASM, it was called). Basically it was then the route for people like me who couldn't afford drama school. Most theatres took on two or three people a year and I was determined to be one of them. I think it helped that I was prepared to go anywhere at all – But sadly, it meant that Karen and I went our separate ways.

My friend Brian Larkman from art school was studying at Leeds University, so one of the places I tried was the Leeds Grand Theatre – and I managed to bluff my way in there. It was the Autumn of 1975. I was interviewed by the stage manager, known to the local crew as 'Will Shakespeare'. He had a finely kept beard and long hair. His real name was Eddie de Pledge.

He asked me if I had any experience as a stage manager and I said: 'Yes, of course.'

'Are you sure?' he said. 'Well, you'd better move to your left or else that piece of scenery is about to fall straight down on your head!'

A year or so later we were stood at the bar, having a drink and I said to him: 'Did you know I didn't have any experience?'

He looked straight at me, laughed and said: 'Of course I did, you almost got killed by the set! I took you on because you looked keen.'

So I got the job and I didn't look back. I packed up and moved lock, stock and barrel to Leeds to learn my craft. I had no idea that ten years later this would eventually lead me to the BBC and a job as one of the most recognisable villains of all time.

CHAPTER 8

IT'S NEVER TOO LATE TO ROCK 'N' ROLL
JOHN ALTMAN

At one time I was torn between acting and trying to become a rock star. My great love of pop and rock music began at a very early age, when I first heard The Beatles perform 'Please Please Me' on what was then called the *Light Programme* on BBC Radio. I was lucky to grow up in the 1960s, those classic years for rock'n'roll.

When I was about fifteen I taught myself to play the drums. The very first drum kit I owned consisted of a cherry-red bass drum, a snare and a cymbal, which I bought from a friend. At secondary school I played drums in a band but soon realised my equipment wasn't much good and I needed the full kit. Around this time I was roadying for a Herne Bay band called Turnstyle – my first rock'n'roll job – alongside my friend Paul Bennett. Turnstyle had been formed from a previous band called Steve and the Corvettes, who had been a bit like The Rolling Stones. Mac, the lead guitarist, was as good as Eric Clapton as far as I was concerned but he would never get the big breaks. His brother, Mark McVey – 'Chunks', after his love of pineapple chunks – the drummer, went on to find fame and fortune with a band called Rare Bird and they had a 1969 hit, 'Sympathy'.

With Turnstyle we travelled all over the UK – up the M1 in an old Transit van. Of course I should have been at home swotting up on business studies but being on the road with a band was much more fun. I remember on the way home once we ran out of petrol on top of a hill on the A2, but as luck would have it, we coasted to the bottom and into the forecourt of an Esso garage.

The boys in the band helped me when I took the train to London to buy a drum kit in a shop off Denmark Street, then the heart of the music business. I traded in my cherry-red drums, cashed in some savings and bought a Premier kit. I paid cash and realised I might have been ripped off because there were no cases for the drums when they should have been included.

I practised while listening to various records by the likes of the Shadows and The Who in my bedroom at 5pm every evening. Chunks would help me with my technique. It was bloody loud and we warned the neighbours. Coming back from the station on his way home from work my dad could hear the drums halfway down the high street but we thought that was the best time to play when people were still up and about – I never got any complaints.

In 1968 I formed a band with Paul Bennett and a bass player called Dave. We played Cream numbers with ambitions of being a bit like them, but the only gigs we ever played were in Paul's living room and my bedroom! Sadly, we never progressed beyond that.

I remember taking my drum kit into the woods one night. Everyone partied, I got stoned and then did a solo that I'm sure must have echoed off the trees for miles around – a wood-on-wood symphony. Over the next few years I practised the drums at every opportunity I could. I remember all-night sessions on the beach in Goa during my trip to India. My love of music continued unabated.

***

IN THE NICK OF TIME

In the 1970s I discovered the magic of David Bowie and decided to go and see him at the Central Hall, Chatham, where I'd seen Jimi Hendrix. In 1973 Bowie toured *Aladdin Sane* with the Ziggy Stardust line-up, including Mick Ronson, Woody Woodmansey and Trevor Bolder on drums. For me, this was the best rock line-up that Bowie ever had and the show was magnificent. Theatrically exciting, it blew me away.

Having met Pink Floyd, Jimi Hendrix and Keith Emerson backstage at that very same venue in 1967 I thought I would go in search of David Bowie. Although I never shook his hand, I did manage to see him through the wide open door of his dressing room. He was sat in front of the mirror, applying make-up, with his colourful hair cascading down his back. Something stopped me from entering the room. Perhaps it was my old shyness, or sensitivity, telling me not to invade his privacy. Whatever it was, I never got to speak to him but at least I'd seen him at close quarters. After his death in early 2016, it will always be a treasured memory.

***

In 1974 I began to teach myself how to play guitar. Paul Bennett sold me his Echo 12-string with a pickup. A beautiful instrument, it was a devil to tune but it sounded fantastic and I still have it. I was living in the gatehouse of Dropmore country estate when I first began to learn. It was hard at first but a joyful thing in the end. No matter where I was, I would play drums and guitar whenever I could from then on. Unbeknownst to me at the time this would prove extremely useful when I met up with The Pip Simmons Theatre Group at Leicester Haymarket Theatre at the end of 1976. In order to be part of the group, an actor needed to be able to play at least two instruments and sing.

I auditioned and spent most of the following two years touring Europe and the UK with them. In 1977 Pip directed. Chris Jordan was the musical director and played keyboards and guitar, Rod Beddall was on bass and lead guitar while Sheila Burnett played clarinet and was the group's resident photographer. Also involved alongside Peter Jonfield were Meirav Gary, Emil Wolk (acrobat), Roderic Leigh and Peter and Joan Oliver. Our set designer, Andrew McAlpine, later went on to do great things in Hollywood, and Dick Johnson designed the lighting and sound. The first tour was a colourful pageant with everything that could be put on stage in an avant-garde fashion. It featured *Dracula* and Dostoyevsky's short story, *Dream of a Ridiculous Man*, set to music and featuring dance. My drumming and guitar technique improved enormously. I no longer had the Premier drums so I went out and bought myself a Tama kit. I recall being egged on by Peter Jonfield to play harder and louder because there weren't enough mics for the kit – today it would be fully miked up.

In 1977, the year that Elvis died, I performed one of my last big gigs with Pip Simmons in the Mickery Theatre in Amsterdam – *The Masque of the Red Death*, based on the works of Edgar Allan Poe. The show included a premature burial, live rats and in the interval we danced blindfold and naked with the audience to the sound of a solo violin. During the run, I lived on a canal boat with a girl called Jude – known to my friend Simon Cutter and I as the 'velvet grapefruit' (a complimentary term, I hasten to add).

Returning to the UK and Maida Vale in 1977, in the summer of punk, I was now in a basement bedsit – 111 Sutherland Avenue, W9, not far from The Clash's Westway. Alongside my acting I became part of the west London music scene. I began to write songs on my guitar while continuing to play drums in a couple of bands, including the UK version of the B52s, and one I formed myself called The Hitmen with Eunan Brady on lead guitar, Gass Wild (formerly of Johnny Thunders and The Pretenders) on drums and John Brown on bass. My rock'n'roll persona was Johnny Rio; all spiky punk hair, black leatherm tight jeans and black Cuban boots.

The Maida Vale scene was later documented in punkzine *ZigZag* by writer Alan Anger under the headline 'Johnny is a Hitman', including the titbit that I had been mooted as a replacement for Johnny Thunders in a new line-up of the Heartbreakers and played a rehearsal before the idea fizzled out and the band returned to the US. The first gig that The Hitmen played, fuelled by amphetamines and Special Brew, was supporting the Bernie Torme band under the Westway at the Acklam Hall. Alan Anger wrote: 'It was a pure "let's-have-a-laugh" night' with Wreckless Eric putting in a drunken appearance on guitar.' It was the first time that I was a frontman in a band, having become fed up with being hidden away at the back of the stage on the drums – I was channelling the spirit of Phil Collins. The gig turned out surprisingly well and the band became a regular feature on the scene.

I also played a garden party gig in the countryside that caused a stampede among nearby cattle (I think we were hired to play for the birthday of a debutante). The band included singer Amanda Donohoe, who would later become a big Hollywood star, thanks to films such as *Castaway* (1986), where she played opposite Oliver Reed. Del Phelan played lead guitar and consumed a vast amount of vintage wine that he found in the cellar of the house. This being the era of punk, the crowd were impressed when I broke a drumstick and kept on playing as the jagged end cut my hand and my kit was splattered with blood. But the punk rock didn't agree with the cows in the nearest field, who stampeded and made a run for it. The police were called and the music for the debutante's birthday bash was swiftly ended by the forces of law, order and chaos.

On Portobello Road in 1978 I got friendly with the late Lemmy from Motörhead. He showed me his collection of Nazi memorabilia. I used to go running alongside the Grand Union Canal with Tony James, then with Generation X and later of Sigue Sigue Sputnik fame. He was living with the writer and broadcaster Janet Street Porter then. I also became friends with Gary Holton from the Heavy Metal Kids, coincidentally a band I myself was to join decades later. Away from Maida Vale I used to go to Dingwalls and the Music Machine in Camden.

Some years later, as a result of the friends I'd made in the punk years, I formed a band called Resurrection with Brady on guitar and Phil Brown on bass, formerly of a band called The Records, who had had a hit with 'Starry Eyes'. We would occasionally be joined on guitar by Ronny Rocker, formerly of The Godfathers and the Angelic Upstarts. Resurrection had a succession of drummers including Ben Matthews and performed quite a few gigs, including Manchester as well as London venues. We also recorded some of the tracks that I had written with Ronny, Phil and Brady, such as 'Twisted Mind', 'Tightrope' and 'Never Too Late to Rock'n'Roll' (I was the lyricist). Tragically, neither Phil nor Ronny are with us any longer – gone to the great rock'n'roll gig in the sky. God bless them both.

Around the same time I formed a band with Del Phelan called Soviet Posters. We recorded tracks for which I wrote lyrics such as 'Too Many Guys at the Party' and 'Directing Films of My Own'.

Sadly, Resurrection and I finally parted company around 2001. This was because I was lured away by promises of solo stardom – the classic sad rock'n'roll story. But I should never have broken up the group because we were really good – tight, exciting to watch, and we wrote some really good material too. I think it was quite upsetting for the other members of the band, particularly Brady and Phil, with whom I'd worked and written for years, but we remained friends and recently I've been writing new material with Brady.

In November 1990, I worked with Iron Maiden's Bruce Dickinson in the TV series starring Leslie Grantham, *The Paradise Club*. I was the bassist in Bruce's onscreen band and we filmed at the Music Machine in Camden. I'd never actually played bass for real, but I only had to mime and the rest of the band thought I could do it for real. I got on well with Bruce and had a memorable time.

Probably one of the highest points ever in my rock'n'roll career was being asked to perform at a gig at the Hammersmith Apollo for the Nordoff Robbins music therapy charity in July 2001. It was a tribute to legendary rock writers Leiber and Stoller, responsible for such hits as 'Hound Dog', 'Heartbreak Hotel' and the track I sang, 'Trouble', made famous by Elvis Presley. I appeared among stars such as David Gilmour, Tom Jones, Meat Loaf, Keith Emerson, Ben E. King, Bob Geldof, Elkie Brooks and Leo Sayer. It was organised by Laurie Jay, who asked how I'd like to make my entrance. I said I'd like to fly in, but the budget wouldn't stretch to that so I walked down the centre aisle accompanied by the insistent opening notes of 'Trouble' – 'da da da da. Tista tist a tist a tist' – and accompanied by a group of heavily-built doormen. Smoking a cigarette, I sported a full-length black leather coat – the very coat that I wore on *EastEnders* when Nick fell off the railway bridge – and shades.

The crowd started to murmur and whisper to one another once they realised who was approaching the stage. I stood in front of the mic, removed the shades and gave them to one of my entourage, took off the coat and underneath I had a black rock'n'roll frock coat suit. After taking a final drag of the cigarette, I ground it into the stage with my black shoe and launched into the song, backed by some of the finest musicians in the world. What a treat that night was!

I continued to keep my hand in with music but I didn't work with another band until 2010, when a good chap called Robin Greatrex, whom I had known back in the 1970s, bumped into me in Waitrose, Kingston.

'I might have an idea for you,' he said. 'What are you doing musically?'

I told him I wasn't doing a lot and he gave me his number. He told me that the legendary Heavy Metal Kids – I didn't know they still existed – were looking for a new lead singer. Previously Robin had managed the band and they had remained friends.

Robin said that I looked like former lead singer Gary Holton would have done if he'd stopped drinking. He wasn't the first to mention that. Gary and I both worked on *Quadrophenia* (1979), when director Franc Roddam said we looked like brothers – apparently he also auditioned for the part of Nick Cotton. Sadly, Gary died from an overdose back in 1985, just a month short of his thirty-third birthday.

Robin arranged for me to meet the Heavy Metal Kids at the flat owned by Cosmo, their lead guitarist, in Chelsea Harbour. I got on well with them, they played me their music and I played them some of mine. The very next day I got the call to say that they'd love me to join and if I wanted to, they were keen to start rehearsing as soon as possible. We did that without delay in a studio down a mews near Putney Bridge. The band still had three original members – Keith Boyce on drums, Ronnie Thomas on bass and Cosmo on guitar. They also had a newer guitarist, Justin McConville. For my part, I didn't try to emulate Gary but rather performed in my own style.

Thanks to Cosmo's deafening guitar I felt very much at home with the band and over the summer of 2010 I learned the full set before we went out in the autumn to play some gigs. I also had some material that I'd written myself, which I knew would blend perfectly with their style. We played the legendary 100 Club in Oxford Street and The Garage in Islington, north London.

One thing that Gary and I had in common was a lively onstage persona. At the 100 Club I gave it my all, hurling the mic stand about and running around the stage. When the gig was over, I came off drenched in sweat. Strangely, Cosmo later asked me not to be quite so energetic, even though their music was so dynamic. Rula Lenska enjoyed the gig.

IN THE NICK OF TIME

During the summer of 2010, we recorded a single with a video, 'Uncontrollable'. By then I was enjoying my time with them but they didn't have a manager and it felt like we were a ship without a rudder.

One of the last gigs we did was in the Half Moon pub in Putney. Not long after that I got a call from Cosmo while at home in Richmond. He said they had decided to reduce the band to a four-piece again. Justin was going to take over duties as lead vocalist. We hadn't had a falling-out, but I guess it just goes to show that you never know what goes on in people's minds. After that call I sat on my bed, feeling rather crestfallen, having put so much time and energy into the past year or so with the band. But there was nothing I could do about it and I had to leave it at that. So I wished them well and I thought, 'There'll be a lot more rock'n'roll to come.' It was just that I didn't quite know where it would come from. As it turned out, I was right and the rock would come in the very attractive and talented form of an all-female band called JOANovARC.

It was in 2011 when I was on a P&O cruise ship heading for the Norwegian fjords. JOANovARC were also on board, performing for passengers and doing a rock workshop for the kids. I met them all – Shelley Walker on lead guitar, Sam Walker on bass, Debbie Wildish on drums, Ruth Gomez on keyboards and Laura Ozhol on guitar – we socialised and became good friends. When we parted company at Southampton they said they'd like me to go and sing with them if I had the chance but due to our respective commitments it didn't happen for almost three years.

In the summer of 2014 they invited me to join them at the Baldock Arts and Music Festival – they were doing an open-air gig in the middle of town. I sang the Undertones' 'Teenage Kicks' and Led Zeppelin's 'Rock'n'Roll' with them. Towards
the end of the second song so many in the audience climbed onstage to jump up and down that it almost collapsed. A great reaction!

Afterwards I had a curry with the girls and we all agreed that we'd had a ball. One of the fans in the audience had recorded 'Teenage Kicks' on his phone and posted it on YouTube. It was a poor-quality clip with bad sound and a lot of artists might have been quite angry about this being released into the public domain. However, a chap called Steve Blacknell, someone I'd met many years before, spotted the video and thought we looked and sounded good together. He had connections at Right Track Records, a subsidiary of Universal run by Colin Peter. Steve suggested to him that the girls and I could put out a Christmas single. It would be good timing because Nick Cotton was to feature heavily on *EastEnders* during December 2014.

Steve Loveday was the producer and a friend of mine, Andre Govia, shot the video. We Christmassed up Iggy Pop's 'Wild One'. Despite getting a few thousand hits on YouTube and being played on Steve Wright's radio show and stations across the UK, sadly it wasn't a hit but we enjoyed working on it.

JOANovARC tour in their own right and are very popular so it's the perfect situation: we work together as and when we can. Our dream would be to play the Whiskey a Go Go in LA together. They look fantastic, we look fantastic together... and they've a lot more balls than many male rock'n'rollers.

***

My taste in music is not confined to rock'n'roll, though. Since the age of thirteen I've listened to the music of the *James Bond* soundtracks composer John Barry. There was so much more to him than that famous guitar riff – which he arranged – well over 100 soundtracks for films and TV series, including *Dances with Wolves*, *Indecent Proposal*, *The Knack*, *Zulu* and *Born Free*. In April 1998 I went with Bridget to see him perform in concert when he conducted the English Chamber Orchestra at the Royal Albert Hall in London.

IN THE NICK OF TIME

Michael Caine introduced him with a great anecdote from the 1960s. He recalled staying with the composer in his London apartment and being kept awake late into the night while he was composing some music. He asked Barry what it was.

'It's a tune for the new *James Bond* film,' he said casually, proceeding to give the actor his first taste of the theme to *Goldfinger*.

I had the honour of briefly meeting the man himself at a drinks reception after the concert. He struck me as a quiet, warm yet humble man. My mother loved his music too. Particularly the 'Somewhere in Time' soundtrack. It was another night I will always remember.

CHAPTER 9

PARADISE IS WHERE I AM
VOLTAIRE

From 'In Defence of Actors' by William Hazlitt:

Actors have been accused, as a profession, of being extravagant and dissipated. While they are said to be so as a piece of common cant, they are likely to continue so… With respect to the extravagance of actors, as a traditional character, it is not to be wondered at. They live from hand to mouth: they plunge from want into luxury; they have no means of making money breed, and all professions that do not live by turning money into money, or have not a certainty of accumulating it in the end by parsimony, spend it. Uncertain of the future, they make sure of the present moment. Chilled with poverty, steeped in contempt, they sometimes pass into the sunshine of fortune, and are lifted into the very pinnacle of public favour; yet even they cannot calculate on the continuance of success… A man of genius is not a machine. The neglected actor may be excused if he drinks to oblivion because of his disappointments; the successful one if he quaffs the applause of the world… in draughts of nectar… Players are only not so respectable as a profession as they might be, because their profession is not respected as it ought to be.

It's funny when you do a book like this and look back at all the junctions and crossroads you've encountered without knowing it. I have spent a great deal of time wondering what would have happened if I hadn't been Nick Cotton, if my time in the theatre had continued without the TV soap interruption and what would have become of my acting path had I stuck to the more classical route. I discussed it a lot with my co-star June Brown. She really understood my conflicting emotions when it came to my love/hate relationship with Nick Cotton – she has the same struggles when it comes to loving her own character, Dot Cotton. I truly believe that June could have been a Penelope Keith or a Vanessa Redgrave if she'd had the 'Sliding Doors' moment we used to talk about. We both joined *EastEnders* because we needed the money and security it brought, but it has meant that lots of other doors have remained firmly shut to us and career opportunities have been limited. That's something I have worked hard to try and overcome but I know deep down a lot of people won't even consider a former East End bad boy for some of the roles I would love to play. I guess something has to give if you are prepared to shackle yourself to an institution like *EastEnders*.

Right from the start I was passionate about the thrill stage work gave me and my love of acting only increased when I started work at the Grand Theatre and Opera House, albeit right at the bottom of the ladder as an ASM. I worked long hours and did whatever was required of me – you name it, I said yes to it. Life as an ASM couldn't have been less glamorous. It involved unloading the rucks, sweeping the stage, putting up the sets and making sure the props were on set at the right time – it was very physical and utterly exhausting, but the crew were great. We had fun.

For me the interesting thing was that we would have a different show up on the stage every week. One week it would be opera, the next it would be pantomime, we had it all: Alan Bates in *The Seagull* and then a variety of shows and concerts starring Elton John, David Essex, Timothy West, Margot Fonteyn, Peter Eyre, Dennis Waterman... It was amazing to think I actually worked on every form of British theatre possible. You had to be physically fit to keep up, often there would be three trucks bringing all the sets in for the first act of Wagner's Ring Cycle for example, and we would have to get it all on stage and then they would bring the second act on the following day and that scenery would arrive in three more trucks and so on. I was trained up to be a flyman, too, by the head flyman, Eddie Flint. This involved attaching the scenery onto bars, and maintaining and repairing the flying equipment. We would build and set up stage scenery and suspended scenery. We raised and lowered suspended scenery during the performance and operated many mechanical elements on the stage. The actors knew that they could rely on us to rescue them in the event of an emergency.

The backstage team were a great gang and they all had nicknames: I was known as Vision, then there was Intellectual Trog, Billy Rose, Will Shakespeare, Ginger Rogers, Effervescence, Jethro, Frederica, Steve 'The Leg', Groping Pedro, Big John, Zebedee, Wiz, Dillon, and Swifty Willy (Godfather of Roundhay). There was also a backstage bar run by a woman called Betty Walsh, where we would all gather after the show and that was our chance to meet the stars. I learned a lot there just watching from the wings or the Fly Floor (writing unclear) and it didn't take long for me to convince a director that I was ready for my first walk-on part in an opera called *Culloden*, which was put on by the Scottish National Opera, and was all about the Battle of Culloden on 16 April 1746.

There was a scene where the soldiers had to hang an actor on a scaffold. He was very nervous and then he actually passed out after he was strung up in a harness, attached to the rope, metres above the stage. During his key song he passed out and while the music kept playing, we had to cut him down, get him backstage and revive him. The audience thought it was all part of the action!

The flymen work on a walkway high up above the stage and it is where all the ropes are. In a big show you may have dozens of different cues, working with 24 bars or more. So, for example, when fly cue 1 goes, you might pull in bars 3, 6, 9 and 8 and take out 2, 7 and 12. They all have taped marks or 'deads' on them so you don't have to keep looking down.

I was involved in the lighting too, operating the spotlights on occasions. Often each show would pass in a blur with me doing many different jobs , but I can honestly say they were some of the happiest professional times I have had.

All of the full time crew were involved in the long-term work of clearing out and cleaning up the backstage area. One day I was in a dusty old room at the top of a staircase backstage when I discovered some photos by Cecil Beaton – I wish I'd kept them now as they'd be worth a fortune. There was an old wooden crate containing more framed photos that had once been hung in the front-of-house bar. Amazingly, one of these pictures was of my grandfather, Johnnie Schofield junior, signed, 'Best wishes to Harry'. This was extraordinary, not least because I was only on my first job in theatre and I could have gone anywhere in the country, yet here was a picture of Johnnie in this very room. The last theatrical link in my family. If I'd had any doubts about embarking on a theatrical career, finding this photo quickly dispelled them – I had indeed made the right decision.

I lived with Brian Larkman and a group of artists in a big house at 68 Cardigan Road in Headingley, Leeds. He was a kind soul – and still is a good friend – and would occasionally lend me his Morris 1000. Driving out of town one sunny summer's day, I spotted a very pretty blonde girl standing at a bus stop near the university. I turned the car round, drove back and asked her if she'd like a lift into Headingley as I guessed that was where she was going. Her name was Jenni Hume and she was a student teacher from Hull. She invited me back to her hostel, where we had some tea and biscuits, and I arranged for her to come and see a show at the theatre. We went for a drink afterwards. That was the beginning of an affair that lasted for the next three years. I will always treasure the memories of the beautiful times we spent together.

Years later, in 2001, I went back to The Grand Theatre, topping the bill as Billy Flynn in *Chicago*. I operated my fly cue 2, which felt like a real full-circle moment. The theatre manager Warren Smith came to see me in Dressing Room 1, the room I had only ever walked past as an ASM all those years ago. You never forget those moments in your career when you really feel like you've made it.

***

For me the real turning point at Leeds was when *Blithe Spirit* came in from the Leicester Haymarket Theatre in 1976. What I hadn't realised, in my ignorance, was that I needed an Equity card to progress in the theatrical world, but I couldn't get it from a touring theatre like Leeds, which has different shows arriving every week. It had to be from a rep theatre, where you have a season of your own shows. In those days it was the done thing that when you finished in drama school, you would go and work in rep and they would give away one or two Equity cards a year.

I got on really well with the Leicester Haymarket crew and their stage manager Susie Copley and studio theatre director Hugh Thomas and told them I needed my Equity card. They let me know that they had a vacancy for an acting ASM and to give them a call. A couple of weeks later I was working on the fly floor, fitting up a show on a Monday afternoon. During a break I ran down to the payphone. Just in the nick of time I rang Susie, and she asked me down for an interview, resulting in my much-coveted Equity ASM job there. I got the job helping to run the studio theatre with the directors Jan Sargent, Hugh Thomas and ASM's John, Leslie and Martin Hazelwood and doing some more walk-on parts. So I was on the move again. I played a German soldier on a train in a war play by John Antrobus called *They Sleep Together*. My line. The immortal words 'your papers please sir!' Or words to that effect. I also worked on Samuel Beckett's *Endgame*.

At Leicester things stepped up a gear as I operated the sound and the lights, looked after the props, and helped to make the sets. All the cues for a Deputy Stage Manager are in what we call 'The Book': it has the whole script typed up on one side in case the actor dries and on the other you have all the sound and lighting cues. For example: 'Act 1 lights full up, cue car arriving at door, birds singing, etc.'.

Other performers at Leicester included Oz Clarke, Belinda Lang and Elaine Paige. Robin Midgely was the artistic director, affectionately known as 'the beard' for the growth that seemed to cover his entire face.

I was only there for three or four months when this incredible theatre company arrived called The Pip Simmons Theatre Group. I had never heard of them but was immediately blown away. The group in 1976 consisted of Pip himself, Chris Jordan, Rod Beddall, Roderick Leigh, Peter Jonfield, Meirave Gary, Sheila Burnett, Peter and Joan Oliver, Dick Johnson (lighting), Emile Wolk (acrobat) and Ben Bazell. They were partly a rock band and by that time my interest in music had been cemented, having taught myself guitar and drums and I had worked on my singing. Visually, I had seen nothing like it in the theatre before – they did an incredible version of *Dracula*. Two girls came on naked and then got dressed to strip music. There was blood everywhere, sex, white doves… It was a pageant of truly exciting theatre. I watched, agog, every single night and every night I noticed different colourful parts of the performance. They were quite self-sufficient so there wasn't a lot to do for them, which meant I could be like a spectator with the best seat in the house. I also jammed with the band on drums and drank with them after the show.

Pip worked under cover; he never wanted to let anyone know who he was, it was like underground fringe alternative rock'n'roll theatre. At the end of the closing week, he came up to me and said one of the company, Ben Bazell, was leaving. He wanted to know if I would come to London and audition in a few weeks' time – he was so laid-back about it. One of the group, Peter Jonfield, had suggested me. I was surprised, delighted and elated to be asked. In many ways Peter was a mentor to me during that period in my acting career and I will always be grateful to him.

So I went down to the Royal Court Theatre at the top of the King's Road, sang a few Beatles' songs which I had rehearsed with Hugh Thomas and then went to a café on the King's Road, where Pip handed me the scripts for *Dracula* and *Dream of a Ridiculous Man* by Dostoyevsky and said we would be going to Paris in the New Year. To me it felt like being offered a Hollywood contract. I happily spent Christmas and New Year of 1976 in St John's Wood learning the scripts and songs I had been given and it was then I realised that teaching myself the musical instruments had been vital. If I hadn't done that, I wouldn't have been offered the part in the group. It all came together like the perfect storm. The next thing I knew we were in Paris and performing at the Théâtre le Palace, Montmartre. It was an exciting gig for me. All the things I loved. Acting, singing, playing guitar and drums. A rock theatre group – I was in awe of them all.

One of the first things I did in Paris was to go off to the rue St Denis. I'd read about it in Henry Miller's *Tropic of Cancer* and did exactly as his novel described – I started at the top end and wandered down. What soon became clear was that the pretty girls were very far away from the top end: the further you went down, the younger and more beautiful they got. I hit the middle and picked a particular girl. I couldn't believe she was on the game really, she was one of the most stunning girls I had ever seen, (she looked like a *Vogue* model), and to my young mind it didn't make sense that she needed to do a job like that. She led me up some creaky wooden stairs in an old Parisian house and there was a woman behind a small box office style window who looked like your average aunty taking the money – I remember thinking it was all quite relaxed and efficient. Up we went and the process was very much a ritual. She made sure I was clean before we had sex and after we had finished, because she was so lovely, I asked her if we could meet again. Predictably she said no but the experience was definitely one I was glad I had had. It was a pleasant interlude, not sordid in any way, and when I got back to the theatre group, I told Pip Simmons, the director, but he was not impressed. I always remember being shocked by his reaction – I had thought him to be a very open-minded guy, especially with the raunchy content of the shows we were performing.

***

In March 1977 we performed *The Dream of a Ridiculous Man* – about a man contemplating suicide who takes a gun out of a drawer and falls into a dream and goes to paradise amongst other places as opposed to killing himself – and *Dracula* at Glasgow's Citizens Theatre. We got great reviews, including the Scottish *Daily Express*, who said: 'Anything goes in this production of *Dream of a Ridiculous Man* … in a mixture of theatre, circus, gospel meeting and strip club, they whip up a variety of emotions with a skill and enthusiasm which show that they are no mean performers. It is a search for paradise on earth with an open invitation to the audience to join the converted of the Pip Simmons Group.

'At one point Meirave Gary is down among the audience singing with fervent religiosity, bearing not only her soul but her breasts as well! Whether this is all justified in subsidised theatre will remain a matter for debate.

'The Lord Provost [a role in Scotland similar to that of a town's mayor], Peter McCann, doesn't think so. He said, "It seems to me ridiculous that I cannot get £2,000 to help disabled children, yet we are paying out public money to support this kind of thing. Someone says, 'This is not a woman taking her clothes off, this is art,' and that is supposed to be all right."

'He finishes, "Well, we drove the Sex Pistols pop group out of town and prevented them from appearing in a commercial place, so are we guilty of double standards?" Despite the protestations of the Lord Provost, the show carried on to the end of its Glasgow run. And as Dostoyevsky himself said, "Dreams are very queer things."'

Despite all the fuss in Glasgow, the nudity was at times comical. For example, when Sheila Burnett and Meirave Gary walked onto the stage naked in *Dracula*, clutching a bundle of clothing, they proceeded to get dressed in front of the audience, accompanied by music written by Chris Jordan that would have been appropriate for a strip routine. While writing this book I've been looking back through my cuttings and some of the reviews have made me chuckle at how critics were baffled by the nakedness in our work. A good example is the *Jewish Echo* in March 1977 on *Dracula*: 'The Citizens' curtain rose at 7.30 pm. The first pair of trousers dropped six minutes later. And continued to drop for the best part of the curious evening … in *Dracula*.

'An actor removing his trousers in the theatre hardly raises an eyebrow these days. After all, Brian Rix did it successfully for decades. Even nude ladies prancing around the stage hardly justifies a paragraph in anybody's first-night notice.

'But when a trouserless actor clambers over the heads of the stalls audience and nubile, naked young ladies sit themselves upon the laps of unsuspecting theatre-goers there has to be some explanation. But if you expect it from this critic then you are in for a bitter disappointment.'

CHAPTER 10

A DREAM. WHAT IS A DREAM? IS NOT OUR LIFE A DREAM?
EDGAR ALLAN POE, 'THE MASQUE OF THE RED DEATH'

Being a recovering alcoholic and having gone through the 12-Step Recovery Program you spend a lot of time looking back and wondering when it was that you tipped the balance from being a normal social drinker to someone out of control. There are always moments when you, perhaps unconsciously, started drinking more and I think this was how it was for me. During my year as a student it had started to creep up on me but I was never excessive or drank spirits regularly for many years to come. My time with Pip and the gang definitely saw it go up a notch, though: suddenly I was drinking more, trying to keep up. We drank socially after work. I had been increasing my intake throughout Leeds and Leicester. Then there was speed, which I began to take to very well. You could drink more, feel less drunk, and kid yourself you were in control.

There were twelve of us in the group and the majority liked whisky, so I taught myself to like it too. They were all older than me and I wanted to impress them and to be accepted. I was like the kid in the group who was desperate to fit in and I felt like I had to be in the bar, showing I could handle it. Somewhat conversely it was around this time that I started to try and keep myself fit. I think I was trying to offset the effects of all that boozing, it was definitely the beginning of my alcoholic ability to live in denial.

It's easy to fool yourself that things really can't be that bad if you can still go for a long run and function well at work – basically if you were together enough to kid everyone around you, it was fine. I was behaving like a rock band on the road – I would have a session in the bar, and then carry on as though I was fine. There was the occasional groupie too. We worked hard and partied hard on many occasions.

Following on from our two weeks in Glasgow at the Citizens Theatre (where I first met Garry Cooper, with whom I would work on *Quadrophenia*), we set out on a car ferry from Newcastle-upon-Tyne to Stavanger in Norway. We consumed most of our duty-frees on the crossing and I naughtily sneaked into the cabin of one of the sleeping members of the group, Steve Johnston, and poured some of his whisky into a toothpaste glass for the rest of us to share. I thought he hadn't heard me but the next day he quietly said, 'I hope you enjoyed my whisky, John,' making me feel worse than I already was after the night's session. Most of us were still inebriated when we were greeted at the quayside in Stavanger by the Lord Mayor, who welcomed us all with a fresh red rose apiece.

The tour included a mental hospital in Denmark, where one of the inmates was so excited by our performance that he clambered onto the stage and tried to join in. He was led away by Peter Oliver, one of the performers.

We performed in Stockholm and then took the long journey south, passing through Germany and then into France. It was wondrous at that time of year to see the change in climate from the snowy wastelands of Norway to the springtime sunshine of the South of France. We did a show at Aix-en-Provence and then spent a few days off in San Remy, once home to Vincent van Gogh. I took a glorious cycle ride across the French countryside and saw Langlois Bridge at Arles, painted by van Gogh.

We then moved on to Nice, performing at the Palace Theatre. One lunchtime we were entertained in the hills outside the town; the wine began to flow and I puffed happily on a joint. The show that evening was rather difficult, to say the least. It was a frightening feeling, as if I was out of control, and I vowed never to drink or smoke dope before a performance again.

Peter Jonfield and I took a day trip to Cannes, where we swam and sunbathed on the beach – at a cost. It was something like £20, a lot of money in those days, just to have access. As the sun went down we noticed some ladies of the night in evidence, plying their trade on the backstreets, and we took advantage. I ended up with a sweet, petite French blonde. Peter went for the discounted version of sex, which was basically a knee-trembler in an alley with a woman he fancied whose leopard-skin attire was akin to Tarzan's mate Jane. As we compared notes on the way back to Nice, he said, 'It was amazing – I never saw anyone whip out the Kleenex so quickly!'

The tour ended with a few days in Avignon before we returned to England to recuperate and prepare for our next production. It was around this time that I was forced to change my name to John Clarkson Stewart Altman (Altman was a surname I had found in the index of a film annual) due to a clash with an elderly Equity member called John Stewart. Altman seemed to be the right colour and it wasn't pretentious in any way. Years later I was to meet the man from whom I took my surname, the renowned film director Robert Altman, whose films and way of working with actors I admired greatly.

***

A great deal of travelling with any form of band can do strange things to your head. We used a massive white Mercedes van and our passengers included doves and chickens. I remember one time Sheila Burnett and I decided to swap clothes before we ate in a café on the side of an Autobahn in Germany. We thought it might cause a stir but no one batted an eyelid.

Sheila and I had a lot of fun together. In our mid-twenties, we were the youngest members of the group. Unbeknownst to the rest of the group I fell for her quite deeply but a long-term relationship wasn't to be. These days she is a first-class professional photographer and married to Chris Jordan. We are old friends now.

***

In the summer of 1977 we started to prepare a show for Amsterdam and the routine was usually the same: Pip would have an idea for a story and we would sit around fleshing it out and improvising. That was the beauty of it – everything was completely original and organic. Once we got to Amsterdam I ended up living on a houseboat.

One of the biggest productions during my time with Pip Simmons was *The Masque of the Red Death*, adapted by Pip from the works of Edgar Allan Poe. As a huge fan of the writer I was thrilled to be involved. I possessed a collection of his poems with a foreword by Dante Gabriel Rossetti.

The production took over the entire Mickery Theatre in Amsterdam, where we created a graveyard and a room populated by live rats. The audience were dressed in cloaks and hoods and led by us, the performers, to each scene in the performance. Simmons was a pioneer of the 'immersive' style of performance that became popular a few years later . In one part, the audience were taken to the graveyard where Roderic Leigh was prematurely buried in a coffin with live rats inside. In the grand finale we took the audience to a pitch-black room and once assembled, the lights came up to a crescendo of Chris Jordan's music and the theatre-goers found themselves surrounded by rats. Screams and gasps ripped through the crowd. Dick Johnston, Steve Whitson and John Ricker were the creative team responsible for the stunning visual effects.

The *Haarlems Dagblad* reviewed the show, concluding, 'This production include well-played music, fantastic costumes and scenery and plenty to laugh at. Horror? Those who want horror shouldn't bother, those want to see a theatre fanatic depict an insane dream should come to Mickery during the next two weeks.'

Peter Oliver, the oldest member of the group, assigned me as a junior to look after the rats. They were relatively harmless, bought from a laboratory somewhere in Amsterdam, where they had been used in experimentation. I learned that there were many different types of rat (*rattus norvegicus* – also the title of The Stranglers' debut studio album) and it was the first time I'd 'worked' with rats – although I would meet a few later on in my career!

The upsetting part about taking care of the rats in the backroom of the theatre was that I had to intermittently kill some of them because they bred so quickly. I was tasked with having to scoop up the little pink baby rats from the cage, place them in a bucket of water and immediately take another bucket with a heavy weight in it and drop it on top of the first bucket. This was, according to the *Peter Oliver Book of Rat Extermination*, the quickest and most humane way of disposing of the young. Almost instantly they suffocated and drowned. As an avid swimmer and water lover I have heard that drowning is one of the least painful ways to die, though I don't know how anyone worked that out. I suppose it's got to be better than being burnt alive or blown up!

***

My final show with the group was *Woyzeck*: it wasn't so exciting or as spectacular as *Masque* but it was a typically Pip style of production in December 1977. It was expensive to mount, as they built a lake outside the Chapter Arts Centre in Cardiff – one of eight sets constructed around the theatre. Some of the scenes took place on a bridge over the water and the audience watched from the edges, having been led from inside the theatre. When the audience emerged, I poured gallons of petrol over the lake and set it alight – once again Pip had created a memorable dramatic moment. I always envisaged him going on to make movies similar to those created by directors such as Ken Russell but for whatever reason, sadly he never did. But Pip Simmons Theatre Group was my drama school and what an unforgettable time it was!

I was sad to leave Pip and the gang, but it was time to move on, and in the words of The Clash, in the year of punk, London was calling.

CHAPTER 11

THEY ALWAYS SAY THAT TIME CHANGES THINGS, BUT YOU ACTUALLY HAVE TO CHANGE THEM YOURSELF

ANDY WARHOL

After leaving Pip I was homeless for a while. I lived on a houseboat in Hammersmith owned and kindly lent to me by Roderic Leigh from the Simmons group. Then I moved on to stay in a flat in Hammersmith Grove owned by another Simmons member, Dick Johnson. The only time I ever had a threesome was in Dick's flat. I met the two young ladies in question at the Music Machine in Camden and invited them back – it was a very pleasurable night!

In the summer of 1977 I moved into 111 Sutherland Avenue, W9, a large basement bedsit with a back garden and toilet. Pip Simmons' musical director Chris Jordan had been renting it before me and when I moved in, I painted the room white. I was overjoyed to finally have my own place and in such a nice area – I lived there for a good five years or so. There were lots of fine pubs, including The Warrington, The Alfred and The Warwick Castle. I was close to the Grand Union Canal and if I'd spent all my money on a night out in the West End, I could always walk home at the end of it .

The occupants of the other bed-sitting rooms, in what had once been a large Victorian family residence, were an extraordinary collection of people. So much so that at one time I planned to write a TV series and call it *111 Sutherland Avenue*. Let me take you on a journey from the basement to the top of the house. Next door to me was an elderly gentleman, Dennis Wright, who tended the garden and acted as a caretaker. A friendly chap, he once showed me a photo in which he was walking down the gangplank of a luxurious yacht with Aristotle Onassis. Dennis had been a doctor but was struck off – I never managed to find out why. Looking back, I feel some sympathy for him having to put up with my regular all-night drinking sessions next door and the sound of the Sex Pistols late into the night can't have been fun. He never complained, even the night I took amyl nitrate and was carrying a mattress upstairs with my friend Hugh Boyson (whom I met on the set of *Quadrophenia*) for someone to sleep on and we kept falling downstairs, collapsing with laughter. Dennis gave me a brass Edwardian desk lamp when he moved out to Luton and I still have it today. I dug all his rose bushes up for him to take too – a surprisingly exhausting task, as the roots had spread out.

Opposite me were a couple known as The Smellies. There's not much to say about them: he worked in a baked bean factory. Above me lived Marlene Phillips from Aberdeen, Scotland, and Len Heymedinger, her English-Pakistani boyfriend. Like me, he was a Tottenham fan. When he was younger, skinheads kept beating him up on his way back from games so he decided if he couldn't beat them, he'd join them and ended up a Cockney-Pakistani skinhead. Opposite them on the ground floor were a Rastafarian and his wife and their baby. He was a bit of a randy Rasta, to say the least, and was having it off with a nurse. We got friendly and I perfected a Jamaican accent in the course of our conversations – though as yet I've not been called upon to use that accent as an actor! My friend Hugh Bryson ended up recording music with him.

There was a huge bathroom on the same floor as the nurse. I used to get very upset when people didn't clean the shared bath after them and I would pin up irate notices – the joys of bedsit living! The bathroom had great acoustics and I ended up recording some music in there with my friend Brady, a lead guitarist from Dublin.

Finally, on the very top floor lived one of Rick Wakeman's roadies with his volatile Portuguese girlfriend. At least once a week they would have a blazing row, ignited no doubt by a combination of his rock'n'roll intoxication and her passionate Mediterranean personality. It always sounded like murder was being committed up there – thankfully, it never was.

There was a highly dangerous crossroads to the right of my bedsit. I'd be asleep or reading a book and there would be a huge bang outside. Immediately I'd know it was yet another car crash outside and I would race out to see if I could help anyone.

After I'd been living in the house for about two years I was woken one night by a brightness in the room. There at the foot of the bed – or rather, mattress on the floor, the fashionable way of sleeping at the time – were a young boy and girl. They could have been twins. The same height, they were dressed in the fashion of the Edwardian times. I closed my eyes because I couldn't believe what I was seeing and thought I might try to get back to sleep because I was very tired. But I took one more glance, the light faded and then I saw that the figures had gone. I often wondered if there had been some tragedy in the house and these children had died young but I never found out the history of the place. Perhaps one day I will do so.

This wasn't the only time I experienced the supernatural. A few years earlier I had returned to my gatehouse on Dropmore estate after a long drive. I parked up and got out into the pitch darkness. There was no light, no stars and no moon. As I walked down the drive I could hear the sounds of a party inside the gatehouse. The place was miles from anywhere and there was no other noise. 'Ah, my art school friends have planned a surprise for my return home,'

I thought. The sound grew louder as I approached the front door but when I opened it, everything became abruptly silent. I was fascinated rather than frightened as I have an open mind about these sorts of occurrences.

Another brush with the supernatural came in 2010. On a hot summer's day in June I drove to Pluckley, Kent, apparently the most haunted village in the UK. I was staying at a hotel called Elvey Farm run by a couple, Simon and Jeff. The next day I was going to open the local Hog Fair. So I settled into the Canterbury suite having overlooked the spooky reputation since the hotel wasn't in the village itself.

I'd just come back from Los Angeles and I still had jet lag. At one point I woke up thinking I was still in LA. I fell asleep again and the next thing I knew, the bed was violently shaking, as if something in the middle was rocking it. When I opened my eyes, a pure beam of bright light was shining down on me from an orb up on the ceiling. The shaking began to die away and I couldn't believe what I was seeing. I remember being bathed in the light, closing my eyes and falling asleep again. Like before, I didn't feel at all frightened but I was certainly surprised and in awe of it all.

The next morning was a bit of a rush for I had to get to the Hog Fair. As I got up, I glanced at the ceiling to see if I'd left a light on but there were no fittings of any kind. A week later, I happened to speak to Jeff, the owner, on the phone and I mentioned what had happened.

'I forgot to tell you. That's probably the most haunted room in the entire hotel,' he told me.

About a year later I did stay there again, this time with my girlfriend Diana, but nothing else occurred.

A far more frightening encounter in Maida Vale was with the earthly forces of law, order and chaos. One freezing winter's night in the winter of 1979, I crossed over the railway tracks at Royal

Oak. I had scored some amphetamine sulphate from a pub on the Portobello Road. Then I walked back alone, wearing some heavy-duty cowboy boots and wrapped up well in a warm coat. As I crossed back over the railway footbridge, I noticed a policeman coming towards me. Immediately I felt paranoid about the gram of speed wrapped in silver paper. The officer said, 'Hello, son. Where are you off to, then?' (There was a fair bit of crime going on in the area near the Westway and perhaps I looked a little suspicious.)

Already I'd had a taste of the sulphate and was feeling highly energised. Without replying, I took off like a rocket. The officer set off in hot pursuit, radio crackling, and he called for backup. I made it through the icy wastelands of the tower blocks and onto the Harrow Road. He hadn't caught me but the run was horrendous. It was a nightmare because of my bulky winterwear – not least the cowboy boots which weren't built for sprints. As I ran past the shops I knew I had to act quickly as I could hear a police car on its way. I reached into my coat pocket, took out the sulphate and hurled it onto the road, where it disappeared into the snow that had fallen that night.

The police car cut me off and I was arrested due to my guilty behaviour. I was taken to Harrow Road police station, where they gave me a thorough search and put me in a cell. They kept asking why I had run away. I just said I was afraid that I might be framed. They kept me there until about three in the morning, puzzling over my attempted escape.

A little voice inside my head whispered, 'Hey, Johnny, why don't you see if you can find that gear on your way home?' So I returned to the parade of shops and looked in the road. There was the packet, flattened and soaked through by the snow. But I knew it would be foolish to retrieve it whatever state it was in and very exhausted, I made my way back to 111.

***

One of the most perfect relationships I ever had was with a blonde actress and model from Hampstead village called Desirée Erasmus. We met at the *Quadrophenia* premiere in 1979 and our time together was devoid of possessiveness, jealousy and any other negative emotions that often arise in relationships. There was no pressure and we both felt very free together. According to my friend Simon Cutter, I once proposed to her but I have no memory of doing that. There was no animosity in our parting – we simply drifted away from one another, after about a year and a half together.

***

I was out one Saturday with Kate Martin and the Sex Pistols were playing on a roof on the King's Road so we went down to see if we could spot them. Admittedly I had the obligatory long hair and was clasping a can of Special Brew, but I wasn't causing any trouble despite my punky look in 1978. Kate went into a shop to get something and said when she came out, she simply saw me being bundled into the back of a police van – they had obviously been sent down and told to arrest anyone causing any problems. I had been leaning against a wall, sipping my lager. So they grabbed anyone they could and then tried to charge me with wilful obstruction. They took me down to the station. Kate followed to make sure I got out OK and then acted as a witness to vouch I hadn't actually been doing anything. The whole thing went to Pimlico Magistrates' Court and in the end I got off but it was a time of the authorities versus us and often we were arrested for nothing.

In fact, the King's Road was the scene of another brush with the law. One very sunny Saturday I was busking down there and the money was flowing in. I was playing my Echo 12 string and my friend Brady was on lead guitar, so we sounded good as we played Who and Bowie songs among many others. Suddenly I saw a big black boot kick my can of lager over and I looked up to see the police there. I nearly lost my temper but cooled it down when we thought we might be arrested for a breach of the peace. It was the opposite from the time we busked underneath the National Terrorist Unit on the Edgware Road. We were playing in an underpass, unaware that the police could hear us in their office up in the block above us. As opposed to the beat cops in Chelsea, who kicked over my can of lager and got stroppy, two guys dressed in suits came down and said: 'We are really sorry to stop your music but unfortunately, it is interrupting all the work we are trying to do up there, so if you wouldn't mind moving along. We would like to say we have been enjoying it, but we are afraid you will have to stop.' We both packed up and went on our way.

***

My good friends, brother and sister Hugh and Hetta Boyson and her husband Marc, were renowned for their parties – both in their Bayswater flat and a country house in Bedfordshire, the Hyde. This was owned by the Boysons' aunt and uncle, Helen and David Hambro – part of the banking dynasty. Those were wild weekends! Mark used to cook up a storm and the partying would carry on late into the night (and sometimes the next morning). Guests included Martin Clunes, Hugh Silver and various other lively characters from the worlds of television and advertising. They were good times I'll never forget.

***

One of the cushiest jobs I ever had was being a prototype for one of the Hawkmen in *Flash Gordon* at Shepperton Studios in 1980. I was used as a model and they carved my shape out of polystyrene – I'm not sure why, I think maybe some of the Hawkmen flying around were props rather than real actors. They also attached wings to me and flew me in the air to test out the action prior to filming.

It was a Dino De Laurentiis production and the art director was his fellow Italian Danilo Donati. He invited me back to his Thames-side bungalow for lunch one day and his driver took us back there. For the duration of the shoot he'd had his apartment in Rome recreated at great expense in his hired home. After lunch, the driver disappeared and Mr Donati made his move. In the style of Benny Hill, he chased me round the bungalow and pinned me to the wall. He was becoming very excited – 'Oh, John-a, John-a!' – while I insisted I wasn't interested. Eventually he took my repeated refusals for an answer and thrust a £20 note in my top pocket – for what reason I don't know. Perhaps the thrill of the chase turned him on. From then on Mr Donati didn't talk to me much and my employment was terminated shortly afterwards – I've no idea why!

***

I was the last to move out of the house in Maida Vale. In fact I was bought out of my place before I moved to Chelsea. Looking back on my time at 111, it was truly wonderful and I have so many great memories. I was young, carefree and I completed several films while I lived there – *Birth of The Beatles, Quadrophenia, The First Great Train Robbery* and *Remembrance,* to name but a few and I wrote many songs too. Towards the end of my time there a girl called Tracey Lewis moved in with me and she became one of the great loves of my life. An actor, Simon Cutter, was one of the many friends I made in the area. He starred as a very attractive Helen of Troy in *Doctor Faustus* in the West End. Patrick Magee was Mephistopheles and one night someone heckled him. He stopped the show, pointed out the miscreant and said in the deep, booming tones of the character of the devil, 'When you sell your second-hand bicycles in the alleyways of Soho, do *I* interrupt you?' I picked up 'his bottle' of red wine at a party in the theatre once, and was severely berated. 'That is my bottle,' he boomed once again.

Eventually Simon moved into a house in South Kensington with the renowned actor Peter Eyre. I had previously met Peter many years earlier at the start of my career at the Grand Theatre in Leeds when he was on tour with the Prospect Theatre Company. An actor's life is often one of extreme contrasts. I recall attending very grand parties at Peter and Simon's house, where I would mingle with the likes of Trevor Nunn, Jack Nicholson, Warren Beatty, Janet Suzman (I had a huge crush on her), Barry Humphries and Lady Antonia Fraser and Harold Pinter. At the end of the night I would retrieve my bicycle chained to the railings outside and pedal back home across London via Hyde Park to my bedsit in Maida Vale.

CHAPTER 12

HE WHO HAS HEALTH HAS HOPE AND HE WHO HAS HOPE HAS EVERYTHING
PROVERB

The first thing I needed was an agent and to be out at the right parties. Having parted company with Pip Simmons and back in London once again, I threw myself into socialising in the hope something would come up that way. Every actor I've ever known has had a moan about his or her agent. Someone once told me that the collective noun for a group of actors is a 'moan' because if they're out of work they 'moan' and when they're in work they also 'moan'! My grandfather (and fellow actor), Johnnie Schofield junior, once described agents as 'bloodsuckers'.

I met the casting director Patsy Pollock at a party for the theatrical designer Andrew McAlpine. We embarked on an affair and she introduced me to a couple of people and ended up putting me forward for *Quadrophenia*. Originally I was up for 'Ace Face', Sting's part. It has long been seen as an era-defining film, based around The Who's 1973 concept album of the same name about a London mod,

Jimmy Cooper (Phil Daniels). Disillusioned by his family and his job as a post room boy, Jimmy finds an outlet for his teenage angst with his Mod friends but he lets this obsession with the mod lifestyle take over his life, falling apart when he pushes it all too far.

Set in 1963, the production had a big cast – many of whom were unknowns like me in their first film role. There was Sting, Ray Winstone, Phil Daniels and Timothy Spall to name but a few. The role of Jimmy was originally intended for John Lydon of the Sex Pistols, but he was deemed such a liability he was refused insurance for the part.

The film was shot mostly in Brighton over the summer of 1979 and, apart from one party scene that was shot in the studio, the rest were filmed on location. Beachy Head, where Jimmy attempts suicide at the end of the film, was the location of a real-life suicide that supposedly influenced the film's ending. I didn't get Sting's part but I was told that they wanted a few actors to be on hand, ready to step in for smaller parts that would evolve as they were writing. They needed a few people they could rely on to come up with the extra lines, like the all-time classic: 'What's that fuckin' rocker doing here?'

The cast was quite extraordinary, really – what you see on the screen is pretty much how I was living. Having sex, drinking, drugging and dancing.

Franc Roddam, the director, was a veteran of documentaries and he brought a great realism to the film. I was thrilled to be part of the production, as I'd loved The Who album for many years. It was a learning curve for me when I played the mod called John. I had never worked long-term on a film before and so I soaked it all up. Some actors say they get bored on film sets, but to this day that certainly isn't the case for me. I was learning about the lighting, camera work and sound, etc. and performing stunts.

When Roddam asked for volunteers to fight with the rockers in the freezing cold sea off Brighton beach, I was only too glad to take part. The deckchairs were made of balsa wood so it didn't matter if you broke one over someone's head. Soon the riots on the seafront on Union Street became very realistic. Dozens of mods from all over the country had come to work on the film and some of the actors dressed as policemen unfortunately suffered a real pummelling at their hands. Not being professional actors, the mods couldn't divorce stunt fighting from the real thing! We were lining up for a second take on Union Street when a little old lady, clutching her shopping bag, scuttled past me down an alleyway and muttered, 'Oh dear, it's happening all over again!' She'd obviously been affected by the real riots back in 1965.

We relocated to London for the rest of the filming and they kept me on until the end. *Quadrophenia* is one of the few productions – including theatrical work – after which I've kept in touch with most of the cast. You don't always keep in touch with everyone, sometimes one or two, but a great bond was formed with this cast. I still have the pleasure of occasionally seeing Phil Daniels, Mark Wingett, Garry Cooper, Phil Davis, Toyah and Trevor Laird.

Quadrophenia went on to become an enduring cult classic and an immersive event attended by Franc Roddam and various members of the cast, myself included, recently sold out at the Apollo in Hammersmith. It all fitted in with where I wanted to be at that time. My social scene was one of actors and musicians. I would hang out round West Hampstead, Maida Vale, Portobello Road, Ladbroke Grove, Camden, Kilburn and Hampstead. I spent my days writing songs and then we would all meet in the Warwick Castle on a Saturday night. Glen Matlock from the Sex Pistols became a friend and Nick Kant (the best journalist on the *NME*) would pop by occasionally.

For me at the time the drug of choice was cocaine, but always with the booze creeping up alongside it. I fell in with a crowd of musicians and artists from Brazil who knew how to get hold of the most amazing gear. So pure and uncut, it was like putting stars up your nose and the universe in your brain!

***

I was at a huge party in a smart mansion block in Maida Vale with the Sex Pistols, Thin Lizzy and Gary Holton, when I saw some white powder lined up on the table. So I snorted a line , waiting for it to take effect. Then I started to realise something had gone wrong. While I knew what to expect from cocaine, this wasn't it and I was sick as a dog. I realised then it was smack that I had just taken. As soon as the drug started to kick in, it dawned on me. It actually felt very similar to the time I'd visited an opium den in India.

***

When the filming for *Quadrophenia* wrapped, I knew that I needed other work lined up – I was desperate to keep the momentum going. As luck would have it, I met Esther and Beth Charkham at another party and visited their offices the next day with a handful of 8 x 10 black and white photos. I went on to do the same for a handful of well-respected casting directors in Soho. Now I had an agent, Peter Crouch, recommended to me by some friends in the business. (I was with him for about four years; he had an assistant called Penny who was good, but he wasn't really hustling enough for me and never seemed to get me much work.)

I knew I had to create my own luck. Esther and Beth pinned my photo to their board and it just so happened that a few weeks later they found themselves casting for a Beatles film and needed lookalikes. They looked up at the board and thought of me. So I went to a general casting where I came face to face with half a dozen Georges, a few Pauls and a couple of guys with noses like Ringo all sitting around, hoping the likeness was good enough. The casting had many stages; the first one was to take Polaroids of everyone and scrutinise the facial similarities. Then they whittled it down and sent scripts to those who had made it through the first round. You were told to learn your scene off by heart and then, one by one in we went and performed. Back then they videoed auditions before sending the videotapes over to America for the final decision.

I had kept some old Beatles Fan Club discs and records so I played them to help get George's voice into my head. Again for this audition, I had an advantage as I played the guitar. As an actor there's nothing more annoying than if you watch someone playing a singer in a film and they are standing there with the guitar simply holding down a G chord, when they're supposed to be playing F, A minor and C as well. It doesn't look good!

The audition was at Wembley Studios and we videoed a scene with three other Beatles and Brian Jameson (who played Brian Epstein). Something special seemed to occur during that audition. Somehow it seemed to click between Steve Mackenna (who auditioned for John Lennon) and the rest of us. We then travelled back into London on the Metropolitan line on a sunny afternoon. We parted not knowing if we'd got the job but Steve looked at me and said, 'I've got a feeling we're going to be seeing each other again, kid.'

'Yeah, I think you're right,' I said.

And he was. Two weeks passed and then we received the call to say we had scored our dream jobs – playing members of the Fab Four.

I was particularly excited to have landed the part of George. As early as primary school, when you had to have a favourite Beatle out in the playground, I'd choose George partly because even then I always thought we looked similar. Like me he was a Pisces. Being the youngest member of the group and overshadowed by Lennon and McCartney, he was a junior member but I always thought his songs were just as good. He proved himself to be a highly talented tunesmith in his own right, with songs such as 'Something', 'Here

Comes the Sun' and after The Beatles, the magnificent album, *All Things Must Pass*.

I didn't mention that I'd secured the *Birth of The Beatles* film when I next visited my agent, Peter Crouch. His first comment was, 'Not a lot about, John. Things are a bit quiet.' I chuckled to myself before telling him that I was going to play George Harrison.

***

When I was seventeen, in 1969, an Italian student called Elena stayed with my family. She was obsessed with John Lennon and wanted to get a letter to him. While she didn't know where her idol lived, she did have an address for George Harrison in Esher, in Surrey. One Saturday, the two of us took the train to London and from Waterloo, travelled to the nearest station, still a two-mile walk from Esher town centre. We only had a vague idea of where he was. A couple of locals pointed us in the right direction and eventually we found his home, 'Kinfauns' on Claremont Drive, about a mile further on.

It was obvious which bungalow was George's – the walls were covered with bright, colourful psychedelic artwork done by the Beatle himself and various friends. We rang the bell and his wife Pattie Boyd answered. I explained that we wanted George to pass on the message to John. She said she was sorry but George was fast asleep, having been recording at Abbey Road Studios all night. They must have been the sessions that would result in the album *Abbey Road*. We left the letter with Pattie and headed home. It would be the closest I got to meeting my favourite – or indeed any other – Beatle.

***

The remainder of the cast for *Birth of The Beatles* included Steve Mackenna (John Lennon), Ray Ashcroft (Ringo Starr), Rod Culbertson (Paul McCartney), Ryan Michael (Pete Best), David

Wilkinson as Stuart Sutcliffe and Nigel Havers portraying George Martin. The director was Richard Marquand. Mike Angelis (of *Liver Birds*' fame) was our Liverpudlian dialect coach. The trouble was he did such a good job with our accents that we were completely incomprehensible to the American market and the entire film had to be re-dubbed! The real Pete Best was technical and historical advisor.

By today's standards the shoot was fast. We started in Liverpool, in the World War II bombsites that were still a feature of the city, cobblestone backstreets and the rundown docks. Soon we found ourselves bonding and as we all played our instruments, we became quite a tight unit on set, having great fun and fooling around as The Beatles themselves used to do.

I remember that dear Pete Best, a lovely man, became quite emotional when we recreated the scenes outside The Cavern Club when fans demonstrated to keep Pete in the group rather than have Ringo Starr (at that time Pete had been working in the local unemployment benefit office). Thankfully, many years later, when *The Beatles Anthology* came out, it featured some recordings that he was on and he finally made some money out of having been a Beatle.

We filmed all over London, including Tottenham Court Road, Twickenham and Ealing. At Twickenham Town Hall Richard Marquand deliberately kept dozens of teenage girls waiting on the dance floor for us to come onstage. Dressed in black leather, we belted out 'Johnny B Goode'. This was the start of the Litherland ballroom gig, one of The Beatles' first big appearances in Liverpool. Richard had told the crowd to go wild and with so much pent-up energy, that's exactly what they did. I was almost dragged off the stage by some of the girls at the front. We got some great footage as early Beatlemania was recreated.

Our Beatle suits were made by a tailor called Dave Wax, who had a shop in Hammersmith (and still does), and had designed the original outfits for the band – I wish I'd kept mine! I still have a leather jacket and a *Birth of The Beatles* bomber jacket from that time.

The next location was Hamburg. Having hitched through Germany and toured there with Pip Simmons, I'd always found the people to be most kind and hospitable. The cast and crew spent just twenty-four hours in the city, during which we had to cover the whole of The Beatles' formative times spent around the Kaiserkeller on a street called the Reeperbahn and other rundown clubs of the early 1960s. We mostly did exterior work and black-and-white stills photography, with the interior scenes shot back in London. The area looked as though it hadn't changed much since The Beatles were there.

We were befriended by an entrepreneur called Klaus, who seemed to have his fingers in lots of pies, including clubs. Once we'd completed the day's filming, fairly late in the evening, Richard Marquand said we were free to do as we pleased for the rest of the night. We took him at his word and met up with Klaus, who took us on a tour of the neighbourhood.

'I will show you an area,' he confided, 'where you will see more beautiful girls all in one place at the same time than anywhere you have ever been.'

We had no idea what he was talking about.

He took us along the Reeperbahn and stepped off the road up an alleyway. We went through a door and seemed to have arrived in an indoor concrete car park lined with chrome rails. Women stood by them, leaning on the rails and waiting to be picked up. Each had a room nearby she could go to with clients for sex. We were stunned at the sight and this was the beginning of a night during which we relived many of the antics of The Beatles themselves in Hamburg. I knew from my research that George Harrison, who was only seventeen at the time, had lost his virginity in the city.

Klaus took us back to his penthouse suite, where he supplied us with champagne and a girl each of our choice. It was a night that none of us would ever forget. We didn't get back to our hotel until dawn.

On the flight back I remember my pulse was racing and I thought I might have a mid-air heart attack – *Donner und Blitzen*! When we reached the UK we all agreed that it was one of the best twenty-four hours we'd ever spent.

At this point I must mention Richard Marquand. He was a very special man, a sensitive director who never lost his temper, even during the most difficult situations. A rising star, he went on to make *Return of the Jedi* – which I also briefly worked on – and then the excellent thriller *Jagged Edge*, with Glenn Close and Jeff Bridges. *Hearts of Fire* was another rock film of his, this one featuring a real musician in the shape of Bob Dylan. Tragically, Richard died of a stroke just before his fiftieth birthday without seeing the release of his final film. I'm sure he would have gone on to greater things if only he had lived longer.

Birth of The Beatles (1979) was released just nine years after the break-up of the original band and was the only biopic to be made while John Lennon was still alive. It opened with the group driving in a car with their manager Brian Epstein and John's first wife, Cynthia Lennon. It was 1964 and they were heading to America for the very first time after having massive success in Europe and they begin to remember the days before they became famous. The film ends with the group in America performing on *The Ed Sullivan Show* to a mass of screaming fans. The songs were recorded by Beatles tribute act Rain.

When I was signed to the Beatles film I thought I'd made it – I distinctly remember saying to myself, 'Hollywood, here I come', especially as it was being produced by an American company and Dick Clark was in charge. I thought there would be a premiere in Leicester Square with a whole red carpet extravaganza, with trips to

LA to launch and publicise it, and that I would at last achieve fame and fortune. The reality was they decided to turn it into a TV film and my much-hyped, red carpet world premiere ended up with the BBC showing it one rainy October night. I was sat on a beanbag in Esta Charkham's flat in Barnes with the rest of the cast. When it was later shown again, in early 1985, by coincidence it went out during the same week as a transmission of the British war movie *Went the Day Well?* starring my grandfather, Johnnie Schofield junior.

Around this time I felt very despondent and so I went back to Peter Crouch to see what else was going on. He just kept saying things were very quiet so I decided to finish with him and instead signed up with Annette Stone.

Things immediately started to happen once I moved to Annette Stone Associates. Based in Harrow, she was young, attractive and energetic and seemed ideal. The first thing she got me was a tiny part as a rebel fighter pilot in *Return of the Jedi*. It was a dream come true and I went to Elstree Studios to spend a few days filming. I met Carrie Fisher and Harrison Ford and remember driving into town with Richard Marquand and George Lucas – a special memory. It was an exciting time and I marvelled at the technical expertise surrounding me. I had one line – 'We're going in now!' or words to that effect– which I delivered from the cockpit of an X-wing fighter. I was seated in front of a huge blue screen, which by the magic of the special effects people would be transformed into a scene in outer space.

***

During my time in Maida Vale I appeared in several films, beginning with *The First Great Train Robbery* (1979), directed by Michael Crichton and based on the true story of a gold bullion train robbed in the Kentish countryside on its way to pay soldiers at war in the Crimea. The late Mary Selway had cast me as a pickpocket alongside one of my favourite actors, Donald Sutherland. Imagine my surprise on the morning of filming as I sat in the make-up department of Pinewood Studios, when Sutherland himself came into the room and asked my fellow pickpocket actor and I if we would like to accompany him onto the set to rehearse our scene. This was taking place on the Strand in London as it would have looked in Victorian times. It was breathtaking to see the detailed recreation of the famous street on the backlot of Pinewood Studios, including shops, pavements and the church at the far end. Dozens of extras were all around, dressed in their period finery.

Our thievery was a slick operation – my friend bumped into our target, Donald picked his pocket and I tipped my hat, into which he dropped the wallet and we walked off-camera. What a treat to work with one of my favourite actors of all time, a consummate professional and also a very nice man! I also saw Sean Connery and Lesley-Anne Down while I was at the studios.

Other films I appeared in around this time were *An American Werewolf in London* (1981), in which I played a policeman, *Memoirs of a Survivor* (1981) with Julie Christie, TV movie *The Scarlet Pimpernel* (1982) with Ian McKellen and Anthony Andrews and the Channel 4 award-winning film, *Remembrance* (1982), with Timothy Spall and Gary Oldman.

I recall a wild Halloween night at The Post House Hotel while filming *Remembrance*, with Gary Oldman and Martin Barrass. They dared me to break into a hotel bar and steal an optic of whisky. Which I duly did. We took it up to my room and got very drunk watching Jack Nicholson get drunk in a film on TV. The next morning I went for a run and my head felt as though the top had come off, or perhaps that it was hinged and kept opening and then banging back down with every step. Painful.

CHAPTER 13

THERE IS A TIDE IN THE AFFAIRS OF MEN.
WHICH, TAKEN AT THE FLOOD, LEADS ON TO FORTUNE
WILLIAM SHAKESPEARE, *JULIUS CAESAR*

Prior to *EastEnders*, in early 1984 I was given a diary by my good friends Tammy, Gemma and Debbie Smith. I decided to take up writing as a form of therapy in what was a lonely and difficult time and I've kept up the practice ever since. Not long afterwards, I captured a telling snapshot of how things were for me at the time:

The best way to spend an English Sunday is in Barbados. (I hadn't actually been at that point). No, seriously, one of the most abysmal ways is to be living on your own, which proves how much I've grown up, although I really don't mind it these days. You rise with a hangover and grope your way out of the front door to buy the Sunday papers at the nearest tube station. When you get there you either find they've sold out of your favourite papers or there aren't any colour supplements, the best part of it in general.

You get home and find there's not one good thing to watch

on the TV all day. You phone up all the people you can think of and they're either out, in bed with a lover or too hungover to meet up. You fancy a drink to console yourself but all the pubs and off-licences are closed until 7 o'clock and it's now 2.10 pm. What to do? Cook up some beans on toast and even read the business section of *The Sunday Times*. If any of you Martians are thinking of landing on Earth on Sunday in England, don't. It will bore you to death.

It was a time of grey skies, rain, endless phone calls to find accommodation and often being turned down for rented property due to not being employed full-time (despite the fact that I had never once missed a rent payment in my life). I remember it being a time of despair, anger and loneliness too.

Early April 1984 – I was sinking financially and looking back at my diaries, the worry is clear when I see the line: 'my finances are fast dwindling, praying for a well-timed play or TV show to come through. I am just as capable as most of the same old faces I keep seeing on TV.' I needed a break from my own mental energy; I wasn't sleeping for more than four hours a night and it was like a steady whirlpool of disappointment. The drinking was starting to get to me, too – I was reaching my limit. It's funny how at these moments when something has to give, it often does, and when you least expect it.

The truth is that Nick was absolutely everything I was not but I didn't really have a choice about playing him. Do I regret saying yes? The truth is that I do at times, when I think about what might have been. It's a strange experience, writing a book. The first thing you quickly discover is that those times have been left tucked away in the past for a reason – in my case, because they were hard times. Despite a great few years doing all the things you have read about, I hadn't yet had my 'moment'. Although I was grateful at the thought of regular income, I didn't think *EastEnders* was 'it' at the time it was offered to me. I have gone back through some of my old diaries and found entries that certainly highlight my thoughts and when committing them to paper, I was definitely very honest about how low I felt:

> The one good thing about my situation at the moment is having Annette Stone as my agent. She has 6 years experience as an assistant to a top agent behind her, she has a very pleasant manner and warmth combined with a mean business streak. She phoned today and asked me to prepare a piece of Shakespearian comedy, which I found pretty tough going. I remember very clearly being tortured by the fact that I wasn't word perfect so I phoned Annette and she was brilliant at dishing out words of comfort on the phone – 'Just do the best you can.' Sound advice for anyone.

I remember that audition so well – I waited an hour to be seen and watched one actor just get up and leave. After all that preparation and time spent, how could anyone simply walk away? When I think back it's hard to describe the debilitating combination of auditioning and flat hunting – the endless flats that were too tiny, too gloomy, traipsing round the agencies and the endless phone calls. Worse still was the fact I knew I didn't have the income to necessarily pay for where I needed to live. After spending time flicking through notes made to myself then, I found a sentence that summed up perfectly what was happening: 'What I truly need is a completely new situation in work, love and living.'

And then, at the start of 1984, things began to look up as my agent began to send me on a series of what I would call serious 'stage' auditions:

IN THE NICK OF TIME

JANUARY 1984

Tomorrow I will be auditioning for Pinkie in *Brighton Rock*. I have decided to learn the scene where he puts a message on a record for Rose. God, I'd love to play that part, I know I could. Work for me would be the ideal therapy at the moment, far more gratifying than a holiday. On a wet and windy day I made my way to the *Brighton Rock* audition. I'd prepared a piece from the book which I thought would stand me in good stead but from the reaction of the director, it was clear it didn't work. I could do with this part of Pinky more than anything at the moment. The therapy of some good hard work would help more than anything. The director told me that playing Pinkie would be tougher than *Hamlet*. I know I could do it.

I'm sure you can tell from this that I was a bit of a lost soul, looking for meaningful work to put to use all the training I'd done, and also be paid some money too. I was also keen to settle down and build a stable life. In short, I wanted to be a proper grown-up, reinforced by the following entry:

JANUARY 16TH 1984

My mother is 64 today and I sent her some precious books to glance through. I hope I can one day find a certain form of relationship happiness like my parents. I am prepared to be patient in waiting to find the right person and when that time comes, I will surely know.

I'd had what I would call these 'half moments' of potential success and it took a while to get over the Beatles film being relegated to TV, and then suddenly there was talk of a new BBC series that was getting a lot of hype – a gritty show, *E8*, as it was called to begin with, was being tipped as the big 'next thing' on TV. It sounded quite unlike its ITV rival, *Coronation Street*. It was to be a bi-weekly drama that followed the lives and trials of specific authentic, East End families.

Annette Stone heard they were looking for actors and promptly put my name forward for one of the original characters. She called me up and said she would like to put me up for a part in a new soap opera. I remember she said, 'You look right for the part of Nick Cotton. I am going to send your photograph and CV to the casting department of *EastEnders* by post.' I was duly summoned to Bush House on Shepherd's Bush Green in the autumn of 1984. When I got there I met director Matthew Robinson, a few of the writers and some people from production, co-creator Tony Holland and most importantly I would eventually meet the great Matriach herself, Julia Smith later on as she wasn't there to begin with.

I would soon find out that, just like Margaret Thatcher, she was the best 'man' for the job – she took no nonsense and spent her time putting her cabinet permanently in their place.

Right from the start the writers had a very clear idea of what Nick was about, and one word summed it up: trouble. I talked it through with Annette and her instruction was clear – go dressed for aggravation! Her advice was to go in jeans, Doc Martens or trainers, sporting a leather jacket and T-shirt. She also advised that I should gel my hair back, wear an earring and look menacing. For me (the boy from Berkshire) the big stumbling block was that they were looking for a genuine East Ender. They had done their research to give the series the authenticity that Northern shows like *Coronation Street* had, both in terms of set, clothing, accents and names – they got a lot of the original family names that still exist in the show, like Cotton, Fowler and Beale, from graveyards in places like Hoxton.

The only recent job I had actually seen through to production at that time was one commercial for Gillette razors. I was a hungry actor waiting on tables in Chelsea . My career had slumped and I needed the cash.. So I got out the *A–Z* and set about recreating a reality for Nick. I looked up an address in Hoxton, memorised it, and worked on my accent.

I went into the audition as Nick . Nick was supposed to be twenty-two whereas I was a decade older, another vital piece of information I managed to disguise, thanks to my mother's genes (she has always looked ten years younger).

So I perfected the restless youth – a bit jittery, a bit paranoid, as you would be if you'd grown up around criminals and bad behaviour. I had played cockneys before and it was my mission to make those producers believe I was a born-and-bred East Ender. To make it not quite a total lie, I concocted an elaborate tale about how, in the 1950s, my family had moved out of the East End, in the overflow, to Reading. So that meant we lived out that way throughout my childhood with my truck driver dad. Imagine my father, who worked at the Bank of England, being portrayed as someone who drove a truck. I'm not sure he ever knew that's how I got the part – probably just as well, really!

I saw getting *EastEnders* as a means to an end and a way out of what was fast becoming financial meltdown. I'd been waiting on tables at a farmers' market restaurant in Chelsea and had just landed a job in a restaurant in neighbouring Fulham, where part of the deal was much-needed and very delicious free food and the possibility of tips upwards of £40 per table (a lot of money then). I got that job just as I was told about *EastEnders* – ironic, really!

As fate would have it, on the very day of my audition Julia Smith wasn't there (as I previously mentioned) when I arrived. The rest of the team were super-apologetic about the inconvenience and asked if I would be willing to come back that afternoon. Obviously, even in those early days she ruled with an iron grip and nothing was decided in her absence even if that meant sending away people who were there to audition at the allotted hour.

I had worked hard to get into character and was steeped in everything I believed Nick should be – keeping up the feeling of menace I had psyched myself into. So, when they asked if I would be willing to postpone I just glared at them, still in full Nick mode, and muttered 'Yeah, s'pose so.' Armed with the script I now had a couple of hours to learn my part off by heart. Someone must have been looking down on me that day for it was one of those rare occasions when it all fell into place. I strode along to Shepherd's Bush Market.

I found a greasy spoon. Ironically, it was similar to Kathy Beale's café in Albert Square, where Nick was to spend much of his time drinking tea and hiding from those he had traumatised. I memorised as much of the script as I could. When I went back in Julia was there. We met for the first time, I stood up and I did the audition and it was spot on. I can't remember exactly what I had to say, probably some deeply profound and kindly words from the first episode like 'What you doing here, you stupid Turk?' or even 'Stuff your poxy pub!'

I acted my way through the whole audition , appearing to be almost like Nick, but not so much that they thought I would be difficult to work with. It obviously worked well because not only did I get the job but on the first day of rehearsal on the *EastEnders*' lot at Elstree, director Matthew Robinson said, 'Oh dear, John! What are we going to do about your accent?'

I switched to cockney mode and answered, 'Don't worry, Maffyew. It's gonna be alright.'

I have no idea if I would have been successful had the fates not conspired to make Julia Smith absent from that first morning audition – perhaps it would have gone to Gary Holton, who was also up for the part – the two of us seemed to circle each other for certain roles and this was definitely one of them. I don't know who else was up for it but a few days later, I heard it was mine.

In the meantime some doubts had surfaced in my head: 'Do you really want to do this?' they screamed. Now, I don't feel so bad writing this because I know other long-term soap actors, particularly June Brown (Dot Cotton) and Pam St Clement (Pat Butcher), have shared the worries they felt at committing long-term to a drama like this. The thing is, from the off you know with strongly drawn characters like Nick that you're at the mercy of the storyline and whether or not the public take you to their hearts. It's a lottery, and being in people's living rooms (twice a week as it was then, but now four times a week), it's so easy to get typecast and if you happen to be playing a 'baddie' too that brings with it a lot of extra limitations.

There was a stigma attached to soaps and it is still there to this day. In the English acting world, whether we like it or not, there are different cliques and sections – it can be terribly snobbish – and my terror of being typecast was ever-present, even then right at the start. It probably seems strange and somewhat ungrateful, given how much I needed money at that time, to say it was one of the biggest dilemmas of my life but it was one of the hardest professional decisions I have ever had to make, and I spent a good week thinking about whether to take it, and talking it over with Kitty Aldridge, my girlfriend at the time.

At the time I was offered the role of Nick it was only temporary and I had no idea that it would last almost as long as the age I was when I accepted the part for the first time. It was a risk, but on the plus side I was part of the very first episode, which is a great situation to be in, so I said yes and took myself off to Boston and New York before I started rehearsing.

A pilot film about the life of John Lennon, *The John Lennon Story* (1984) produced by Imagine Films, was being made in Boston and once again I would be playing George Harrison. Luckily, my nephew Sean James was staying with me at Sydney Street. We had stayed up until 5am and I didn't hear the phone alarm call. If it hadn't been for Sean, I would have missed the plane. Luckily, South Kensington is on the same line as Heathrow. At the airport I jumped all the queues, ran down all the walkways and made the flight, sweating profusely, with my heart pounding.

I stayed at the Plaza in Boston with Midge Weissman (who played Paul McCartney) and Garry Gibson (John Lennon). Keith Entel directed us. Filming went well and then I travelled on Amtrak to New York with Keith Hughes . I nearly got arrested by a train guard because students were jumping off the train and running across the tracks to avoid paying. He thought I was helping them but luckily Keith came to my rescue. Arriving by night at Penn station, New York with its lights seemed like a sea of jewels. My first impression was that it was much more than I thought it would be from films and TV – bigger and louder. Somebody back in the UK had said it was the best time of year to be there and they were right: it was 75 degrees in October 1984.

I stayed with my friend Karl Kholer near the Lower East Side. It was so exciting at long last to be in New York. Along with my visit to Boston I was loving being in America. Karl had several cats and kittens in his apartment and they would wake me up in the morning, tickling my feet.

On my first day, while Karl was still asleep, I looked at a map and naively decided to go running in Battery Park, deeper on the Lower East Side. I noticed the roads weren't quite so well made up and there were no white faces to be seen at all. Nothing untoward happened but when I got back and told Karl where I'd run, he said, 'What? John, you know how dangerous it is down there? You're lucky to still be alive!' I told him not to be so silly and later I took him on a run in the same area just to prove it was safe. Which it was, although we did have some fruit and vegetables thrown at us along the way!

My many adventures included a breath-taking ride in a helicopter round the skyscrapers, lots of parties, dancing, art galleries, a boat trip around Manhattan and seeing the Statue of Liberty. I met a lovely girl called Debbie, and we dated throughout my time there,

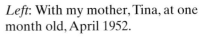
Left: With my mother, Tina, at one month old, April 1952.

Right: After a swim with my dad, Cecil, Herne Bay, Kent, 1964.

Left: Leaving Dover for India in September 1969, aged just seventeen.

Above: My mother and father at 19 Beltinge Road, our home in Herne Bay, in the early 1980s.

Above left: A night in London's West End with my wife, Bridget, in 1986.

Above right: With my dear granddaughter Lily, aged one, in 2015.

Below: Three generations: Rosanna, Lily and Tina at my niece Jaqui's wedding in Whitstable, Kent, in 2015.

Above: Resurrection, the best band I ever had. Left to right: Phil Brown, Ben Matthews, 'Johnny Rio' (my rock 'n' roll persona then), Brady.

Below left: On the road with the Pip Simmons Theatre Group. (*© Sheila Burnett*)

Below right: Group, 1976/77, having a ball – seeing Europe and getting my Equity card.

(*© Sheila Burnett*)

Above left: As George Harrison in *Birth of The Beatles*, 1979.

Above right, upper: 'The Fab Four' – first Polaroid shot of the line-up.

Above right, lower: Left to right: Ray Ashcroft (Ringo), Steve Mackenna (John), Rod Culbertson (Paul), John Altman (George).

Below: As Midwink in the 1995 BBC1 television series *Black Hearts in Battersea*, with Roger Bizley as Captain Dark.

Above left: My first panto. Playing the Wicked Queen's henchman in *Snow White and he Seven Dwarves* at the Newcastle Theatre Royal, December1985.

Above right: *Peter Pan* in Lewisham, 1999. Appearing as Captain Hook, with June Brown as Captain Hook's Ma.

Below: Me (back row, centre) as a member of the Leeds Grand Theatre stage crew in 1975. My first job in professional theatre as an ASM/flyman.

Above: In the UK tour of *Bouncers*, 2003. Left to right: Christopher Connel (Les), John Altman (Lucky Eric), Nigel Divaro (Judd), Andrew Dennis (Ralph).

Below: As Billy Flynn in the first UK tour of *Chicago – The Musical*, 2001–2.

Nick Cotton (the full pose!).

'Mrs Thatcher leaves the back door of No 10 Downing Street. Accompanied by her bodyguard.' (Endercards. Theres no end of em).

'On The Square.' 19.4.2001 Endercard

Polaroids from my EastEnders collection.
Above left, upper: With June Brown, 6 October 2000.

Above left, lower: On the Square with Frankie Fitzgerald (Ashley Cotton), 19 April 2001

Above right: June and me (Nick and his dear old Ma), 2009.

Below: '*EastEnders* mania': at Parkside Youth Club, Herne Bay, in autumn 1987, the golden years.

and my old friends Hetta Boyson and Marc Scherman also joined me. On a clear blue golden day I made it to the top of the World Trade Center. Utterly breathtaking! The lift travelled at 20mph and I hardly felt the rise, just a slight popping in my ears.

I attended a gala premiere of Prince's *Purple Rain* (1984). Everyone wore outrageous costumes and I had on what I called my spacesuit and we all danced in front of the screen.

I called my agent to check on the BBC role and Annette confirmed, '*E8* is still going ahead.'

E8 is the Hackney, London postcode that was then the show's title. What more could I ask for? I was having a ball in New York and I would soon be heading back to the UK to perform in a brand new BBC TV series.

CHAPTER 14

YESTERDAY IS HISTORY. TOMORROW IS A MYSTERY. TODAY IS A GIFT
ALICE MORSE EARLE

I was sad to leave New York – America had made a big impression on me. There was a huge thunderstorm as my plane took off but we got back safely.

I received a postcard from Debbie in New York on 24 October 1984. She wrote: 'New York wept at your departure. After all that beautiful weather, your plane took off and the sky opened up and poured for hours. Now it's drizzly, cold and gloomy. So you see, the city you love so much also cares for you. I miss you. Love, Debs.'

My worry about taking the job and my on-off relationship with Kitty plunged me into a deep depression, which couldn't have been worse timing. Again my diary makes very clear my state of mind then:

The character I have to play will do me no favours in the future, I am sure of it. Thank God it is only 3 months. I suppose I will have to go through with it. If I'd read the script before I had signed the contract, I think I would have turned it down. Here's hoping I can grow to enjoy it but I know it is going to be hard. I talked it over with Kitty and we agreed that I can't back out now. I remind myself that Michael Caine took an upper-class part after *Alfie*. I must do the same.

But my mood has lifted somewhat in my diary entries following the first day:

NOVEMBER 13TH

I had a night of cooking and an early night, I then rose at 6.45am after a restless night and went for a 3-mile run. Travelled to the BBC at Elstree for my first day on set, which turned out to be a great day.

NOVEMBER 19TH

At Elstree today, Nejdet [Ali Osman] and I were the first actors to be filmed for *EastEnders* – 'An historic moment,' as Julia Smith, the producer, said. Freezing cold in my small, leather jacket – my scene was sorted on the second take – good to have finally started after so long. So good to be working during the dark, winter days.

I think people assume when you join a soap that the money is instantly brilliant – I certainly thought it would be better than it was, but during this period of having signed the contract and doing long hours of rehearsing, we only earned £100 a week. I couldn't wait until we started recording because that meant the money would increase. I was still signing on and felt guilty and worried about the consequences if I got found out but I had little choice when I was in such debt and Christmas was just around the corner. My mother called not long after I started the job and offered to lend me some cash, but I declined – I had enough debt as it was without adding her to the list of people I needed to pay back. Although I was very grateful for her offer.

Then something happened at Elstree that brought me up short and made me realise that I really needed and wanted this job as Nick – Jean Fennell was given the sack for being difficult about her part and for generally not fitting in. It definitely had the desired effect of pulling us all back into line and making us realise how hard this business can be sometimes. When *EastEnders* was first screened on BBC1 on Tuesday, 19 February 1985, very few people would have realised that only the last-minute sacking of another actress enabled Anita Dobson to play the part of Angie Watts. Jean Fennell was a true East Ender born in June 1951 and raised in Ilford, and seemed ideal for the role of landlady, but during rehearsals for the first cluster of episodes it became clear to Julia Smith and the co-creator Tony Holland that she wasn't right and so she was just fired. Rumour has it that Jean had a very definite way of presenting herself. She felt Angie should be elegant, but Wardrobe and Julia believed she should be more 'out there', more flashy and bling-like.

The truth is that your job as an actor is to do what is expected of you and to give the performance you are employed to give, not always the one you would like to give. The scriptwriters give you lines and write your character in a certain way for a reason. But the story goes that Jean wouldn't be directed, wouldn't go with it. It was a real lesson to us all – about how ruthless the producers and directors could be. It also shows how much actresses like June Brown have earned their stripes in order to be allowed to influence the writing and shaping of their characters – after six episodes Jean hadn't in any way earned the right to kick up a fuss. You have to be established before you can go into battle. Angie Watts was such an essential character, she had to be spot on – she definitely wasn't someone you could experiment with.

My diary entries certainly reflected a keener desire to please after Jean's sacking. By the end of November 1984 I had learned all of my lines for the first six episodes of the show.

[DECEMBER 1984]

I had lunch at Elstree and met the cast again in the portakabin. It was a wasted journey as we didn't rehearse. Shreela Ghosh [Naima Jeffery] told me that my bum had been the subject of a discussion between Gillian Taylforth [Kathy Beale] and Anna Wing [Lou Beale]. Well, really!

Annette Stone came to lunch and met all three directors and Julia [Smith]. She said that she didn't want me to be typecast as a result of *EastEnders*.

***

I suffered the night after a party at a friend's house in Chelsea. Guests included Simon Cutter, Kermit (she was a socialite) and comedian Peter Cook. I walked – or rather staggered – home and fell onto my bed fully clothed. At 5am I briefly woke up and then got up properly at 8.30am in a mad panic. I made it out of the house in ten minutes flat and just caught the shuttle bus to Elstree.

All day I felt rough and vowed to give my system a break from the heavy drinking. I longed to feel normal and there was so much to do in the build-up to Christmas. In the Green Room at Elstree we played a game with colours that was supposed to give us an analysis of our characters. I also kissed Gretchen Franklin (Ethel May Skinner) and she blushed and for a moment looked like a little girl. Leonard Fenton (Dr Harold Legg) also kept us amused in the Green Room by throwing his voice and making animal noises. He could, without moving his mouth, make you believe there was a sheep hanging around the corridor outside the room or there was a dog in the corner. Leonard Fenton was the first to admit he was bad with props. During a scene in the Beales' bedroom, having tended to her, he stood up, snapped his briefcase shut and walked out of the room taking her bed cover with him. It had caught in the briefcase; what's more, there was Anna Wing (Lou Beale) in her negligée for all to see!

I befriended most of the early cast, especially Linda Davidson (Mary Smith, the punk) and Nejdet Salih (Ali Osman). One of the reasons why many of the actors became quite close was that we were all sailing on the same ship – heading into uncharted waters. None of us knew whether we would be a success or swiftly cancelled. Most of us had a positive feeling that we would do well. Although I got on fine with most people, my closest friends were Oscar James (Tony Carpenter), Wendy Richard (Pauline Fowler), Peter Dean (Pete Beale, whom I nicknamed 'Pete the Potato' when I was Nick. He ran the fruit and veg stall on Albert Square), Gillian Taylforth (Kathy Beale), Shirley Cheriton (Debbie Wilkins), Gretchen Franklin (Ethel Skinner) and Tom Watt (Lofty Holloway). I remember Linda was very impressed by my Liverpudlian accent when she caught a broadcast of *Birth of The Beatles* that went out while we were filming. Coming from a Scouser I took this to be a real compliment.

***

Les Grantham began to give me lifts to and from Chelsea in his BMW, often accompanied by Bruce Springsteen's 'Born in the USA' or some Bob Seger. We picked up Gretchen Franklin one day and she described herself as the Faye Dunaway of her quiet street in Barnes.

***

14TH DECEMBER 1984

The word came to me via Matthew [Robinson] that Julia [Smith] approved of our performance today – which was a huge relief in so many ways for all of us. Through the studio nerves are running high. Sadly, I missed Annette's first ever get together with her clients, but work comes first. My first fight scene went really well and I must admit to a weird satisfaction in punching my hand through the glass in the door. 'Stuff your poxy pub!' were my lines. The make-up girls were really amused by the whole thing – they are good fun and we had a real laugh. We are broken up now until the 29th. Felt half-happy that we were wrapping up and half-sad that my routine and rhythm would be interrupted.

On 17 December I got a note from Julia Smith via the director of the first two episodes, Matthew Robinson. She told me not to make Nick quite so heavy. I must have made him X-certificate evil.

'She's right,' I wrote in my diary, 'so I will take it down.' I made a note to myself about status games, citing Max Stafford-Clark, then director of the Royal Court. I'd learned this in his workshops – how to adjust the volume of your performance, the intensity. But I was so happy to be working and I made up a quote for myself: 'There is a power within and without. If you ask, it answers. It's just a matter of being calm and wise and listening. It takes years.'

**

In the early days of the show we would take a shuttle bus that we could get from BBC Television Centre in Shepherd's Bush. One of our initial tasks as an ensemble was to have a photo call on set. I noticed that the crew seemed terrified of Julia Smith but I remember feeling no fear at that time: she was the boss and she knew what she wanted. Later that day I drove back from the studios with Oscar James, who played Tony Carpenter. Oscar was a gentleman and was quite heavily into Buddhism and often promised to take me to one of his meetings. Our characters Tony and Nick were great adversaries in the programme.

Our first day of shooting in the studio was on 19 December 1984. I took the shuttle with Leslie Grantham and rehearsed in the morning. I had a fight scene in The Queen Vic with Nejdet and Leslie. It went well and I enjoyed punching the glass in the pub door. We played the analysis game again and the make-up girls were much amused by it too.

I was invited to a party by the director Matthew Robinson (brother of Tom, the singer) but I was working too late to attend. 'Still,' I wrote in my diary, 'think how healthy I'll feel tomorrow.'

The exterior Albert Square set was known as 'the Lot'. It was built on the same plot that *Auf Wiedersehen, Pet* was filmed on. One viewer even noticed that the tower blocks in the background were the same in both series! It could be freezing cold out there and one day the temperature got me down – I was only half in the show that day and I wanted to be alone. The facilities weren't very good at that point. There was no heating at all for an hour and I wondered if they were deliberately trying to give us all colds and flu. For myself, I felt alone and rather distant all day.

The final studio day for the year was on 30 December. I had a restless night, dreaming of fights, East End pubs and bags of jelly – I wonder why? It seemed the majority of the cast had had similar experiences as we headed into the final day of recording. I still get that to this day – I never sleep well before beginning rehearsals in the theatre or filming. Anita Dobson and Leslie Grantham (as Angie and Den Watts) seemed to click. We gave Anita a round of applause at the end of her first day of rehearsal.

I avoided the dreaded portakabin where we had to wait to be called for our scenes on the Lot and spent the morning in my dressing room, reading the Sunday papers, rehearsing my lines and dozing. The whole cast turned up for lunch, having been assembled for a photo call featuring the 23 regulars, so that excluded me. It's strange to think back now but there were comparatively so few long-term cast members than there are these days. I think the entire cast must be around 55-strong at the moment.

That day I completed my take in the Indian supermarket first time. I could hardly believe it, but it felt fine so I had no complaints. It was just so good to be working even though the Lot was once again freezing and it was drizzling outside.

The following day I didn't do any filming and spent my time playing billiards and reading. After champagne for cast and directors, Andrew Johnson (Saeed Jeffery) drove me to Marble Arch and I went on to a big New Year's Eve party at my friends Hugh and Hetta Boyson's flat in Queen's Gardens. There were streamers, blue faces, broken coffee tables and endless wine.

The year 1984 ended on a high – I had a job, albeit a temporary one, and so I decided to put looking for a partner on hold and to throw myself into my work while I could.

***

Early in the New Year of 1985 I heard that BBC1 controller Michael Grade had okayed the first two episodes, which must have been a relief to Julia Smith, the producer. The freezing cold spell continued – it was the coldest I'd known it for years. Towards the end of the previous year there was a plentiful supply of winter berries, traditionally the sign of a hard winter. It was true that year and I was thankful to have something that would keep me busy throughout this time. I would wake up curled at the top of my bed because the bottom half was so chilly in my Chelsea basement.

I told director Matthew Robinson that some people – mentioning no names – were not off the book (they didn't know their lines) when doing the run-through in front of the producers. He assured me he'd make sure everyone was word perfect in future and couldn't believe they weren't.

After filming I was driven to White City by Oscar, along with some of the other cast, encountering mad motorists on the way. We left Gretchen at the bus stop and she said, 'You'll often find me here.' Gretchen Franklin was quite a character and would always come out with classic funny phrases. I was once at The Queen Vic bar between scenes next to her as she clutched her Little Willy – the legendary pug – and I reached out to stroke the dog. It bared its teeth and growled.

'He's a good judge of character is my Little Willy,' said Gretchen. Sometimes she would kick her legs in the air and demonstrate what a good dancer she used to be.

In 1991 she informed the cast that she had already paid for her funeral in advance – which as it turned out was still fortunately many years in the future.

In choosing a dog for the family at The Queen Vic, Julia made the mistake of asking Leslie Grantham what he thought would be an authentic breed for an East End landlord. With a sense of humour dryer than a desert wind, he said, 'One of those giant poodles.' He didn't think they'd go out and buy one but that was precisely what she and Tony Holland did, and that was how the very docile Roly became the second canine cast member. Julia used to keep him at her place most nights. At the time of writing, the present owners of The Queen Vic have a bulldog, which is far more appropriate – as would have been an Alsatian or a Rottweiler.

***

My diary entry for 9 January 1985 on set read: 'I put on tight leather jeans, bluebird tattoo on my neck and dagger earring. Wendy Richard and I shared the same high spirits but we both feared that they might lapse. Oscar James gave me a wise quote or two to read tonight. Sandy Ratcliff dried on take two. I wish she would leave it alone, whatever she takes, because she doesn't need it. A good actress onscreen – screwing herself up in private. I left mid-afternoon and made my way to the snow-covered Elstree station platform. I was in a really bad mood for the rest of the day. Have I brought my role home? No. It was just one of those times when the biting cold bit on.'

The next day, 10 January, I wrote: 'I finally caught up on my sleep and very much on form for recording today. Rehearsed well in the morning and waited around for the rest of the day, talking with Gary Whelan (who was playing the detective investigating Reg Cox's murder), an Irish guy also known as Whiplash and talked with the make-up girls. There was chaos in the studio. Julia Smith and Vivienne Cousins, the director, were arguing throughout the recording and we only completed one episode. I never even got around to doing my scenes. It was a disappointing end to a potentially satisfying day. Apparently, Julia had reduced Viv to tears at one point. Viv's too nice and easy-going to work with Julia. I actually think Julia likes people to stand up to her when she becomes aggressive. Sandy R had her lines written on a piece of paper for a scene about a chain letter in the café.'

***

Gary Whelan (DS Terry Rich) and I shared a mischievous sense of humour. I was due in at 2pm and he got someone to leave me a message saying that I was actually due in at 11am. I scrambled about, made my way into the studio and was told that I was three hours early. Eventually I got my revenge when Gary was supposed to come over for dinner in Chelsea. He failed to turn up for an Italian shepherd's pie supper that I'd cooked for him, so I put it in a Jiffy bag, sealed it up tight and posted it to him. He opened it at breakfast two days later and said it looked disgusting.

Gary's nickname, Whiplash, came from Nejdet in recognition of his propensity for being quick to go out on the lash. He came up with a plan for instant fame – a streak in front of Lady Diana. The result would be arrest, a small fine and your face and member syndicated around the world!

***

By the time we got to read episodes nine and ten it was clear to me that my character was getting worse. I thought that Nick was now becoming a part I could really sink my teeth into. It was fun to play the villain although I was nervous that I might face aggression from people on the street when it went out if anyone confused me with the character. After reading through the latest scripts, I drove back to BBC TV Centre with director Viv Cousins. I felt sorry for her after that argument with Julia – and she was on her way to see her then. As she put it along the way: 'To collect my cards.'

It looked as though my final two episodes would be with a different director, although in fact Viv did survive the encounter and returned to the set. I had to shoot a scene with her in the snowy Square as Nick sat in a BMW. She and her assistant were in panic. Shortly afterwards she was sacked and Peter Edwards took over.

Peter was very organised and worked at a fast pace – as you need to do on a soap opera. But it wasn't all work: during rehearsals I put a cigarette in the mouth of the toy baby being used as a stand-in for a real child and rested a pint of beer on his high chair, which caused some amusement. Despite the doom and gloom of the storylines, on the *EastEnders*' set there was always time to lighten the mood with a few laughs.

Work on the show proceeded quickly according to my diary and, on 14 January, I wrote: 'A fast-moving day at Elstree with Peter Edwards, who is so in control. A happier atmosphere pervades this week in the cast, all through him. He has a clear eye for the camera, the performance and the feel of it all. A sensitive soul, in control. Time passes so fast in the studio when you're creating the TV land world for the eyes out there. My character becomes more grotesque as time moves on but I manage to retain "me" when I leave. I do feel exhausted when I return home and rather spaced between me and Nick Cotton.'

As the end of my stint in *EastEnders* approached, I wrote: 'There are moments when I walk alone down the roadways of the studio when feelings of pure happiness come over me. I feel so glad to be working. The red lights are flashing, which indicates that filming is taking place and smoke is curling up from the steel chimney and inside, away from the freezing cold, three dozen people are creating some magic that will be seen by millions all over England. Perhaps it's because I know I will be leaving on 22 February that I'm savouring every tiny moment, working hard and loving it. A good company to work with. David Scarboro [Mark Fowler] is opening up at last and everyone is falling into line with their parts.'

On the Lot I recorded a trailer for the launch with Julia Smith. She let me make up my own words and I came out with, 'I'm Nick Cotton and don't forget it.' I looked directly into the camera and jabbed my finger menacingly at the viewing public.

As launch time approached, I found out that David Scarboro and Sandy Ratcliff had been called up in front of Julia. Someone in the cast wouldn't live and let live and had made a complaint about them. They were both very angry that whoever had complained wasn't there to confront them. Sandy drove me back to White City – it was clear to me that she was really dedicated to her task.

On 29 January 1985 cast and crew were shown the first two episodes at Elstree. Watching was quite exhausting. It was hard to be neutral about something that I was so close to, but I felt sure that the show would do very well. Everyone else seemed happy too. We drank champagne and orange and Julia told me that I would be back in August. I noted in my diary her comment – 'You will have a mother when you return.'

Oscar James and I did a radio interview in character before he drove me back with Adam Woodyatt (Ian Beale) and Letitia Dean (Sharon Watts). I held Letitia's hand – but I knew then, as I wrote in my diary, 'that it would be fatal to embark with her even though she was very fanciable.' That same day I wrote, 'Les Grantham [Den Watts] seems to be pissing a few people off. Foolish person.'

The next day we prepared for a scene in which I was to be beaten up and I tested special make-up before shooting other scenes. Julia Smith seemed happy and I was pleased myself, knowing she wanted me back. At last I felt I had a chance to shine and I was giving it all I had. In the car on the way home, Wendy Richard (Pauline Fowler] said I was very strong. I reflected that it was funny that I had been so reserved about the show in the beginning. My mother and father were delighted that I had made some success of a very precarious profession.

Julia would often catch Nejdet and I chatting together and wonder what we were plotting. She always seemed to find us in the most unlikely places. As I was approaching the end of the show I began to worry that Annette wouldn't find me any more work and I surely didn't fancy returning to the dole queue.

Gary Whelan (DS Terry Rich) and I heard a rumour that Julia wanted us permanently because of our acting. We were quite pissed off because in the end we were not even in the press release for the launch – we weren't mentioned in the *Radio Times* and there wasn't a photograph of us. After all the time and effort we had put in. The rest of the cast were surprised too. I felt we'd been put in the back row by Cheryl Wilson, one of the producers, but now we were being omitted entirely. My mother was also disappointed and angry. Julia got to hear about it and that was the main thing as far as I was concerned. Gary and I were owed a big one after this, I felt.

In early February I had a drink before doing an evening shoot. It threw me and made the job twice as difficult. I resolved not to do it again and found it hard to believe some actors regularly work with booze inside them. Midway through the recording, Julia Smith asked to see me in the corridor. She apologised – after a fashion – for not putting me in the *Radio Times*. When I returned in the summer I would have the full treatment, she promised.

I sent Valentine's cards to Anna Wing and Gretchen Franklin and one to Peter Dean to cheer him up (he was a bit heartbroken at the time).

Inevitably, as with any big group of people who spend a lot of time together, there was an active rumour mill. In early 1985 it was said that two attractive young cast members had got it together in their dressing room and when Peter Dean (Pete Beale) was sent to hospital with chest pains people were soon saying he'd had a heart attack. Soon afterwards he was released, having been diagnosed with nothing more life threatening than bad digestion. Lovely Leonard Fenton (Dr Harold Legg) was said to be having marital difficulties – nothing more was said about that one.

David Scarboro continued to have problems on the programme. Peter Braham, one of the top stuntmen in the business, was called in to choreograph a fight in Ethel's front room that occurred while Nick and Mark Fowler were attempting to rob her. He had the swagger of John Wayne and had stood in for the legendary actor when he filmed *Brannigan* (1975) in London. Peter had done everything from *Bond* to war movies but he and David Scarboro just did not see eye to eye.

***

I will never forget how on 19 February 1985 we all celebrated the airing of the first episode – it was a far cry from the glamour you might expect. The big launch involved twelve of us all huddled round an old steam-driven television in the corner of the Elstree canteen. The writers and production crew had laid on a few pints and some bags of peanuts and we were thrilled – it felt like such a huge deal but it couldn't have been any more low-key. The recent 30th Anniversary had 2,000 people gathered around a 50ft HD screen with cocktails and a vodka stream ice sculpture! I don't think the significance of the whole thing really dawned on me until about a week after the initial launch episode aired. It was the following Sunday, back in the good old days of the omnibus episodes, and I decided to go out for a run down Sloane Street. As I ran down towards the river, I passed a TV shop and saw a scene from the show beaming out from the shop front window. It made me realise that my life had changed for good. That, and being called 'Nick' in Waitrose on the King's Road!

I led the way on Nick's look, voice and vocabulary but as an actor the one thing you can't control is the way the public will react and whether they take your character to their hearts. The truth is in many ways as an actor you are only as good as the others around you, the other actors who feed into the consciousness and DNA of your character. They help your character to grow and adapt and there is no doubt Nick's personality and my own scope as an actor was greatly enhanced by some of the working partnerships I had on *EastEnders*. The most important relationship and pairing for me was with June Brown, Nick's long-suffering 'Ma'.

Dot Cotton (now Branning) is an institution. Working with June Brown was a constant joy – she was wonderfully particular about her scripts and like a terrier when it came to protecting and preserving the Dot she had created. I remember endless scenes being re-written by her, a menthol cigarette hanging out of the corner of her mouth. It could be the smallest of things – that Dot was right-handed so would reach for her Bible with that hand rather than the left. That Dot wasn't ostentatious when it came to jewellery but remained devoted to her pearls and cameo pins; that she was not of the trouser-wearing generation, more a stockings and skirts woman and, like the Queen, she never went anywhere without her handbag.

Nick was always complicated. I am aware there aren't many actors lucky enough to have a partner in performance so revered and skilled as June and I know Dot and Nick are the characters they are due to the spark we have together. I have always loved Nick's edginess, simmering-below-the-surface evil – his love of tormenting the mother who adored him and laments about the fact he was her 'little angel' when he was young.

***

As I have said, on 19 February 1985 the show was launched and broadcast for the first time. The *Daily Mail* splashed the cast's earnings over a whole page. As a result, Gretchen Franklin and Sandy Ratcliff ended up having a row later that day, although I forget exactly why – I guess one of them must have found out she was earning much less than the other. Poor Nejdet ended up in hospital with back pain. I too was suffering with pain down my neck, back and arms. Pre-launch tension, I think, although we had all been working very hard and I was still doing a lot of running.

Work continued on the show during the day. I got notes from Julia Smith and Peter Edwards: 'Put on the viciousness,' they suggested. 'Be nastier.'

'No problem,' I thought. 'I can do it.'

Looking back, it surprised me that hardly any of the cast turned up at the launch party that night. Peter Dean, Anita Dobson, Gillian Taylforth, Sue Tully, Letitia Dean and Ross Davidson were the main guests. Compared to the 30th Anniversary, it would have seemed somewhat underwhelming. We watched the 2015 show on an enormous HD screen when back at the start of it all we had to huddle around a two-foot box, with a twenty-inch screen, from the days when Radio Rentals were the last word in technology.

My only criticism was that the sound in the market was too loud. By 8pm, when the show finished, the BBC had received 98 complaints from Glasgow and Manchester (perhaps these were *Coronation Street* fans trying to sabotage the soft southerners), mostly about the violence – which, I'm proud to say, was in part due to my character.

The overall opinion from the reviewers was that we had turned out a really good programme and the viewing figures were very good indeed and from then on they began to rise. Julia Smith and Tony Holland had created a hard-hitting soap unlike any other on the TV at that time and I think it excited the viewing public. The following day, my good friend Kate Martin and her son Ollie Fitchie came in. I was delighted when Henry the floor manager took Ollie into one of the scenes in the cafe.

During this same period of filming I was injured on set. This was my final scene in the run, the one that had been rehearsed with Peter Braham. My agent Annette Stone had come to see the show at work. Even in rehearsal it hadn't been straightforward to get right and on my first take I smashed my hands into a picture frame. As I pointed at Gretchen Franklin I saw blood flowing from the top of my right hand.

They kept filming and when we completed another take dear Tom Watt (Lofty Holloway) took me to Barnet General Hospital for an X-ray and some stitches. But this was my last day and so I headed back to the studio, picking up flowers and drink on the way. I wasn't sad to be leaving – I was exhausted and I needed a break.

I spent the evening at the studio, saying goodbye to everyone. I gave out flowers for the girls and sets of drinking glasses to Demelza and Martin, my dresser. Along with David Scarboro, Peter Dean and Gillian Taylforth called in for a vodka and then it was time to go up to the control box to see Julia and Tony, Morag, Jillie Fraser and Allison.

Julia said they had worked out with my agent that I would come back earlier than expected – June 1985– and that I would be 'a reformed character'. I thought it sounded like a great change for me.

Back home I drank Bacardi and fell fast asleep. It was a couple of days later, on 23 February, that I recorded my reaction to the newspapers' discovery of the years that Leslie had spent in prison –

'I eased my way gently into the day and then in the local newsagent's headlines screamed out about Leslie Grantham's murder rap in Germany many years ago. I couldn't help but feel sorry for him in some way. He must feel like disappearing fast from the face of the Earth. The papers can be very cruel.'

Things are very different now. Back then there was much more of a feeling of being in it together for the long haul – these characters were being created for a show no one knew would succeed. But there were other shows that had enjoyed longevity and I knew the BBC wouldn't have been making such a fuss and spending so much money if they didn't think it would work. There wasn't the turnover of younger actors then that there is now and the pressure was different as it was only twice a week. When you suddenly double the number of episodes airing every week, the pressure to up the ante on more characters becomes harder to manage, I believe. That's perhaps when storylines become outlandish and improbable. Back then there was a small circle of trust between the powers that be – Julia Smith, Tony Holland and the scriptwriters, they sat around, coming up with new characters and storylines. This still happens today. I remember going into the forward planning offices and seeing a wallchart, perfectly arranged, with storylines stretching ahead up to 18 months in advance, with Polaroids of character's faces attached to timelines and plot ideas. They understood the way to keep an audience hooked – like the poisoning of Dot and Ashley's death. Those were storylines that grabbed the viewers and got the all-important media hype and tabloid speculation at fever pitch. Suddenly I was being papped shopping for groceries or buying petrol. Some of the cast loved it, even engineered it, but not me – especially later on, but I learned to live with it.

I based Nick on various n'er-do-well characters I'd met during my time in London. At the beginning he was an out-and-out baddie – he just seemed to rob and kill people! Not only that but he bullied Lofty and upset most of the residents of Albert Square. For these reasons alone Nick Cotton was never going to be a permanent member of the *EastEnders* cast: a soap is unable to have a permanent baddie in its midst because it cannot be sustained. Villains either have to dip in and out, die or get rehabilitated – you only have to look at what happened to Phil and Grant Mitchell to see that. They arrived on the Square as the equivalent of the Kray Brothers and then the next thing you see a few months later is Phil giving Arthur Fowler driving lessons!

Nick appeared in the very first episode in February 1985 and he pre-dated Dot (something that is easy to forget as they have always gone so hand-in-hand). June Brown actually joined in July 1985 and the idea was for Dot to try and get him in line. A great character is the combination of your own real experiences and relationships as well as the nimble ability to get under the skin of the person you are playing and really mine their mental and physical space. Nick was a racist, obviously a concern, and he didn't care who he shoved out of his way – he even roughed up poor Ethel Skinner (Gretchen Franklin) as he tried to rob her.

For Den (Leslie Grantham) and Angie (Anita Dobson), the divorce papers storyline and Angie's drinking became much talked about. The programme generated an unprecedented level of hype and any misdemeanour was picked over at length. The characters, both on and off the air, were dissected in the tabloids as a form of sport.

***

Nerves ran high towards the end of 1984 when we were rehearsing but not yet filming, like being in a bubble and not really being able to see the fruits of your labours. It was hard, the early starts and the commute to Elstree. I would always begin the day with a long run so that I arrived on set fresh and raring to go. There was a huge sense of relief when word came down that Matthew Robinson and Julia Smith approved of your performance, especially as they had shown their muscle in sacking Jean Fennell.

A typical day at *EastEnders* in those times would consist of arriving at the studio at 8 o'clock, taking a run into the countryside, showering, having breakfast, checking my lines and then rehearsing in a building with a mocked-up version of the sets. They put taped markings on the floor and plain wooden furniture to represent the pub or whatever scenery was needed. All morning we would rehearse – usually on a Monday – and in the afternoon we performed a technical run on the proper set.

We waited on our various sets or in the bar at The Queen Vic until Julia Smith, Tony Holland and the rest of the crew involved in the particular episodes of that week would come round and watch us perform. There were then only two episodes of *EastEnders* in a week, Tuesdays and Thursdays. I've often thought the quality of the earlier programmes was higher because we had more time to concentrate on each individual character. It was tough but less of a scramble to put the episodes together.

When they moved on to have four episodes a week they dropped the off-set rehearsals so we would go straight in front of the battery of cameras and do what is called 'rehearse-and-record'. Pretty frightening for any newcomers to the programme!

There were times when I was amazed that they managed to get it done 52 weeks a year – quite an operation, and that includes Christmas. To allow the cast and crew to get a decent break over the festive season they created a filming schedule called 'double banking'. We'd have to do an extra 8 episodes over a month or so, in late autumn, and those would go out while we took our break.

Filming entailed plenty of hanging around. Sometimes I would be called for a scene at 9.30am and not film again until 3pm. But there were always lines to learn and fan mail to answer. No sooner had I memorised my scenes, than another envelope appeared with more lines to be learned.

Once cast members were locked into *EastEnders* it was like being on a treadmill and a lot of the cast called it 'the factory'. For myself, I nicknamed it 'St Julia's' because it was like being at a school with Julia Smith as the stern head teacher. Incidentally, the show's 50th episode was marked on 4 July 1995 with a champagne reception hosted by Julia in the bar. She wore a white suit and was sporting a silver '50' badge on her pocket. Looking back, she must have been so proud, bless her, that her baby was now a fully-grown child, and up and running!

I had really become accustomed it all quite quickly. Going back to the end of 1984, I signed off as follows:

Turned on the Christmas lights in Regent Street with Letitia Dean. Got a car home, which felt amazing, found even more cards on the mat, which was cheering.

CHAPTER 15

DREAM AS IF YOU'LL LIVE FOREVER. LIVE AS IF YOU'LL DIE TODAY
JAMES DEAN

Life settles into a routine quickly. Having been so unsure about the impact of joining the show, I couldn't wait to get back to it in January 1985. There was particular excitement that the bosses had finally listened to the plight of the workers and provided us with a brand new smoking room. Most of the cast were avid smokers – I was very happy to have had that written into Nick's character.

The way in which Nick smoked his cigarettes became increasingly dramatic as time went on. He gripped the cigarette end as if his whole existence depended on it, sucking the life from it in a way that meant business. The fact we didn't have to keep going outside for a smoke was a massive plus, especially in the freezing cold and snow. I remember Sue Tully, who played Michelle Fowler, taking up the habit again just two days later after she had given up as part of a New Year's Resolution. One morning in the smoking room with me and she was straight back on them.

Julia Smith and Tony Holland insisted on gritty storylines

and snappy editing as the basis for this new British soap opera. I clearly remember the contrast to series such as *Coronation Street* – *EastEnders* hit you between the eyes with its faster pace. The only well-known face among us was Wendy Richard, famous for playing Miss Brahms in *Are You Being Served?* She didn't suffer fools gladly and nor do I so we got on well. I became good friends with her and her husband John.

She showed me a simple method for memorising lines, which I had never used before. Mark up your own lines in the script with a highlighter pen and use a card or any piece of paper to work down the page. Once you get your first line, go down to the second line and so on until you reach the bottom of the page. Repeat until you know it off by heart. It was a foolproof method that I still use to this day. Thank you, Wendy, I still miss you!

There was great excitement among the actors because we all felt that we had created something special and we couldn't wait for the public's reaction once the show was broadcast.

My first contract on the Square lasted no more than four months. I was just getting used to being on TV when my time was up. During those first few months, Nick wreaked havoc and somehow I managed to get away without a backlash from the great British public. Despite everything, they seemed to take this bad boy to their hearts.

In the end I would go on to appear in 237 episodes of the show. By March 2016, *EastEnders* itself had racked up 5,248 episodes. But for now Nick had pushed it too far and he was run out of town by the institution that was Pete Beale. It was a case of Walford uniting to see the back of the destructive yob the viewers had grown to hate. And it was the end of Nick, at least for now, but leaving the show at this point allowed me to concentrate on a far more exciting prospect in my life – I was about to meet my future wife, Bridget Poodhun.

***

Nejdet Salih (Ali Osman) and I had become very good friends on set and socialised a lot away from Elstree. One Monday, 25 March 1985, we had been out shopping together in Covent Garden – it was just after I left *EastEnders* for the first time. I had bought a Bryan Adams album, *Reckless*, which had one of my favourite tracks, 'Run to You', on it. Nejdet insisted I didn't go home on my own to listen to my album, he kept on saying, 'You must come to Swiss Cottage. There is a beautiful girl called Bridget, she is going to make a wonderful curry and I want you to meet her.'

I remember feeling so tired – you know that feeling when you just want to be in your own home? I was desperate to get back to Sydney Street, but he was so insistent that I went and I just remember walking into that flat and seeing her and she looked so beautiful, she was extraordinary! The evening passed in a haze of curry and wine and I remember kissing her on the cheek in the kitchen – I was just taken over by this urge to be close to her. She liked my Bryan Adams album, which we played. I gave her my number and I invited her over to Chelsea the following weekend.

Bridget had no idea who I was or that I'd been in a new soap that was taking off; she herself was an actress and had done some nursing in the past .

The next Sunday was the day after I'd been out to celebrate my 33rd birthday and split my leather trousers with Nejdet on the dance floor at the Streatham Bowl. I'd been longing to see Bridget again and was looking forward to it. I paid for her cab from Swiss Cottage and her company seemed so good. When I looked into her eyes I felt my heart beat faster. This was someone special, with similar tastes in food and music. It was raining, but we ignored it and drank wine. I cooked a meal and felt so relaxed with her that it seemed almost strange.

'She's Singapore, Egypt and India rolled into one,' I thought to myself.

It was the perfect way to round off what had been a mad birthday weekend.

***

Bridget was ten years younger than me but we fell for each other hard and that whirlwind year of courting was one of the happiest times of my life. When I think back (and read my diaries from then), my one big wish was a happy and settled private life – I was so keen to find 'The One' and make a home of my own. I am someone who needs love in my life and I didn't feel complete without it; meeting this beautiful girl was my chance for a happy ever after.

At the time I was living in my Chelsea flat, inherited from an artist friend of mine, Karl Kholer, who had trouble with his visa, meaning he had to go and live in New York. I moved from Maida Vale in 1983 to look after 67a Sydney Street for him. With it came this beautiful black cat, Cleo. The owners of the house, Francis and Olive Brown, lived upstairs. Their son-in-law was the first Canadian astronaut. When Bridget appeared on the scene, Cleo was not happy at all. She used to jump up to the top of the wardrobe and glare over the top at her. One time we were lying in bed and Cleo just sat there, giving us an evil look, and then she jumped straight down onto the bed, aiming for Bridget. Eventually I had to re-house Cleo in the village of Nonnington in the Kentish countryside.

Bridget eventually introduced me to her family. Reverend Lambert and Ivy Poodhun and her two brothers Jerome and Julian. Bright and friendly people. We got on well. They had come over from Durban in South Africa a few years before in the late 1970s.

***

During the early days of my relationship with Bridget, I was sent to Northern Ireland to make a series called *Dispatches* for BBC Belfast.

It was about some young soldiers caught up in the Troubles. Lots of actors refused to go there because it was so dangerous.

We were on our way to the centre of Belfast and not far from the airport when soldiers stopped the car.

'Oh, it's you,' they said, waving their machine guns in my direction, 'What are you doing here?'

I explained that I was there for another BBC series and they let us go on our way.

We stayed in a hotel near Lisburn on the outskirts of the city that was surrounded by barbed wire and had a security box at the entrance. As I had fairly long hair, I was allowed into Belfast city centre but the other actors had traditional British military-style haircuts and so they were confined to the BBC studio and hotel just in case they were kidnapped or shot at.

I had lunch one day at the BBC when Bridget had joined me. An alarm went off and we looked out of the window to see the entire area had been cleared and a robot was moving down the street to check a car feared to have a bomb in it. On another occasion I saw the remains of a Transit van flying high in the air, which had been blown up in the financial district of Belfast. I had been in Lisburn when it went off but I still heard the distant boom and saw the debris of the explosion floating down, like paper fluttering down in slow motion. A day later I saw the destruction it had caused: a whole street with all its office windows blown out.

When filming was completed, Bridget and I decided to take a drive down to the southwest coast of Ireland. We'd both seen *Ryan's Daughter* and being romantics wanted to see the beautiful beaches of Dingle depicted in the movie for ourselves. We took our hired Ford Sierra on a gorgeous trip, sampling the Guinness in Waterford and seeing many wonderful sights and meeting some warm-hearted people along the way.

I wanted to show off my driving skills to the new love in my life on the flat, sandy beach of the Inch Peninsula. However I didn't know that the tide was coming in and it was becoming extremely wet underneath the sand. The car became embedded and I couldn't move it. I ran to the only other people around, some young German tourists. Being helpful and practical as Germans often are – and here's a tip for any would-be beach motorists out there – they got me to take the floor mats out of the car, placed them tightly under the wheels and with the tyres gripping the mats, slowly edged the car back onto the dry part of the beach. Bridget and I were so grateful for their help and offered to buy them a drink but they wouldn't hear of it. Our journey continued and she and I became even closer.

In a small fishing village called Baltimore we took a pre-dinner stroll through the town. Outside a local pub we saw a chalkboard: 'Playing tonight: Noel Redding and his missus'. Sure enough, it was the same bassist who had once performed in the Jimi Hendrix Experience. After his set we had a drink with him. How extraordinary to have met him once again, the last occasion being at the Central Hall in Chatham in 1967! He'd fallen on hard times and spent some of the latter part of his life playing these small gigs in Ireland – he certainly wasn't the millionaire rock star that he might have been.

***

11 DECEMBER 1985

Away touring in Newcastle and things are a bit up and down with Bridget. We spoke on the phone tonight and it wasn't so jolly. I miss her a lot more today than I have but she didn't sound very happy when we spoke and I sometimes feel I am too nice and easy-going. I was at a market and was hit by an endless stream of autograph hunters. Did the dress rehearsal and was told that my entrance needs to be stronger, so a long way to go before it's perfect and my performance is improved.

IN THE NICK OF TIME

21 JANUARY 1986, NEWCASTLE.

B was none too pleased with me in the morning – she said I could hardly stand up when we arrived home last night. I wasn't sick and I didn't have a fight or a hangover. She's worried about me making a fool of myself in public, which is fair enough.

24 JANUARY 1986

Bridget has gone out and said she won't be coming back as we rowed over the fact she wouldn't show me a letter she had received from an ex. I know she is pregnant but these stubborn, pathetic moods were apparent before she conceived and I hope for our sakes she grows out of them soon. She can be so sweet and then the most annoying person on God's earth.

Our courtship was short but very intense and Bridget and I were married in February 1986, a year almost to the day after the first episode of *EastEnders* aired. My parents were thrilled – I'd had a lot of affairs over the years and my heart had been broken many times, but here was a girl who ticked all the boxes and I think everyone was relieved. She was beautiful, smart, had a lovely voice and was a great cook. We loved the same things, even the same music. I was also lucky that, despite the fact she was Indian, she was a Christian, not Hindu or Muslim, and her father, Lambert, was the Chaplain of a hospital in Sussex and eventual Canon in Chichester which made it easier for us to marry. I got on well with her parents and two brothers, and was welcomed into the family with open arms.

We were married at the Chelsea Register Office. I was so nervous that I forgot my flies were undone and the official discreetly told me, 'Mr Altman, you might wish to adjust your trousers.' Afterwards there was a service in St Lukes Chelsea conducted by Bridget's father. We had a wonderful honeymoon in Eilat. Bridget was pregnant at the time of our marriage but that wasn't why we did it, we just knew we were destined to be together. The pregnancy simply sped up what would have happened anyway. It was a mark of the increase in my fame that the paparazzi were installed outside the register office and all along the road on our wedding day, trying to get the money shot. We kindly obliged.

During the early days of my relationship with Bridget, when we lived in Chelsea, we were on our way to South Kensington station one day in 1986, when a newspaper vendor shouted out, 'Oi, Nick! Who's been a naughty boy then?'

I looked down and saw 'EastEnders Nick in Love Storm – Nightclub Bust-Up' spread across the front page of the *Sun*. Up until that point we had been enjoying a very happy day and I couldn't believe what I was seeing. Then I remembered: we had both been at the Hippodrome on Leicester Square more than a week earlier. I was asked to present an award onstage. During the evening, Bridget and I had an argument – about what, I know not, but something petty, I'm sure. She walked away from me into the ladies' toilet. I followed her to finish the argument. The next thing I knew, a doorman had grabbed me by the shoulder, bundled me downstairs and kicked me out of the fire-escape door onto the pavement outside.

Unbeknownst to me, poor Bridget had exited the ladies' only to be told by the doorman: 'Don't worry, miss. I got rid of 'im for you.' She was cross and told him that he shouldn't have done that and we spent the next half-hour trying to find each other. I re-entered the building through the stage door and presented the award. Bridget found me and we went home and forgot about the whole incident.

The club was owned by Peter Stringfellow. The *Sun* heard about the incident and a front page was born.

Once we'd seen the story and we knew everyone else would have done too, Bridget and I had to ring round the family and let them know that everything was OK and we weren't splitting up. That was the tiresome side of being in the public eye. I know I was no Al Pacino in terms of status, but when you can't even pop out to get a pint of milk without being verbally abused or asked for an autograph, it's hard to imagine what it was once like to anonymous. It's so hard to explain, but walking down the street and no one looking twice is something precious, and impossible to get back once it's gone. Unless you go somewhere like South Africa, as I did twice, where it was a joy not to be recognised.

The time after I first left the show and when Bridget was pregnant became like a gap year from *EastEnders* – I went off and did a pantomime in Newcastle. It was my first pantomime, playing the wicked Queen's henchman in *Snow White*. Dana was Snow White and Ted Robbins and Mike Newman also starred. It turned out that the stint in the soap that had so worried me actually did me no harm at all and got me some regular stage work. By December 1985 my diaries were full of a sense of freedom at no longer being associated with *EastEnders*:

> No longer in the show and it is quite a relief. I look forward
> to the future.

The work was sporadic and perhaps I was missing the rigour and routine of regular employment, so it was a double-edged sword when *EastEnders* got in touch with my agent Annette again to request me back for a short-lived storyline. So, in March 1986, I headed back through the Elstree gates again. It was a weird sensation really, so much had happened in my life and I felt I had changed a lot – I felt more mature, more responsible, calmer, less worked up and nervous.

I was met by Julia in the canteen: she greeted me very warmly and seemed happy to have me back (she had a quality that no matter how you feel, the minute you see her, you want to please her). Not all the cast seemed happy, though. I also had a lovely chat with Bill Treacher (Arthur Fowler), who told me that being married makes you realise all the soap stuff is just a load of old rubbish – that the so-called fame and glamour is nothing compared to a happy home.

I had a fight scene with Ross Davidson (Andy O'Brien) and Linda Davidson (Mary Smith). Meanwhile there were all kinds of rows and complaints going on in the cast. The BBC didn't treat us at all well, I thought. We had to share cramped dressing rooms and employ our own secretaries – or, in some cases, mothers – to answer our fan mail. I was sure this didn't happen in commercial television or in top-rated drama in the US. Also, Julia had her favourites, which caused bad feeling among the rest of the cast.

You could make a soap about the birth and rise of a soap, I thought. The interpersonal goings-on and the changes that people went through with the show being a success would make riveting viewing. In her usual dry fashion Gretchen Franklin (Ethel May Skinner) told me: 'If you write it, make sure it's a tragedy. No funny lines.'

***

Shortly before I went back to *EastEnders* I met up with June Brown for the first time at Elstree. Julia and Tony were away so I got an update on the story from another top gun, Morag. I wrote in my diary: 'June Brown will be playing my mother, Dot Cotton. She seems warm and friendly. Her daughter, Louise, was there. She's also a Pisces and I have to say I did find her very attractive.'

At one time I was torn between Bridget and Louise, although I remained true to Bridget. Anyway, I left the studio looking forward to working with June.

Appropriately, on my first day back, the rain lashed against the windows and thunder crashed ominously around the buildings as I visited the Green Room. It was good to see everyone again and they gave me a warm welcome. I wrote in my diary: '[Producer] Matthew

Robinson thinks I should cut my hair short. We'll see what Julia and Tony think about that.'

I took lunch with Les Grantham (Den Watts), Shirley Cheriton (Debbie Wilkins), Paul Medford (Kelvin Carpenter) and Oscar James (Tony Carpenter).

Afterwards I met June Brown as the lift doors opened and she gave me a lift home. It was good to be back.

A few days later I started filming and Julia Smith decided to have my hair cut very short to increase the shock effect of Nick's return. The wardrobe department reported my jewellery and boots had gone missing.

At the end of the day, Sandy Ratcliff (Sue Osman) gave me a lift in her new classic car. I made the mistake of asking how fast it would go and she put her foot down on the accelerator on the North Circular while my own foot frantically worked an imaginary brake. Visions of broken glass and twisted metal filled my head. Somehow we made it safely to Finsbury Park. Leslie Grantham was another fast driver and lifts with him to Elstree would also be manic but I felt safer with him. I didn't own a car yet.

I soon discovered that June Brown was quite a chatterbox. Gretchen Franklin summed it up nicely when I asked her one day how June was: 'She hasn't drawn breath all morning,' she said with a mischievous glint in her eye.

Nick's new police nemesis was DS Roy Quick, played by Douglas Fielding. Fair-haired and red-faced, he was a good contrast to me, as Antonia Bird noted. She was also new to me – an actor's director rather than a technical person – and would take the time to work closely with us.

I always got on well with Anita Dobson (Angie Watts) and our scenes together were enjoyable.

After a day's filming with Anita I gave Sue Tully (Michelle Fowler) a driving lesson. It was a little hair-raising at times due to the way she'd drive across the centre lines of the pretty country lanes around Borehamwood.

My relationship with June Brown deepened the more we worked together. She was another one who drove me home and I remember thinking she was a wise person; she was well liked by the rest of the cast too.

It wasn't long after I returned when I saw a scene that I played with Leonard Fenton (Dr Legg) had been cut to the bone by Julia and Tony. It was my favourite moment of the two episodes I was involved with and as an actor I felt insulted that it had been cut to ribbons – a feeling shared by much of the rest of the cast. I felt bad for Leonard and the writer as well.

The run-through for the producers wasn't too good. It was under-rehearsed and I wrote in my diary: 'Julia had the look of thunder about her. It's amazing how we ever put the whole thing together.' The 'producers' run' was normally a serious and sombre affair but there was a lighter side when Leonard Fenton performed one of his animal sound effects and fooled a security guard into thinking there was a dog loose in the studio. Gretchen and I joined in with our best sheep and chicken noises. At that point Julia told everyone to shut up. Sometimes this job was more like being back at school.

My diaries from this time make interesting reading:

17 MARCH 1986

I had just two words to rehearse today: ''Ello, Ma', which gave me time to talk to everyone and suss out the atmosphere.

25 MARCH 1986

Struggled with the amount of lines and the way we were being expected to learn them, so was relieved to know that June [Brown] had the same trouble – she has been in the business a great deal longer than me so it was a huge comfort to know it wasn't just me being inadequate. Really starting to see divisions in the cast now – there was annoyance with Anita [Dobson] for taking a Saturday off to do a PA [personal appearance], but really this is Julia's fault – these jealousies and rifts. For my own part I am glad that I stand back and merely observe. No point getting involved in other people's rows, is there? I am here simply to do the work and do it well. It was clear that Julia had had a hard day but I think she was cheered up by our clairvoyant tea-party scene. It feels weird to be gearing up and getting back into the rhythm but knowing I will be gone in a few weeks after all that effort.

29 MARCH 1986

We ran a little late due to June's eye for detail. We all got a bottle of wine for having to put up with the rescheduling due to Anita taking the whole day off for a PA – they should not get in the way of the job and the result meant that we would all be under-rehearsed for the producers' run on Monday.

3 APRIL 1986

I managed to finish all of my scenes, even though it was a mad rush at the end as the wardrobe and make-up people were missing. Julia was not pleased and quite right – they should have been there right until the end. Good old June shook them up a bit when she got hold of them! It was my last day so there didn't seem much sense in getting involved.

Around this time I had started to do some personal appearances that paid really well, sometimes you could get around £500 a night for just the one gig, though mine was one with a difference as I did a whole stand-up villain routine. I got into a pattern and knew how to handle them – I would go to the gig in a stretch limo with Roger Burnett, my friend and P.A. organiser, and have a few drinks to get me in the right frame of mind for the rest of the night .

I'd get there and my job was to wind up the audience. Dressed in a leather jacket, with all the Nick gear on for full effect, I would insult them with certain catchphrases like: 'Up yours, the lot of you!' or 'Got any drugs?'. After doing this for a while and really winding them all up, I would shout 'Sod the lot of you, this music is crap!', grab the DJ and pretend to throttle him (all set up). The doormen would then come and drag me off the stage, through the crowd and out of the exit door, staging my 'eviction' in a very thorough way. I would then re-emerge in the VIP area and sign photos for fans and have some pictures taken, etc. I was once up for PA of the Year – I was really putting my all into it because people wanted a slice of Nick Cotton. Once with Ross Davidson in Swansea it was like *Eastenders* mania. The fans almost pulled us off the stage screaming and crying out.

I nearly did come a cropper in a particular club when I went into the manager's office to discuss how it was going to be when I got on stage. One of his doormen took his job very seriously and as the boss explained how he had to fake me being dragged off and 'chucked out', the doorman said: 'I'm sorry, mate. I can't fake it, I can't do that – I would have to hurt him!' We had to find another doorman who could act.

I have a vivid memory of being paid in cash and coming home one night and chucking the money all over Bridget as she sat up in bed. It was the most phenomenal feeling, to have all that cash in my hands for a few hours' work, and I was being paid to drink from a free bar too.

***

I was in and out of *EastEnders* and it was an eye-opener to see how much had changed in just a year. It's funny what happens to a group of people once they become institutionalised: everyone pretty much started out on the same level, but egos kicked in and suddenly it was every man for himself. I remember the original Mark Fowler, David Scarboro. A moody and talented teenage actor who struggled with fame, he latched onto me and so I tried to help him when he confided in me. David and I had many scenes together as Nick was hell-bent on leading Mark down the slippery slope that he himself was heading for. Between scenes I got to know the actor quite well.

I was thirty-two at the time and I found fame. It suddenly turned my life around, but I had managed to deal with it and secretly I think I'd longed for it, deep down inside. David found it very difficult when people shouted 'Oi! Mark Fowler. Alright, mate?' as he walked down the street. He was a warm-hearted but introverted soul. Unlike today no one at the BBC was there to advise or help any of us when we became celebrities and we were left to deal with it on our own.

David's moodiness annoyed several of the cast members but I could see what was going on in his mind. He had a James Dean-like character – a natural-born rebel with whom I could identify. I made a point of meeting up with him when we weren't filming and trying to rescue him from his despair and depression. I did my best to save him, and it was with great sadness that I learned, having split up with his girlfriend, he had committed suicide at Beachy Head in his car, accompanied by all his beloved Elvis records.

When I left Nick at BBC TV Elstree I prepared for my next role, definitely my most biggest and important part: I was about to become a father.

CHAPTER 16

THE ARRIVAL OF A NEWBORN BABY IS
THE EMBODIMENT OF HOPE
PAUL WILSON

During the summer of 1986 I'd been cast in a national tour of *Whodunnit?*, a thriller by Anthony Shaffer. My co-stars were Sandor Eles of *Crossroads* fame, Jack Douglas from the *Carry On...* films and his wife Su, Roy North of *The Basil Brush Show*, Lynda Baron from *Open All Hours* and Nicholas Smith from *Are You Being Served?*

Just before rehearsals began, Bridget and I set off for Dorset down the M3. The sunset was beautiful and just before nightfall we reached Lulworth Cove and the Cromwell Hotel, which was small but clean and comfortable. The mounds of the Purbeck Hills stood out like two large breasts to our right. I was so shattered that I immediately fell fast asleep. In the morning our first views of Dorset through the window were of blue skies and green hills, with a long, chalky path to the top. The hotel owner had noticed that I was rather exhausted the previous night and he gave us a much-needed breakfast before I phoned another hotel in Wareham, a converted priory, just by the River Frome. I wrote in my diary: 'We have a four-poster bed on

Saturday night!' It was a far grander hotel but this was a treat for Bridget, who was weeks away from giving birth. Soon I would be off on tour and this was one of our last chances to be alone together.

We looked around Lulworth and gazed across at the clear blue sea. There were lots of day-trippers about and we would have had to walk a long way to escape them. It was out of the question for Bridget at that point so we headed off to Wareham and settled into the luxurious hotel, which was very tastefully decorated.

The mood was broken by a phone call from my agent Annette Stone. I had raised money in support of a boy called Kevin Canning, who had cystic fibrosis, and she was ringing to let me know that he had passed away. I'd never met him but his early death certainly affected me and I went on to raise hundreds of pounds for research into the condition when I later ran the London Marathon in 1988.

We rarely made it out of the suite, named after the nearby beauty spot Durdle Door, and we slept until early evening. In my diary I wrote: 'The wind and the rain came up from the south-west and a blackbird sheltered in the yew tree beneath our window.' We had dinner in the converted cellar beneath the hotel and on the way Bridget spotted the actor Edward Fox being turned away at reception! The food was exquisite and the service impeccable – it was the best meal we had enjoyed in a long time.

In the days leading up to our holiday I'd been working non-stop and in my diary the next day I wrote: 'A bad night's sleep full of strange dreams. Still paying for my 48 hours awake.' But I was extremely glad to be away from the hustle and bustle back in town. I wrote in my diary: 'Bridget looks beautiful and baby looks like the fruit on a tree which is ripe and ready to drop at any time.'

On the Sunday we drove across Dorset. It was a gloriously sunny day that we spent on the Isle of Purbeck. We passed through Corfe Castle and Swanage and ended up having lunch at the Manor House on the clifftops above Studland Bay. Bridget said that the dunes and the beach reminded her of South Africa. Back at the hotel in Wareham we slept on the lawn in the sun and then had a new suite for the second night, called the Purbeck. It too had a four-poster and a spa bath – I was glad that I could provide this luxury for my wife.

I did a run along the Frome and we spent a quiet evening relaxing in the suite. We also had dinner in the room – we felt we couldn't have asked for anything more. That night we made love beautifully and fell into a deep, contented sleep.

When I got back to London I heard a quote that seemed very apt. It was someone from Kuwait on the TV who said, 'A child is like an uncut diamond. Education is the polishing of that diamond.' I love a good wise quote. It seemed so right at that time.

On my return to town I went straight into rehearsals for *Whodunnit?* and continued over what proved to be a very hot August. It was an uncomfortable time for poor Bridget, now about to give birth at any minute. Luckily, our basement flat in Chelsea was reasonably cool.

The tour was to open at the Taunton Brewhouse Theatre and both Bridget and I were both on tenterhooks as it was a long way from central London. My agent, Annette Stone, arranged with the production company that should Bridget go into labour, they would put on an understudy. Sure enough, a day or so after opening, I received a call in Taunton on 28 August to say that Bridget had been taken to the West London Hospital in Hammersmith in preparation for the birth.

The cast wished me well and I set off as soon as I could up the M5 in the blue 520 BMW that I'd bought from a friend of Leslie Grantham. It was a bright sunny morning and the full capabilities of the German car took me the 160 miles or more to Hammersmith in just two hours twenty minutes.

Bridget was in agony when I arrived. But she had a radiance about her. They gave her an epidural as she had been suffering since the day before. Pat was the midwife, a lovely lady who came from Trinidad.

At about 2.30am the epidural wore off and Bridget's contractions became more regular. She held on tightly to Jerry, one of the midwives, and me. I told Bridget it was 3am and she informed me she didn't want to know the time! At 3.03am precisely, on Friday, 29 August, out came our baby – it all seemed so quick. Before I knew it, they had placed the child on Bridget's stomach and Pat handed me a pair of scissors. I cut the cord and tiny drops of blood splashed on my fingers. As I held Bridget's hand I kissed them away.

As the medical team swept baby aside my first remark was, 'What beautiful ears!' Not at all like mine which are quite large. I glanced at my child being measured and checked. We had a lovely baby girl, although the cord had become wrapped around her neck and she was a bit blue – a small, blue thing. As I held my daughter, Bridget was in agony and our baby was wailing then things calmed down.

We had already decided to name her Rosanna Ivy Tina Altman (the middle two names were after her grandmothers). A mixture of Bridget and I , she had a thick thatch of strong black hair, large brown eyes, shell-like ears and kissable lips. For the record her weight was 6lb 2.5oz, she was 19in long and the diameter of her head was 13.5in. Her temperature was 37°F. The nurses kept coming in to see 'the most beautiful baby on the ward.' Lambert and the family came up from West Sussex. So Bridget was in good company.

I was back on stage on Saturday night .I didn't sleep and I was so tired that I fell over at Victoria station on my way back to Taunton . The doctors gave us permission to take Rosanna to Glasgow for the next date on the tour. I was so pleased that my wife and daughter would be with me and they accompanied me on the rest of the tour over the summer.

In Glasgow, Lynda Baron – a lovely lady to work with – was the first person to babysit Rosanna. As the production progressed we became good friends with Sandor and Jack and Su Douglas too. Our friends on tour would kindly look after Rosanna so that I could take

Bridget for a night out, or so that she could catch up on some much-needed sleep. Rosanna was a good baby and those were happy times for the three of us.

Poor Sandor came a cropper in Brighton when he forgot that we had a matinee on a different day that week! We couldn't contact him so a camp young actor called Richard Waites was forced to go on and with very little rehearsal had to read from the book. He looked nothing like Sandor but we made it through the performance. The missing actor arrived at the front of the theatre just as the matinee audience was exiting. An elderly lady spotted him and said, 'Sorry you weren't in it, dear, but the young man who took your part was word perfect.' Sandor, who was both charming and sensitive, was mortified.

At the end of the first act, Sandor – the 'oily Levantine' (the original name for the play) – was beheaded by an unknown assailant. The severed head once bounced onto a sloped stage – known as a 'rake' – and rolled into the audience, causing consternation among the patrons in the front row.

On a following tour that we did of the production, Bernie Winters took over from Nicholas Smith as the detective. He was questioning the cast in the Key Theatre, Peterborough, when we all got a terrible fit of the giggles – 'corpsing', as it's known. It was the most widespread case of corpsing that I'd ever experienced in the theatre and the audience caught it too. Everything calmed down but unfortunately, Bernie's very next line (delivered from that most comical of faces) was: 'I don't think you lot are taking this very seriously.' And off we all went again.

Touring was pleasurable, seeing beautiful countryside on the way. The downside was that we didn't get much in the way of expenses and couldn't always thoroughly check the digs we had booked. I remember one time – on the first tour with Bridget and Rosanna – we checked into a hotel on a road leading out of Birmingham.

I thought it was a straightforward, two-star hotel for businessmen but when I got back from the Alexandra Theatre I saw a couple of women running down the corridor clad only in T-shirts and knickers. From behind closed doors I could hear the gentle thwack of someone being spanked.

We checked out the very next morning.

Eventually the tour run came to an end and we went back to London and to a very happy domestic time at 67a Sydney Street, Chelsea. We still had quite a good social life and some excellent professional babysitters. We were still renting from Olive and Francis Brown, who owned the entire house. When we returned with Rosanna, Olive said 'I can see that Bridget definitely hasn't been straying.'

***

During the summer of 1987 Bridget and I decided that we definitely had to move from the basement in Sydney Street – there wasn't enough room now that we had Rosanna . Through the *Evening Standard* we found a beautiful 1930s flat, 8 Townend House on the High Street at Kingston, with a great view of the Thames. When we first went to see it, the sun was shining on the river, casting a golden light into the flat. We knew immediately that this was where we would like to live. We could never have afforded somewhere bigger in Chelsea and here at last we found and owned a spacious home of our own and Rosanna had her own bedroom, also overlooking the river. In fact, when we arrived to take our first look at the flat, Rosanna, uncannily, toddled straight into the room that was to be hers. We moved in just two days after the great hurricane that devastated huge parts of the country in mid-October.

We missed the hurricane entirely, still being in the basement flat when it hit on Friday, 16th. The first indication of what had happened was waking up to a power cut. When I left the flat that morning I saw trees and fences were down all over Chelsea. Waitrose was also without power and the local newsagent had a candle in the window. I saw a motorbike that had been blown over in Stewart's Grove. Branches and leaves littered the streets. The power came back on in the flat just as Rosanna happened to jab her finger in the direction of the light switch, causing us to joke that she had superhuman powers.

It wasn't until we drove to Kingston to the new flat that we realised the full extent of the damage, though. It was like passing through a war zone. There were police everywhere, trees on top of cars, trees buried in houses, broken iron railings and one tree that had missed a garden but snapped off a lamppost. Parts of England's heritage had gone forever – I heard that there's only one oak left in Sevenoaks, Kent. It was later reported that 18 people had died in the storm and around 15 million trees were destroyed; the total bill came to £1.5 billion.

CHAPTER 17

ONE JOY DISPELS A HUNDRED CARES
CONFUCIUS

In February 1988 Bridget's parents, Lambert and Ivy Poodhun, kindly offered to pay for the three of us to accompany them and Bridget's brothers, Jerome and Julian, to South Africa. I bought my first video camera for the trip. Rosanna was then eighteen months old and the Poodhuns wanted to take their first grandchild to visit the rest of the family – it would be my first visit too.

There is little jet lag as South Africa is virtually on the same latitude as the UK. We had just three hours' sleep after packing before our early start to the airport. Everything seemed to be in place, down to the last phone call. It was a clear sky as we approached Heathrow but disaster struck at Security: Bridget didn't have her passport. I thought she'd taken it; she thought I'd got it. She took a cab back to Kingston but we had less than ninety minutes before take-off and the round trip was at least forty minutes. I sat with the rest of the family, waiting anxiously. All of our connections would be messed up and we were in danger of having to abandon the trip. Bridget phoned in a panic because she didn't know where to look, but once she'd calmed down, she found the passport and got back with five minutes to spare.

Her father Lambert was a calming influence as we waited at Passport Control. Then we ran all the way to our gate with Rosanna perched on a luggage trolley – she was having a great time. We made it, hot and sweaty, on board the plane. I don't think I've ever prayed so much in such a short space of time!

'It was like a bomb was set to a timer,' said Bridget, 'and we had to stop it.'

With seconds to spare, we did. We ended up waiting nine hours in Lisbon but it didn't matter as we were on our way.

Lambert, a Man of the Cloth, always travelled wearing his clerical collar. In times of difficulty he can work wonders and I later discovered that he had had a word with the pilot, who gave us an extra few minutes to catch the flight.

We stayed near Durban in a luxurious house in Reservoir Hills owned by Bridget's Uncle Raj and Auntie Shirley; also with her cousins, Leon and Miranda. Their dog was called Tammy and Rosanna really enjoyed playing with her. There was a swimming pool and a Mercedes in the drive. Raj was a very successful barrister and his house was extremely pleasant, with fantastic views across the valley. The thunderstorms were spectacular to watch from such a great height.

We were kept busy, visiting relatives most days. The hospitality was second to none and Rosanna was adored by one and all. We went to the coast where, with apartheid still in force, I should technically have been on the white beach while Bridget (of Indian descent) and Rosanna would only have been allowed on the 'coloured' beach. I was allowed to join them in their area and gazed over at the whites-only area. A flock of black birds flew overhead and settled on their beach. I wonder what the authorities would have made of that?

Bridget told me that as a child there had been benches she wasn't allowed to sit on. There was a miniature version of Durban, Mini-Town, made for kids but only whites were allowed and she'd always wanted to see it. How sad that must have been for her. Hence their move to the UK.

I had a great time on that holiday and swam in the sea off the Wild Coast, risking the local sharks. It was such a beautiful country and had every kind of region, from alpine to desert climates. I just thought what a pity it was that the country was in the grip of apartheid.

Later that year, I ran my first London Marathon to raise money for research into cystic fibrosis. I had trained quite seriously, with my neighbour, Chris. Our longest run was from Kingston to Putney and back on a route of about twenty miles. What an experience! It took me into another dimension, mentally and physically, and I remember the joy as I finally reached the Embankment on 25 April 1988 and spotted Bridget, Rosanna and Chris at the barriers. I ran over to kiss Bridget and Rosanna and seeing them spurred me on to the finish (I completed in four hours fifteen minutes).

I ran the London Marathon again in 2008, this time with the actor Gary Webster – known for taking over from Dennis Waterman in the reboot of *Minder*. This time around I managed five hours fifteen minutes, which I didn't think was too bad – I'd only put on an hour in twenty years. As I reached Buckingham Palace a man shot past me and called out, 'I'm not letting that bleedin' elephant beat me to the finish!' I looked to my left and sure enough, there was someone in an elephant costume lumbering along beside me.

I've often wondered why on earth people dress up to run that far – it's hard enough without extra weight! One year someone even ran it in a fully weighted diving suit (I think he took a few days). In 2011 my friend Eddie Kidd completed the marathon in 43 days, an astonishing achievement following his motorbike accident in 1996 that had left him paralysed and brain-damaged. Family and friends, including Ray Winstone, Joe Pasquale and I , cheered him along the way.

***

Back in 1996 I had participated in a less strenuous charity fund-raiser when a leading charity called NCH Action for Children contacted celebrities such as Jenny Agutter, Tony Adams, Barry Cryer, Michael Aspel, Christopher Biggins and I . They asked each of us to provide a poem for a book called *For the Children*. At the time I was still living in a 1930s flat, 8 Townend House in Kingston. We had been there for eight or nine years. Having had the experience of writing songs over the years (basically poems set to music), I knew I wouldn't find it difficult to pen a poem but what would the subject be? Lo and behold, the answer was just outside my window, flowing constantly every day – dear old Father Thames! It had played a big part in my life, as I was born and raised in the Thames Valley and learned to swim in a tributary of the Thames called the Loddon. This was my inspiration for the first – and so far the only – poem I have ever had published:

THE RIVER

Outside my window,
This old river flows.
Fast down to the sea
She carries her woes,
Of flotsam and jetsam,
From cities and towns,
Once clear but now muddy
This old river frowns.
Once there was swimming
And dipping of toes.
Yet now comes pollution,

IN THE NICK OF TIME

As each chemical grows.
Dead fish float on seawards,
Past Richmond and Kew.
If you lived in this river,
Your corpse would be blue.
So take heed corporations,
Who don't have a care.
Your neglect is destroying,
This water so fair.
For now I just watch,
As the sails glide on by.
And the fishermen's lights
Are like stars in the sky.
I pray that this river
Will flow on forever.
To cherish its beauty should be
Our endeavour.

CHAPTER 18

BE THE CHANGE THAT YOU WANT
TO SEE IN THE WORLD
GANDHI

I'd had a break from *EastEnders* and then my agent called to say they wanted me back again. If I'd been single I'm not sure I would have said yes to it again – I still had dreams of a Hollywood career and more serious parts. But I now had the responsibilities of a mortgage and taking care of Bridget and Rosanna, which I would continue to do for many years. I had no choice but to return for purely financial reasons.

So I returned with a brand new storyline and my onscreen 'Ma'. When June Brown was cast my real mother, Tina Stewart, told me she looked more like my mother than she did – a great compliment for the casting department. It was to be the beginning of one of my best professional relationships and the start of a deep and treasured friendship.

Sometimes I would question how the elderly cast members were treated. For example June Brown used to drive herself in well into her late seventies and it was only after much consternation and a lot of negotiation that the producers agreed to pay for her car. Poor old Anna Wing (Lou Beale) used to pay for her own taxis.

Lots of people think if you work on a soap you are treated like royalty, with cars and other perks, but that simply isn't the case. I will never forget when *EastEnders* was at its peak in the mid 1980s and we were on the nation's TV screens and often all over the red tops and poor Anita Dobson (Angie Watts) was fighting her way in on the tube with fans right in her face and made her journey almost dangerous. It wasn't a civilised way to start the working day, that's for sure. Actors crashed their cars driving into work due to sheer tiredness.

It was far better financially when the omnibus set-up was still in place, which meant getting 80 per cent on top of your original salary. But then they disbanded it and in 2015 rearranged the payment structure. Luckily for my last comeback it was still under the old contractual terms and was paid in the old-fashioned way.

Julia Smith ruled with an iron fist. If you displeased her she didn't even waste words telling you, she would simply cut you dead. I lost count of the number of people who would be plastered over the tabloids (usually the *News of the World* on a Sunday), and then come in on a Monday morning. They would pass Julia in the corridor, nod and say 'Morning, Julia', only to receive a stony look and deathly silence. She could make or break the atmosphere with the tilt of her head or a single glance and I certainly came a cropper when I tried to take her on during this particular return.

When I got word via the cast that there were plans to make Nick and George 'Lofty' Holloway (Tom Watt) gay, I couldn't imagine anything more ludicrous. My issue was never the idea of a gay relationship, not for one moment – it was the lack of continuity. Nick hadn't entered the soap gay, far from it, and neither had Lofty, the amiable Queen Vic pot man. He and Nick were not great friends. In fact Lofty had always tried to avoid Nick, who bullied him at times. It is one of those examples of knowing your character inside out and being very aware of what's passable and what doesn't work at all. Every actor wants to be involved in a ratings booster, but not at the expense of all the hard work he has put into building a credible character that makes sense to the viewers. Treat the fans as idiots at your peril – they truly believe in these characters who make their way into their living rooms every week. To the hardcore supporters they are real. Once you lose the fans by doing something that doesn't sit right, you can never get that trust back.

The rumour carried on for a few more days. So I went to find Julia. She was sitting in the BBC restaurant in Elstree with a group of writers and producers. So I walked over to her and said: 'Can I have a quick word, Julia?'

I was met with the dead-eye stare so familiar to so many, but I felt it was important so I came straight to the point.

'It's just that I've heard a rumour that you might be making Nick and Lofty gay. To be honest, I just don't think that's a good idea. I don't think it will work.'

She was busy so I didn't really hang around for a full response. I just said my piece, turned around and left. Low murmurings began as soon as I backed away from the table but I didn't hear what was being said. Many weeks later someone told me that Julia simply turned to one of the writers and said: 'Write him out.'

And that was that, I had received the grand order of the Julia Smith boot! True to her word, my stretch was shorter than might have been intended when I signed on the dotted line a few months previously, but I was determined that Nick would remain just as he had always been.

***

In the summer of 1988, with Julia Smith in the Director's chair , our *EastEnders* cast and crew relocated to a motel in Ashburton on the edge of Dartmoor. Work continued as normal in Elstree while Leslie

Grantham and various others including myself went to a special location: namely Dartmoor Prison, a Category C men's prison. A wing that was soon to be redecorated had been allocated to us for a couple of weeks to be used as the fictional Dickens Hill Prison, not far from Albert Square.

Each day we set off in a minibus from the motel to the prison, winding our way across Dartmoor. We sang songs as we went, laughing and cracking jokes, but as soon as the prison doors opened and we entered the 'airlock' (the space between the outer prison doors and the interior doors), everyone fell silent. No one had told us to be quiet, but for some reason we were. The prisoners threw pornographic magazines out of their windows at the women on the catering trucks in the yard below and I remember seeing the glint of shaving mirrors as the inmates tried to get a better view of what was going on.

Once the doors had closed we were confined for the whole day with few distractions. There were no mobile phones then. This was an intense period of filming as Leslie Grantham was going to leave and needed to record as many episodes in as short a time as possible. Later he told the press he'd recorded 90 episodes in five weeks and then took the rest of the year off.

The cells in our wing dated back to Napoleonic times and, according to one of the real guards, Americans often visited to see the graves of their ancestors from the time of the American Revolutionary War (1775–83). They laid flowers on the graves and when they'd gone, the Governor repurposed them to brighten up the prison. When one group unexpectedly came back for a second visit, he had to hurriedly gather the blooms up and return them to the graves.

Through a door at the end of the wing we could see some of the real inmates. A depressing sight, they looked drugged and had not a hint of brightness in their faces. I wrote postcards home while sitting in one of the cells and after a few days I was not the only one who began to feel as if we were doing time for real. It must have been particularly strange for Leslie, as he had served many years in prison in real life. I never let on to anyone that I too had done some time!

I had several scenes with Mr Grantham and in one Nick confessed to 'Dirty' Den that he had killed Reg Cox. In the original story Nick had been cleared. He thought that Den would be impressed – but he wasn't.

I recall a young actor, playing a prison guard, was nervous at working with Leslie Grantham. He kept drying (something that happens to all actors occasionally). It was agonising to watch because we couldn't leave the set, being inside the prison, and take after take – directed by Julia Smith – was shown on the monitors. Sadly, many of his lines were cut. I myself dried a bit later, filming a scene on the walkways.

'Cut!' called Julia. 'Not another one who doesn't know his lines.'

'Don't worry, Julia,' I said. 'I'll be fine next time.'

Leslie could see that I was slightly upset and it was one of the few times that he showed any affection towards me. He put his arm around me and said, 'Don't worry, John. She's an old bag, just like Ethel.'

'Thanks, Leslie,' I said and I instantly felt a lot better because he had made me laugh. We went on to do the scene perfectly.

Because we were away from the studio, Julia became more relaxed off-set. One night I actually got to have a proper conversation with her at the hotel bar. I must have mentioned to her that a lot of people were in fear of her very presence because of how strict she could be. 'When I was a little girl, John,' she confided, 'I was aware that I had a "dark side". If I did something naughty – or broke something – my mother would reprimand me. "It wasn't me, Mother," I'd say, "Ms Jones did it." And she is my dark side.'

A few days after I returned to Elstree, I wrote in my diary:

June [Brown] agreed with me that our homecoming scene is badly written and that it hasn't been blocked very well. Tony Holland was at the Square and I told him I had a couple of ideas for future storylines and he said to write them down. Oscar James [Tony Carpenter] had a bust-up with Julia and is leaving in the summer. He has been treated very badly, not only in his and Sally's storylines [Sagoe, who played Sally Carpenter, Tony's wife]. We filmed the beating up of Mehmet [Osman] on the Square in the middle of the night – it was bloody freezing! Tom Watt and Leslie Grantham were pissing around in rehearsal as usual. There have been so many changes to the set, 3 new houses, a railway bridge and community centre.

The changes June and I made to our script were agreed. Les Grantham is pissing me off with his 'Nancy Boy Cotton' quote. It is his own personal vindictiveness and I just think he needs to leave as soon as possible. Tom Watt – I worry about him. Bill [Treacher] and Letitia [Dean] haven't changed a bit – they are so professional.

People often ask me who my most annoying co-star was, or who I disliked the most and I would have to say Leslie Grantham. He was an oddball – deliberately provocative and tricky, and although we never had a blazing row there were times I wanted to punch him! Once, in a fight scene, he deliberately pulled a chunk of my hair out. I like to think he just got carried away, but sometimes the darker side of Leslie would emerge through his character Dirty Den and it was hard to judge what he was thinking and what he would or could do. He wanted to be kingpin and didn't like the fact there was a new boy on the block getting all the attention. The young girls liked me and the older cast, like Wendy Richard, and June Brown, and Barbara Windsor later on, I got on well with too – I think they liked the fact that I worked hard and took it seriously.

There really wasn't much opportunity to fall out with any of my co-stars – the way that Nick's scenes were filmed and due to the very isolated nature of his relationship with Dot, he didn't really interact with the other characters very often. I thought that they never examined what Nick had been up to off-screen; that the viewers were never shown his other life, and strands could have been developed on the show, although there was one special episode, *The Return of Nick Cotton*. He was certainly a character who could have been up to anything, which is why I enjoyed his prison scenes so much – they allowed the strict parameters to be stretched a little.

***

It was a hard time of juggling my family life and work and it meant that the childcare was mainly left to Bridget, though I did what I could when I was home. Rosanna and I had such a lovely bond. She was now saying 'Dada' and running around – she had such a sunny and happy nature, she hardly ever cried. Bridget was now working part-time. We loved our flat and our daughter was happy; we felt very blessed.

CHAPTER 19

COCAINE IS GOD'S WAY OF SAYING YOU'RE MAKING TOO MUCH MONEY
ROBIN WILLIAMS

I was constantly going in and out of *EastEnders* over the years and grateful for the work at the time, but I observed that some of the regulars who were once so pleased to have found success in the programme were now complaining about it, and they told me how awful it all was. In turn I would tell them: 'You should try signing on at the Kingston Job Centre and being out of work for a few months.' They had nothing to say to that but it must have given them food for thought.

I always tried to be the consummate professional: if you mess up the system it costs money, if you are late, it costs thousands of pounds. There are 500 people who work on that show today and they've got it down to a fine art. If one cog doesn't turn then it's a disaster for everyone down the line. I tried to introduce some rules to my drinking too – I never took it to the studio and I really don't recall any long nights in the studio bar afterwards at that time, because I drove. The truth about me, booze and drugs is that I was a bit schizophrenic – I could have ingested who knows what the night before but the next day I would be running for miles to get it out of my system.

I think I was quite compartmentalised really – if there was an affair or something unsavoury going on among the cast or crew, I was always the last to know. The job was the main thing for me – concentrating, getting it right and being invited back. A bit like Bill Treacher – go in there, do the bloody job and leave the bad behaviour to others, then go home to my wife and daughter. There were some real characters there, and I loved standing on the sidelines and watching the sparks fly at times. There were a few, like Wendy Richard, who had a real reputation for a sharp putdown. I was one of the lucky ones who got on well with her but my God, you didn't want to cross her, God rest her soul! She didn't stand for any nonsense. Whenever I came back, she would always say: 'Thank God, we've got a real villain back on the premises, not just those pretenders!'

I used to take that as a compliment.

**

Nick's reputation only grew worse with each episode. That meant being in Make-up could take ages. It was the heroin scenes in 1991 that really required time and effort from the brilliant make-up boys and girls, especially Françoise and Martine. When I watch them back, both the heroin addiction in 1991 and the actual death scene in 2015 – well, they are magicians! They even painted my teeth green. How about some soap awards for the makeup department?

I think the heroin scenes were some of the most dramatic of my career, and I'm proud of the impact we genuinely made by airing such a gritty storyline. One of the most affecting addiction stories I have ever heard was from a guy whom the writers hired to come in and advise me. He was a drummer and had been addicted to heroin.

Determined to kick it, he did this by locking himself in a room in Richmond upon Thames with a couple of bottles of whisky. In the clearest terms he described what Nick would have gone through to get clean. What cold turkey actually was, and how the body was affected – banging on the door, pleading, etc. I injected all of that into Nick, mentally and physically. Your legs can't relax and all you want is to be able to get out of your body. Searching for respite, you inch your legs up the wall, hoping for some reprieve, no matter how fleeting. You look at the clock and the hands don't seem to have moved, so you take another shot of whisky. Shivering, shaking, vomiting, wanting to die – all you want is another fix, whatever the cost. I recorded everything he knew about addiction and how he had kicked it with the help of whisky.

What they did to Nick on the show was actually a form of torture as he didn't get any outside help, and the residents of the Square paid the price. We saw that it is dangerous to tackle such deep-seated addictions without professional help – Dot was too proud to commit him to hospital, believing a mother's love and God's guidance could fix anything. But it backfired on everyone, because when Nick did eventually escape, he went on the rampage and murdered Eddie Royle (Michael Melia).

I remember very clearly being on set during those heroin storylines and looking like a complete physical wreck. Sue Tully (Michelle Fowler) was always witty whenever I bumped into her in the corridors – I would look an absolute fright but would still be wearing my favourite aftershave. She would breathe in as I passed, take a puff on an invisible cigarette (imitating Nick) and say: 'John, it doesn't seem quite right... Your fragrance!'

On location in west London during this time (dressed as the down and out that Nick was supposed to be), I decided to walk around between takes under the Hammersmith Flyover looking pretty dreadful. I had grown my hair and beard to try and make it look as authentic as possible and I thought it would be a good idea to put the disguise to the test and beg, to see if I could pass the authenticity test. No one recognised me as Nick Cotton but people avoided me like the plague – no one would come anywhere near me.

I'm not sure if it was being in costume but I got the devil in me in the front seat of the car, trying to get back into the studio at the BBC Centre. The BBC security guard took one look at me as we reached the studio gates and said, 'No way, you can't come in here, mate!' I deliberately started lolling about as if I was going to be sick and he refused to let me in. The runner had to phone the office to get them to tell him to let me in.

There were certain things in place – you saw the tourniquet being bound around Nick's upper arm and all the accompanying paraphernalia laid out, but you never saw the actual 'heroin' or the needle go into the arm onscreen because that was deemed too much. Despite the fact it was tastefully done, I vetoed Rosanna from watching any of those drugs scenes – I didn't want her to see her father playing a smack addict. It was gruelling doing those scenes and to shake off Nick after a long day's filming, I would shower and then get in the car and put on Classic FM. I found it soothing. It also made a change to get fan mail for Nick that was about more than how badly he treated his 'Ma'. There was one letter that summed up just how hard-hitting the storyline was. It said: 'We love Nick Cotton. Seeing him on heroin, we ain't never going to touch the stuff.'

As an actor you can't ask for more than that. You are, hopefully, saving lives.

In my time I have experimented with quite a few drugs so I guess for that reason I am fairly open-minded. I always thought that by now, in 2016, if you were of sound mind and had been checked out by your GP and you wanted a bit of coke or hashish, you would be able to get it out of a government-licensed machine. I've never understood what would be wrong with the idea of putting your credit card into some kind of vending machine and retrieving cocaine or weed. It could be monitored so that you could only take out a specific amount per person, per week.

**

After some years with Annette Stone, the agent who had sent me along to the *EastEnders* audition, for which I was very grateful, I decided it was time to move on. I went to Kate Sharkey at ICM in Oxford Street, one of the biggest agencies in the world. Things went well with her, but unfortunately for me she got pregnant and retired from the business. I was then taken on by Paul Lyon-Maris at the same company, which did not work out.

So I moved to Roger Carey Associates in Chiswick and became good friends with him and his wife Primi, who was born on the same day as me, 2 March. We shared many good times together and some very fine curries – not least because Roger was part Indian. He found me some great jobs, including *Chicago – The Musical*, and Matthew his assistant was great fun and a hard worker. As so often happens in this business, though, things began to go too quiet and sadly we parted company some years later, by which time his offices were in Pimlico. He's now based at Shepperton Studios.

Next came Harris Pearson – Mel Harris and Paul Pearson, recommended by the well-known casting director Kate Plantin. It was Paul who looked after me until the pair split and then he joined David Daly on the King's Road, which became Daly-Pearson. I moved with him because he knew exactly what I wanted and we agreed on most things. When he became independent at the start of 2010 he formed London Theatrical with fewer clients so that he could concentrate more on people such as myself, Faye Dunaway, Joss Ackland and Rula Lenska. And yet, once again, things went very quiet and I was recommended to see Malcolm Browning at International Artists in the West End. We got on well, he was thrilled to take me on, but he didn't produce a single job for me.

I went for a curry in Teddington with Paul Pearson and a couple of days later he phoned and said that while he shouldn't mention it, there was a part for a paparazzi photographer in a new film at Pinewood – *Photoshoot*. I gratefully accepted his offer to audition even though the convention in the business was you couldn't be represented by more than one agent.

The script was sent to me, I memorised it and auditioned at the Spotlight office off Leicester Square. They offered me the part and I told Paul I would accept. I was cast alongside Debbie Arnold, an actress also represented by someone in Malcolm Browning's office, and someone in the office at International Artists mentioned it in passing to Malcolm. He had no idea what was going on and was very confused. That afternoon I was on the train to Cardiff for a charity gig with Jane Cotton (daughter of Bill) when I decided to call Malcolm and tell him it was over. We parted company there and then on the phone, and I was back with Paul Pearson at London Theatrical, and I have been with him ever since.

Showbiz... Don't you just love it?

CHAPTER 20

**THE PEOPLE WHO GET ON IN THIS WORLD ARE THE
PEOPLE WHO GET UP AND LOOK FOR THE CIRCUMSTANCES
THEY WANT, AND IF THEY CAN'T FIND THEM, MAKE THEM**
GEORGE BERNARD SHAW

I can honestly say that ten years of marriage to Bridget wasn't
always a bed of roses but there were many happy times. We
shared the joy of bringing up Rosanna in our flat in Kingston, we
holidayed in South Africa, Gibraltar, Marbella, Castle Combe and
Lynton in the West Country, we had picnics in Bushy Park, and I
was with my daughter for most of her formative years. Although I
worked extensively, we took Rosanna to most of the major cities in
the UK when I toured with *Whodunnit?* and also with a play about
Marie Lloyd called *Up in the Gallery* in 1989. When I kissed Marie
Lloyd (Adrienne Posta) onstage, little Rosanna got up and turned
her back on the performance.

The *News of the World* paid for the three of us to go to Orlando,
Florida, when Rosanna was about six. It was an all-expenses trip
that included a penthouse suite in a hotel for a week, a Chrysler car
and VIP tickets to all the attractions – Universal Studios, MGM and

Disneyworld. In return, they took hundreds of photographs but when they ran the story it was tiny – the size of a postcard with just one picture of me posing with Jaws the shark!

Rosanna was just the right age for the trip – any younger and she wouldn't have remembered it at all. We spent the entire week in the theme parks. There was so much to see and do. It was completely different to anything I'd experienced in the UK. Compared to ours they were so much more advanced – Universal made the biggest parks at home look like a fair on a village green.

The *Back to the Future* ride was particularly amazing. We were in a DeLorean car in the pitch-black darkness. The hydraulics rocked the vehicle and shot it forwards towards a screen that made it look as though you were going through the iconic clock from the movies. *Star Wars* was equally thrilling. We were hurtled through outer space on a joyride piloted by two droids. Our VIP passes gave us the added advantage of being able to jump all the queues. We learned a few trade secrets – such as the multiple Mickey Mouses and other characters at work at any one time. I was in the Disney park office one day when an official on the telephone said, 'Get another Mickey down to the gate – the one down there has passed out.' It was extremely uncomfortable to be dressed up as those lovable figures when the temperatures hit 80° Fahrenheit or more. The characters were not permitted to be out too long; they were also forbidden to talk to anyone – hearing Snow White with a Mexican accent or a deep Southern drawl would be alarming for any impressionable young fan.

Rosanna took a shine to the Ewoks from *Star Wars*. She had three of them in toy form. Someone stole them from the edge of the hotel pool and she was particularly upset because she'd made a home for them in the safe in our hotel room, complete with grass. The things you do for your children – on the last day I had to rush to the studio shop to get replacements. We've still got this batch!

***

Bridget and I were deeply in love for many years and we had a great passion running through our relationship. When things seemed to be going slightly wrong, I whisked her away to Paris because as much as we loved Rosanna, we needed a couple of days alone. On birthdays we would always make scrambled eggs and smoked salmon for breakfast accompanied by a glass of Buck's Fizz for one another.

Our flat had a log fire and there was nothing cosier than lying beside it during the winter months. It was blissful. Rosanna was always our number one priority and being our only child, she became slightly spoilt, but that's only natural.

***

My friend Julie Peasgood, the actress and presenter, was working for a radio station in London. She asked me if I'd like to go to Antigua for her holiday programme. Two years earlier a hurricane had devastated the island and the inhabitants were keen to publicise the fact that everything was back to normal. Armed with a Marant tape recorder, I flew to the Caribbean for the very first time.

I stayed at the Sandals couples-only resort. I arrived when it was dark and heard the night-time sounds of the jungle mingling with the sea lapping on the shore. They had given me the honeymoon suite in an exclusive bungalow apartment on the far left-hand side of the resort on the beach. Flowers decorated the bed and I was pleased to see a full complement of alcoholic beverages in the drinks cabinet. However, I was going to stick to the vodka only. Bridget had hoped to join me as a surprise, but it didn't happen. So, there I was, in paradise on my own.

I had breakfast on the terrace and the waiter noticed I was sitting alone.

'Wassap, man?' he asked. 'Had a row with the missus?'

Randy Wilkie, the manager of Sandals, helped me to explore the island over the next ten days. It has 365 beaches – one for every day of the year. I've always loved the sea and all things aquatic and I quickly fell in love with the Caribbean.

I went on a short scuba-diving course, and then swam down quite deep over a wreck out at sea. What a wonderful experience that was! However, two foolish Spanish tourists on the dive didn't obey the instruction not to touch the coral, and towards the end of the dive they cut themselves and left a trail of fresh blood in the water. You probably know what I'm going to say next – cue *Jaws* music! As I loved the water so much I was the last one to climb out of the boat and I didn't look behind me. As I swung my legs round to heave myself out, I glanced down into the water and just below my feet the dark grey silhouette of a large shark swept past – I guess you could say I was inches from being its lunch. Heart pounding, I quickly clambered onto the deck, relieved to be in one piece. I didn't mention it to the Spanish tourists – they didn't speak English anyway.

I moved on from Sandals to a resort on the Atlantic side of Antigua. The sea was much rougher there. There was a fascinating place where the sea swept over the rocks, which were peppered with holes and made a sound like flutes being played as it did so.

The owner of the resort was a large, loud, ex-US Marine. He said he was pleased with the hurricane because it churned up so much sand that his beach had increased in size by a factor of three. Sandals was the more luxurious of the two resorts and this one was much wilder, but I got to know and enjoy the wildness.

A local Antiguan organised a walk from the resort to the rocks, pointing out various herbal remedies along the way such as aloe vera, whose leaves could be squeezed to get a substance that healed cuts. He was a fascinating man and quite a character.

I soon got to know 'Caribbean time' – it was all very laid-back. Everyone was routinely an hour late for meetings, up to and including the Minister for Tourism.

Captain Jack took me on a catamaran ride, out across the sea, stopping off at a desert island. I'd never seen the sea so crystal-clear or walked on such a perfect beach. It was amazing! All thanks to being in *EastEnders*. I felt blessed.

***

I began a fresh run of six months on *EastEnders* on 3 May 1991, coincidentally a year to the day since I'd left the show. Nick was down and out at the time and I spent an hour in Make-up to look suitably rough. Michael Melia (Eddie Royle) joked that I would have the record for sleeping and lying down in the most locations around the Square. I was certainly pleased to get rid of the ugly make-up at the end of the day's filming.

I was friendly with Ron Tarr – 'Big Ron' – one of my favourite extras. He became a popular member of the cast. At one point I had to sell some classical CDs to him. Of course Nick knew nothing about the genre and mispronounced most of the composers' names. When he tells him the cost, Big Ron leans in and asks, menacingly, ''Ow much?' He swiftly gets a discount.

Michael Ferguson, the then executive producer, spoke to the cast about drugs in the studio after newspaper rumours – no names were mentioned. It was a busy time. I had the first discussions about the death of Charlie Cotton (Christopher Hancock), who was not best pleased, judging by the card June Brown received from him. Dear old June, good-hearted as ever, tried her best to persuade the producers to reverse the decision but to no avail. I too had a talk with Ferguson – I felt what the writers were doing was wrong, because we all worked so well together as a family and he was much loved by audiences. Finally I asked story editor Andrew Holden about the axing of Charlie and he said that it was the only way that Dot and Nick could be reconciled at this point in the story. I never quite believed that, to be honest – I thought it was another gratuitous death to boost viewing figures, just as they would do again with Ashley Cotton (Frankie Fitzgerald), much to the chagrin of June and me, not to mention Nick himself. With the exception of Dot, Cotton family members did not have a particularly healthy lifespan, it seemed. As it turned out, a few years later Chris Hancock and I would work together again when Nick was haunted by the ghost of Charlie.

Towards the end of June 1991 we got a new studio at last, which was given a full press launch with much fanfare. Very smart it was too. We had our own toilets, showers, phones and brass plates with our character names on the doors. Adam Woodyatt (Ian Beale) took me to see the rooms for the noisier – i.e. younger – members of the cast on the ground floor (we were on the floor above).

Just a couple of months after Chris Hancock's departure, Michael Melia was axed from the show. Nick had been locked in a room by Dot and Pete Beale, hoping he would come off heroin, but he had escaped and murdered Michael's character, Eddie Royle. I got on well with Michael and I would sometimes give him a lift as we lived near to one another. He had recently bought a bigger house and taken on a larger mortgage because he thought he would be in the show for some time.

The episodes featuring Nick's heroin addiction were extremely harrowing. However I received a lot of praise for the realism with which I portrayed his withdrawal.

My daughter came up to spend a day at the studio and they needed a little girl to be on the swing in the playground. Rosanna, then five years old, got to be an extra, and when the episode went out over the summer of 1991 we watched her scene with Michelle Gayle and Daniella Westbrook. Her line was, 'Please would you push me?' I was thrilled that so much of her scene made it to the final cut. The following day we were at the local video shop when some children began to stare at me through the window. Rosanna, a high-spirited girl at times, poked her tongue out at them and they ran away.

She would often add a bit of comedy to a situation. At an animal park as some young children passed a pony showing a prominent penis, a little girl shouted, 'Look, it's doing a poo!' Rosanna's response was equally loud, 'No, that's its willy!'

Everyone fell about laughing.

***

In the autumn of 1991 we were visited at the studio by another John Altman: renowned saxophonist and composer. He wasn't impressed by the set but I bought him lunch. He and Adam Woodyatt (Ian Beale) lived near one another and they talked cricket. John was at Elstree to do *Top of the Pops* with Eric Idle, singing, 'Always Look on the Bright Side of Life'. He and I have worked together on many occasions. I sang with his band at The Pheasantry on the King's Road. The evening was entitled 'John Altman Presents John Altman'!

After I left *EastEnders* that November, I went up for a play called *Abiding Passion* with Helena Bonham Carter and Rosemary Leach. At the read-through I found Helena very easy to get on with (and she smoked Silk Cut, which was a bonus for me) and the main point of our first meeting was to see if we clicked. In the end the play never happened, but I did enjoy our brief day working together.

***

In December 1991 I was starring in *Aladdin* in Barking alongside Page 3's Gaynor Goodman, Trevor Bannister (Mr Lucas in *Are You Being Served?*), Bob La Castra (Eddie Buckingham in *Neighbours*), Ward Allen and Roger the Dog and TV presenter Ross King. From the off I suspected that Paul Randall, the producer, might have a touch of the Nick Cottons about him. He had a shifty, dishonest aura and a cold, clammy handshake.

A week into rehearsals we found out that all the money he had been given by the Borough of Barking and Dagenham to stage the pantomime had mysteriously disappeared. Therefore, he owed the cast, band and crew a substantial sum. Dressed as Abanazar, the wicked Egyptian wizard, I recall pinning Mr Randall up against the wall of the foyer in the theatre, demanding to know where our money had gone. He wouldn't say. It transpired that he had used the thousands of pounds that had been given him to pay off some debts he had incurred.

Of course, the rest of the cast and I were devastated to hear this news, especially the poor wardrobe lady, who had invested her own money in making the costumes. I don't think she got a penny back – and she was a lovely woman.

I remember the launch of the production, where the snacks consisted of some stale crisps, Twiglets and flat lemonade, as well as warm white wine that would have been more useful for cleaning silver.

The show was on the verge of collapse, with Randall owing a total of between £20,000 and £40,000, and we feared we'd have to close. The Equity union mounted an inquiry. Luckily, Barking and Dagenham Council came to the rescue and although we didn't do the full run, we were able to put on the panto for two weeks.

Once we had finished the show and I was back in my flat in Kingston with Rosanna and Bridget, the incident kept preying on my mind: Randall owed me £4,000 and I was determined to get it back. As far as I was concerned he was the Grinch that had ruined our Christmas. As an actor the money from a panto can keep you going for months if other work doesn't materialise. Plus commuting to Barking from Surrey in the middle of winter had been a stressful experience. But it turned out he couldn't be prosecuted by the Fraud Squad, who were called in, because the council had actually given him the banker's draft in the good faith that he would use it to pay the theatrical company. As the law could do nothing about it, in desperation I turned to other methods to extract the £4,000 fee.

A friend of mine gave me the number of two Essex car dealers who were adept at retrieving unpaid debts. Although I never met them in person we talked on the phone and I explained the situation. I told them how much was owed and gave them Randall's office address. When I asked them if they required a fee, they said they would extract any extras from Mr Randall – 'With you being a bit of a celebrity, I suppose you won't want us to break his arms or legs.'

'As much as I'd like you to, I suppose you'd better not,' I agreed.

So the two gentlemen from Essex paid Mr Randall a call at his office, sat on his desk and I'm not sure what else went on, but they asked him if he'd like to pay the money back. Randall said he didn't have any money so they dragged him off to the cash machine, where they discovered that he was telling the truth: there was nothing in his account. Apparently, he burst into tears at some point in the meeting and begged them not to harm him in any way and they didn't.

'We couldn't get a penny out of him,' the men told me afterwards. 'Sorry, John.'

'Thank you very much for your help,' I said. 'I'll have to pursue other avenues' – which I did. Unfortunately, my experience with Paul Randall was to take an even darker turn. I decided to confront him after hearing he planned shows with Rod Hull and Emu, Latoya Jackson and Petula Clark. One rip-off was enough – I was determined not to let him get away with it again.

I asked Bridget to drive me to Randall's home in Worcester Park, a few miles from where we lived in Kingston and we set off with Rosanna in the back. It was a damp and foggy night. As we approached Randall's street over a crossroads there was an almighty bang, as if a bomb had gone off, and everything went black. As I heard the screeching of brakes, I was flung all over the place and my head smashed into the car roof. It happened in seconds and all I could see was darkness.

IN THE NICK OF TIME

The next thing I remember was hearing Rosanna crying. The car, a Suzuki Alto, which I'd bought for Bridget's birthday the previous year, was a write-off. A car had hit us at speed on the badly lit, foggy crossroads, where the road markings had been virtually wiped away over time. We had spun 180 degrees and had ended up facing in the opposite direction on the other side of the road. Trembling, I somehow managed to get out of the car, pull Rosanna from the back seat and help Bridget out. They were shaking but thankfully not badly hurt.

I walked over to the woman in the other car to see if she was OK. She was in a state of shock but unharmed and her car hadn't suffered nearly so much damage. It was very dark but I could see that Bridget had a nasty bruise on her left leg and I had two gashes on my knees. Blood was trickling down my face from a cut on my head. By the time the police arrived, shock had turned to anger: my wife and daughter's lives had been put at risk, and all I could think about was getting to Randall.

After making sure that Bridget and Rosanna were OK, full of anger I made my way to his house on foot. When I got to the front door, I was ready to deliver a tirade of abuse but I had promised the police that there wouldn't be any trouble. Much to my surprise the door was opened by his father, who was totally sympathetic and told me that I wasn't the first person to call about money. Perhaps he was hiding under the bed or in the garden shed, but I never got the satisfaction of confronting him there that night.

I walked back to the scene of the accident and the police kindly drove me to Kingston Hospital to join Rosanna and Bridget in the casualty unit. The doctor said that if we hadn't been wearing seatbelts, we'd be dead. I thanked God my family were safe and sound. Bridget and I emerged with just a few cuts and bruises, while Rosanna was untouched apart from the shock of it all.

Weighing up everything regarding Paul Randall, particularly in light of what his father had said about other creditors banging on their family door, I realised it was extremely doubtful that I would get a single penny out of this no-good shyster. However I had listened to a programme on BBC Radio 4 called *Face the Facts*, presented by John Waite, brother of Terry Waite – a respected investigative journalist. His programme had exposed many n'er-do-wells, crooks and fraudsters. I made contact with his production team at the BBC and explained what had happened to me with the Barking pantomime.

Face the Facts showed great interest in the story and John Waite interviewed me. I said that Randall might have pulled the same stunt on other artists in the entertainment world. John and his team thoroughly investigated Paul Randall's activities and unearthed a history of similar events. It transpired that he would book artists into a venue, take full payment and pocket the money, knowing full well no one else would see a penny. He had even ripped off an elderly double act called Pearl Carr and Teddy Johnson. Randall mainly operated in the UK's coastal resorts. After his activities were fully exposed on *Face the Facts* he was blacklisted by Equity and entertainment venues across the country. His 'business' folded and as far as I know, he never resumed his career as a producer.

Years later, long after I'd put the whole sorry saga out of my mind, I bumped into him working in a supermarket not far from my home. A rather forlorn figure now, he offered to pay back a small percentage of the debt in cash, in return for me signing a document that would discharge his obligation and allow him to set up in business again. Out of the goodness of my heart and feeling, for some reason, a certain sympathy for this person who had made such a mess of his life, I agreed. Much later still, I discovered that he had died, a lonely alcoholic, in a block of flats less than a quarter of a mile from my own front door.

***

During the summer of 1991 I embarked on a film for Channel 4 called *The Ghosts of Oxford Street*. Also featuring Tom Jones, Sinead O'Connor, The Happy Mondays, Kirsty MacColl, Rebel MC and Leigh Bowery, the film was directed by the legendary manager of the Sex Pistols, Malcolm McLaren. I was to play the role of Thomas De Quincey, author of the Victorian book, *Confessions of an English Opium Eater*, published in 1821.

I felt I was more than apt for the part, having had my own experiences with opium during the heady days of the late 1960s and early 1970s – notwithstanding visits to a Chinese opium den in Calcutta during my epic journey across India at the tender age of eighteen. And with the part of Nick Cotton, I had certainly carried out plenty of literary research into the subject of opium – although I hasten to add I never became addicted because I always used to throw up after taking it.

McLaren, as far as I knew, had little experience of how to direct a feature film. This came to the fore when he asked me to learn reams of Victorian dialogue and then suddenly changed his mind and decided not to use the convoluted passages, which was rather frustrating. I remember sitting in the back of a car memorising it at two in the morning, only to be told it was no longer needed. As an actor on a soap this often happened, but not with such lengthy and difficult passages.

Luckily for me, I was partnered with Sinead O'Connor, who I'd always had a bit of a crush on. She was to play Little Annie, for whom Thomas De Quincey had a deep fondness. We even got to kiss at one point, which was a delight – kisses onscreen as Nick Cotton were few and far between.

We shot scenes of Thomas running after Annie in darkened London streets. My lasting memory, apart from the lovely Sinead, was of the all-night shoots. They were exhausting, but given we were the ghosts of Oxford Street, seemed appropriate. Leaving my car where I was learning my lines one night, Malcolm McLaren led me across Oxford Street and into Selfridges for one of the scenes. He told me how Gordon Selfridge, who had gambled away his entire fortune, was once seen on a bench opposite, gazing at the great store he had previously owned. He turned to the person sitting next to him and said, 'I used to own all of that.' The person replied, 'Yeah… of course you did.'

Malcolm led me into the basement of Selfridges, where I made an amazing discovery. He took me through a large stock room filled with shoes and then through a hole in the wall that led to what was once a London street complete with pavement and the frames of ancient, Dickensian shopfront windows. There were cobwebs everywhere. Inside one of the shops, they had set up a table and chair, with a candle burning and paper and pens for Thomas De Quincey to relate his story.

***

In the summer of 1992 I took Bridget and Rosanna on a trip to Gibraltar with the Lord's Taverners, the UK's leading youth cricket and disability sports charity. The aim of the weekend was for a celebrity cricket team to raise as much money as possible by playing against the combined armed forces of Gibraltar. We stayed in a beautiful old colonial hotel called The Rock as guests of the army, navy and air force. From the moment we stepped off the plane, their generosity knew no bounds. I quickly realised it was going to be a challenge to stay vertical for the entire weekend: champagne for breakfast, wine with lunch, cocktails at sunset and wine over dinner interspersed with lashings of rum from the navy. It proved too much for many of us but I took it steady and made it to every event.

I was there with friends and colleagues including June Brown, Chris Tarrant, Bill and Rosa Tidy and Michael Melia. We had dinner in the caves of the great rock on the Saturday night, by which time gaps were already appearing in the company assembled at the table. One celebrity didn't even make it up to his room one night and collapsed on the sofa at the bottom of the stairs.

Relaxing by the pool on the Saturday afternoon, I said to Rosanna, who was six, that she shouldn't run along the poolside with the towel wrapped round her – it was far too big. She said, 'Don't worry, Daddy, I'll be careful.' I turned back to the conversation at the table with Bridget and the other guests and a little while later was interrupted by a splash. June Brown, who was facing the pool and me, said, 'I think that was Rosanna, dear,' and I leapt to my feet.

Sure enough, she was nowhere to be seen. I ran to the pool and jumped in. She'd fallen in, gone straight to the bottom, bobbed up and was now struggling. I took her in my arms and got her out. Thanking June profusely, I dried off my daughter but I couldn't be cross with her – I was just glad she was safe and sound.

God bless June!

***

In August 1993, after leaving *EastEnders*, I made a film called *The Higher Mortals*, in which I played Mr Thomas, a schoolteacher, with Susannah York as Miss Thoroughgood, the head teacher. My character was a million miles away from Nick Cotton, which made a refreshing change, and it was a joy to work with Susannah York, whom I had watched on the Odeon cinema screen as a boy.

***

One of the saddest occurrences during my married life with Bridget was the loss of her dear brother Jerome. I'd always got on well with my wife's family – and I still do, even now we're divorced. Often I will go to help Ivy and Lambert with their garden in Hayward's Heath, Sussex. I also have a good relationship with her other brother, Julian.

On 24 March 1994 I was ready to start work, singing a song in a music-hall production at the Wimbledon Theatre. I was just about to put on my costume when Bridget phoned the stage door. She told me to sit down and the first thing that came into my head was that something had happened to Rosanna.

Bridget told me there had been a fire at her family's house that morning in Jerome's bedroom and they hadn't been able to save him. A month away from his twenty-fourth birthday, he had so much to live for – a flat of his own that he was about to move into, good friends and a loving family.

The director let me go and I drove straight home to Bridget and Rosanna – ironically on the way at one point I had to pull over for an ambulance and then had to follow a funeral procession at another. It was a beautiful sunny day, but now it seemed very grey. We drove straight to Hayward's Heath to comfort Ivy, Lambert and Julian. Rosanna, then eight, was very sweet with Ivy – she is such a caring soul.

Lambert had burns to his forehead and scorched hair from trying to save his son – Julian had pulled him back from entering Jerome's bedroom during the fire. Julian himself had tried to go back upstairs but the intense heat and the smoke were too much. Eventually Jerome's bedroom window itself blew out. The chief fireman was still there and told us that he wouldn't have suffered too much, as he would have very quickly fallen unconscious.

The press got hold of the story and knew the family were related to me so they kept trying to phone me. I remember thinking what ghouls they were. I bought flowers and we laid them on the lawn – later, the fireman kindly took them into Jerome's bedroom. At the end of the day I left the family with Bridget and Rosanna, and we returned home to Kingston. The day seemed like an awful dream that we would eventually awake from.

As we drove I tried to concentrate on the good times that I'd shared with Jerome and the Poodhun family. Ivy created wonderful dinner parties; they'd been so loving and helpful when Rosanna was born; we spent summer days in their garden and then there was the trip to see the rest of the family in South Africa.

The cause of the fire was never conclusively pinpointed. However, the Fire Service said there could have been a can of cleaning fluid left on top of Jerome's computer while it was still on, and it could have become too hot and exploded. A couple of days later I visited the room and looked at the corner where the computer had been. There were signs that the fire had been at its fiercest there, and I also knew that Jerome had a weak heart. He'd been fitted with a Lazarus box – a kind of pacemaker – and I wondered if that had played a part in his death. To this day he is still deeply missed. A young man so full of promise, who was taken away from us far too soon.

***

During the 1990s I was doing an advertising campaign for Linda Beatty, the casting director at Saatchi & Saatchi. Amazingly, their offices even had a pub, called The Pregnant Man. This was the title of a birth control advert in the 1980s. I played there with my band Resurrection. Through Linda I struck up a friendship with Gareth Hunt, a delightful and talented man who made a name for himself through *The Avengers*. Over the years we often met up to discuss our various projects that we hoped to get into production, such as a game we invented called *Road Rage*. Unfortunately, nothing ever came of it. Tragically, he died of pancreatic cancer in March 2007. A sad loss. He was one of the good guys.

***

At the reception following a Leicester Square film premiere in 1992, I met the very charming Cynthia Payne, otherwise known as 'Madam Cyn'. She had run a brothel in Streatham, south London, and came to public attention when her business was subject to a police raid. They found elderly gentlemen there, who paid with

Luncheon Vouchers and were then attended to by various young ladies. Cynthia herself became something of a celebrity, and eventually a bit of a national treasure.

My father, with whom I shared a bawdy sense of humour, was highly amused – as were many others – by the antics at her home when all was revealed in the late 1970s. He had a fondness for naughty seaside postcards and limericks, especially after a few drinks, though he would never recite them to my mother. I was sure he would be very pleased to get a signed photograph from Madam Cyn herself.

During my next visit to my parents' house in Herne Bay, I presented him with the gift and he was indeed amused, particularly as she'd inscribed the photo, 'With fond memories to Cecil of the wonderful days and nights we spent together at the house in Streatham. With lots of love from Cynthia xxx'. Of course, the nearest to Cynthia's house my father had got was probably passing through Streatham station on his way home to Herne Bay in Kent. The photo swiftly disappeared into Father's office without my mother seeing it.

The office was his domain and his alone, apart from when Mother dusted and hoovered. During one cleaning session, somehow or other she came across the card in his desk drawer and was not best pleased with what she saw. She refused to speak to my father for the next couple of weeks.

After Father died in the summer of 1995, I found some of his collected limericks, neatly typed up, among his possessions. They still make me laugh to this day and in homage to him I'd like to share the best with you:

There was a young man from Herne Bay
Who set sail for China one day
He was pinned to the tiller
By a sex-starved gorilla –
And China's a fucking long way!

There was a young sailor named Bates
Who danced a fandango on skates
Till a fall on his cutlass
Rendered him nut-less
And practically useless on dates.

There was a young lady from Bude
Who went for a swim in a pond
A man in a punt
Stuck his pole in the water
And said, 'You can't swim here – it's private.'

***

During the summer of 1995, when my father was very ill, I had embarked on a children's TV series called *Black Hearts in Battersea*, based on the Joan Aiken novel. I played Midwink, alongside Celia Imrie, Ronald Pickup, Annette Badland, Philip Jackson and William Mannering. The entire production was shot on location at various castles and country estates. In the vast space of an old airship hangar at Cardington, Bedfordshire, they built a huge set which was a re-creation of the houses and streets of Victorian London.

Father had cancer of the pancreas and dementia. I'm not sure which is worse but I do know that seeing him look at my mother and ask, 'Who is that lady?' was a very sad moment. Thankfully, he didn't linger. He died during filming and for me it was a relief that he went when he did. I'm sure he was at least glad to know that his eldest son was fully employed at the time.

It was on 1 July that my father passed away at the age of eighty-four. At the time he died I was showering in the hotel in Bedford, and I felt a pain in my chest; my brother William was driving and felt something strange within. I was preparing for a day's filming on *Black Hearts in Battersea*, and I didn't know Father had passed away until I got back to London that evening. In our kitchen back home Bridget asked me to sit down and I knew what she was going to tell me.

The next morning I set off for Kent to see him in the Chapel of Rest and put a cross on his chest – it was strange to see him like that, as if frozen in time. I said a prayer and kissed his forehead, which was cool to the touch. I was very sad that I hadn't been at his bedside when he breathed his last. Apparently the doctor told my brother William, 'He's not in good shape, he's very distressed. This can't go on.' William agreed and so they gave him an extra shot of morphine. Father glanced at the photo by his bed of Bridget, Rosanna and myself. He pointed to me and said, 'That's my boy.' I never realised how much I'd miss him. I travelled back to the location to find out I wasn't needed for filming after all, so I returned to the hotel and had a few glasses of vodka on my own, releasing all my sadness in floods of tears for quite some time.

The next day was bright and sunny and I took a walk along the river. My father was gone. Without him life would never be quite the same but I always treasure the memories of a good and loving man. Occasionally, when I've done something stupid, I can still hear his voice reprimanding me.

'Don't be a bloody fool,' he says, in his deep, well-spoken tones.

***

One of the perks of my sudden rise to fame through *EastEnders* was that Rosanna got to meet some of her idols, such as Ant & Dec, when they were pop stars. We also attended star-studded premieres of children's films. One of the most special was *Pocahontas* in 1995. We watched the movie in Leicester Square and then walked to the Embankment and boarded a boat to Greenwich. The seventeenth-century world of Pocahontas in New England had been recreated in a huge marquee. Rosanna, then nine years old, was overjoyed by it all and we still remember that night.

Years later I performed in a musical called *Pocahontas* in Gravesend. This was the final resting place of the real Pocahontas. She had become terribly ill on her journey back to America and was taken off the ship in Kent.

***

In 1997, I was in a children's series called *Knight School* and stayed in the Marriott hotel while filming in Birmingham. I'd had half a bottle of wine and got up in the middle of the night to go to the toilet. Being sleepy, I made for the door that would have been in the direction that led to the bathroom at home. The hotel door slammed behind me and I realised I was in the corridor in my underpants, staring down at an orange and brown swirly carpet. What else could I do? I took the lift to Reception and asked the concierge to let me back in my room.

'This is so embarrassing,' I said in the lift on the way back.

'Not to worry, it's nothing compared to some of the sights I've seen,' he replied.

***

It's been interesting to look back at how distressing I found my time behind prison walls, and also to remember another significant time when I stepped through some prison gates, which was much later, after I had found fame. It was to visit Reg Kray at Maidstone Prison, after Roger Burnett, my agent for personal appearances, organised a visit there. Reg wanted a few celebrities down there to visit him and brighten up his day. Every prisoner was supposed to have just one visiting table allocated to him, but Reg had about four. Barbara Windsor (Peggy Mitchell) was there, as were a few other characters from the series too, and we all being considered to meet the legendary man himself.

It was obviously an amazing moment, but it was also helpful

as I was being considered to play Ronnie in a Kray movie called *Gangland 66* and had thought a visit down there would be the ultimate research – talk about going the extra mile! Ronnie had just died of a heart attack and it was an extraordinary moment to meet his brother. Whatever that 'thing' is, that superstar presence, Reggie had it – it truly felt like I was meeting a movie or rock star. Reg wandered over and took a seat in front of me. He had a neat, flat zip-up briefcase and he meant business – he was fit as a fiddle without an ounce of fat on him, short-cut grey hair and piercing blue eyes.

I passed him a packet of tobacco (which I had been asked to bring) under the table and it disappeared past the guard instantly, we had a chat about *EastEnders* for five minutes or so and then shook hands, before he got up and went on to the next table. Another prisoner took his seat. He shook my hand and said: 'Hi, I'm Terry. I'm the guy who shot up the ceiling in the bank in Knightsbridge five years ago, nice to meet you.'

The film was never made, unfortunately.

CHAPTER 21

'TIS BETTER TO HAVE LOVED AND LOST, THAN NEVER TO HAVE LOVED AT ALL
ALFRED, LORD TENNYSON, *IN MEMORIAM*

So when did the cracks in our marriage start to appear? I'm not sure I can say – I often think it's like alcoholism, you don't see trouble creeping up on you and you can't quite pinpoint where it really started to go wrong. Drinking aside, which was obviously a key factor, I think we simply fell out of love – all those things you believe you will have in common forever often turn out to be wishful thinking. They are born out of huge love and lust during the first heady days of a romance you are desperate to make last. We were definitely that couple: we wanted to spend every minute with each other, couldn't stand to be apart, thought we couldn't live without each other. Our courtship and early marriage were some of the happiest times of my life, and the end of our relationship nearly broke me.

I know I wasn't easy, but then neither was Bridget and she certainly knew how to wind me up. That's the thing about spending years being so close to another human being, you can end up knowing them better than you know yourself, and that can be good and bad. The one thing designed to drive me to distraction was the silent treatment (I no doubt deserved it after one too many benders, I'm sure, but it was my weak spot). It could go on for days and being ignored was, hands down, the thing that pressed my buttons the most. But I think, in the main, we just stopped talking. We had all the usual pressures of a young married couple and my being in a soap opera didn't change those – we had a young daughter, a mortgage, bills, and no regular wage coming in because that's the way that actors live. People shouting 'Nick Cotton!' on the street didn't pay the bills and in between my times on the show, things were often lean.

The truth is that we drank quite a bit to distract us from our problems – it started out as being the way we communicated and had fun, but then it got dark and numbed us both, particularly when it came to blotting out the pain we both felt about not being able to have another child. It remains a deep sadness of mine that we couldn't give Rosanna a brother or sister. Instead of discussing it and grieving for the big family we couldn't have, we drank our way through it. There isn't much deep and meaningful talking you can do when you've passed out on the sofa.

I suppose we stopped loving each other, though I did try my absolute best to make it work, but we never stopped caring for each other, and we still do today. The eventual decision to give up the booze was very much a last-ditch attempt to show both Bridget and Rosanna the kind of man I could be when I wasn't under the influence. There wasn't one big dramatic 'moment' to the break-up, more a gradual erosion of all the good we had had, and it does astound me what human beings can put up with in the name of 'holding it all together' and 'trying to make it work'. I was only once unfaithful during our marriage and in a late-night, drunken truth-telling session, I confessed all and felt a huge sense of relief to shrug off this remorse and the huge guilt I'd been feeling. For the last couple of years of our relationship it was a very unhappy household indeed. There was a complete communication breakdown all round.

Later, as part of my 12-Step Recovery Program, we discussed it in more detail. I needed to work hard and make amends. Even though the marriage was over, it was still important that Bridget forgave me. Obviously my drinking didn't help the delicate state of our marriage, but I don't think it was the final nail in the coffin. In my opinion, it takes two to make or break a relationship. There is no point fighting alone to salvage a union that depends so much on closeness and mutual respect. Sometimes you just have to admit defeat. I remember a friend once saying to me, as I told him I was going to fight for my marriage: 'You can only fight if the other person wants to be hung on to, otherwise you are just punching the wind.' Wise words indeed! However at the time I made up a music tape for Bridget with 'Unbreak My Heart' by Toni Braxton and 'Say It Isn't So' from Blood Brothers, hoping it would change her mind.

The unravelling of my marriage was the hardest time of my life – there is nothing designed to make you feel more like a failure than watching your home life crumble. Everything we had built with love was turning sour. There is so much I could say about what really happened. Let's just say that it wasn't only my liking for drink and cocaine that caused the toxic atmosphere within what was once a loving home. The year 1997 was when everything came to a head. Bridget was working in town. I wasn't in regular work so my days lacked the rigour I needed. Even when there was very little going on I always tried my best to maintain a structure, though. I would get up, take Rosanna to school, go for a swim, come back and clean the flat or go shopping, then do some kind of work and admin throughout the day. Later, I would pick up Rosanna, cook, watch TV with her and, towards the end of our 'marriage', wait for Bridget to come home from work in the hope that we could have a family evening together. This happened less and less towards the end and eventually, she sometimes just stopped coming home.

By 1997 my social scene was filled with a lot of drinking and cocaine taking, and none of it helped the unsteady feeling surrounding my situation, that feeling you get when you know you are clinging onto what you have by the skin of your teeth. Throughout 1997 Bridget and Rosanna had spent a long time begging me to give up the booze and fags – I think they could see the damage that all the substances had done to our situation. It can't have been easy for a ten-year-old girl, when all she and her mum wanted was for things to be normal.

As the marriage crumbled we spiralled into despair. I was no angel – I know I drank too much, smoked too much and spent too much time contemplating our financial situation and maybe not doing enough about it – but Bridget too was not blameless. Our late-night drinking sessions, where once we would sit up for hours discussing everything, often ending in us making love and marvelling at how lucky we were to have each other, began to end in unpleasant exchanges and low morale. The silences started to last longer, the insults hurled were more hurtful. Pillows down the middle of the bed became the norm. Separate beds followed until Bridget just stopped coming home at all, preferring to stay with friends. Sometimes with Rosanna. The destruction wasn't just confined to us, though: I lost count of the number of times Bridget's parents would come up to 'have a talk' with us about our intolerable situation, what it was doing to Rosanna, to us all. They begged us to sort out our situation but we were locked into this hideous cycle of not wanting to make the final move to end things.

After hoping against all hope that we could sort things out, I suppose the hope died and was replaced with a depressing practicality about the situation. I think I just realised that I felt so much better when Bridget wasn't there and I began to look forward to the nights she didn't come home. A lot of the situation was my own fault, but there is no doubt that I felt belittled, unloved and without a purpose. I wanted a normal family life for our daughter and yet she was being raised in an unpredictable, unstable household and who knew what damage that was causing.

The day I vowed that I had had my last drink was 4 April 1997. That same week, the Grand National was cancelled due to threats from the IRA and Hale-Bopp – said to be the comet of the century – passed Earth. This was while Bridget and Rosanna were on a two-week cruise of the Mediterranean with Lambert and Ivy.

I remember it so clearly: I went to the pub and had two pints and then attended my first 12-step program meeting, in Richmond. Came home, drank a couple of large vodkas and sat up crying. That night I put it in capital letters in my diary: THAT WAS MY LAST DRINK. I poured the rest of the vodka down the sink. Full of self-loathing, I paced the flat like a mad thing, remembering the old drunk I saw outside the pub the previous night and how that could be me in a few years if I wasn't careful. I vowed to sort myself out and the next day, I went to my second meeting. It was then that I shed real tears and I just couldn't stop. By the end of that week I had been to five meetings and it was so strange, I kept having these out-of-body experiences. I felt as though I was surrounded by golden light; it seemed to me that my God was giving me strength.

It was the end of that week when I finally admitted defeat and agreed to give Bridget a divorce. Her parents came up to mediate at the final showdown and they took Rosanna back to Sussex with them. When the end of the marriage was made official in the summer of 1999 we were as amicable as we could be about it. Bridget and I signed the papers in a solicitor's office in the City of London and then went to see *Being John Malkovich* at the Academy Cinema.

By now I had run out of steam when it came to pretending I couldn't salvage my marriage, but I knew I could save myself. I was sick and tired of being sick and tired – I was fed up with the rows and my relationship with Rosanna was at a very low ebb indeed. She had begged me to stop drinking and stop smoking – my own daughter told me that she felt drinking was at the heart of all that was wrong in the household. Give Bridget her due, it was she who suggested I start the 12-Step Recovery Program – she knew things were out of control.

In the lead-up to stopping completely, if I couldn't sleep I would get out of bed at 3am and have a massive swig of vodka, as if that was the answer to all my problems. Instead of just getting up and going to the loo or trying deep breathing, I would take a shot to obliterate the world and my worries and then return to bed, happily falling back into a coma. I had a few tricks that allowed me to carry on kidding myself – I would finish a whole bottle but leave a thimbleful at the bottom because that meant I hadn't drunk the whole thing in just one evening.

I had strict rules about how I would drink, all designed to kid myself that I had some control. When I was working (I never called in sick, though I wasn't always at my perkiest some days), I would wait until the evening to get wasted. I soon learned that the best thing to do was to drink heavily after a big meal (there's nothing worse than throwing up on an empty stomach, being sick on bile was very debilitating). I was extremely fastidious about how I presented myself, though – no matter how rough I felt in the morning, I would always shower and shave, clean my teeth and use a mouthwash.

I remember so clearly standing outside Rosanna's Montessori school, feeling proud that no one could tell just what a bender I'd been on the night before. I was the model dad there, dropping off my daughter first thing, smiling away with all the other parents. Clean and in control, I didn't have a problem – like everyone else I just liked a drink. It was only years later that I heard that a woman there I had really liked and got on well with was heard to remark: 'John's a lovely guy and but he does smell of alcohol in the mornings.'

Over the years I went through so many phases – from sherry to lager via cider and Carlsberg Special Brew and Tennent's Super Lager. I went into the realms of wines and champagne, culminating in vodka. It was clear and I was able to kid myself it was a clean drink and I believed no one could smell it on my breath.

In the end my intake went beyond excessive. I would go up to London for lunch, have a few drinks and then move on to a bar, where I might meet some fellow drinkers and then head into the park with them for some more drinks. Remembering I was due home for supper, I'd make my way to Waterloo for a few drinks at the station bar, phoning home to say that I was held up but would be back home as soon as possible. I'd take miniatures on the train back to Surbiton (the nearest station to my Kingston home), and when I reached my destination I'd decide that the best way to avoid looking drunk was to go for a pint in the deluded belief that it would somehow sober me up. I would walk along the river to Kingston and fall in through the front door. As these things do, it all came to a head.

Bridget insisted I attend a 12-Step meeting, so I did – my first one was in Chelsea. I enjoyed the meeting, everyone seemed very friendly and we went for a coffee afterwards, but as I drove back through Richmond Park I thought to myself, 'I don't need a 12-Step Program – I can give up drinking on my own.' I did stop for a few days but it didn't last long. I'd chosen to go to Chelsea because I didn't want anyone to see me going in Kingston, although that was nonsensical. The meetings are all completely anonymous and so too are the locations.

When your face is hitting people's living rooms four times a week, there isn't really anywhere to hide, to be honest but I am lucky that the 12-Step Recovery Program has so much respect that people have been happy to honour my privacy as much as anyone else's. I think that is partly due to the fact that all sorts of people from all walks of life find support and courage in those gatherings.

It has, without doubt, been my saviour, but I have known some people become obsessed with it in a most unhealthy way – I suppose it's easy to see a crutch that gets you through the most turbulent times and cling on for dear life. But the correct way to see the program is as a bridge to normal living. It's about giving you the tools to take back control and move forward.

I do believe that I had it in my genes to be a drunk – my grandfather, William Stewart, was asked to retire early from a cable ship company due to his drinking issues, though we never talked about it as a family. I just liked the buzz of alcohol and good cocaine and it was definitely a form of escapism, and cured my shyness.

Being drunk is the ultimate escape from reality, like having a protective shield around you and watching life just bounce off you. There isn't a day that goes by when I don't remind myself how lucky I am, as I could have ended up like poor old George Best – I'd like to say I got out of the lift on the third floor, the basement is a wet brain and a liver transplant.

Life sober and clean is a joy, and so much easier, and I wake up happy and relieved every single day. And still do. All thanks to my Higher Power and the 12-Step Programme.

CHAPTER 22

A TAVERN IS A PLACE WHERE MADNESS
IS SOLD BY THE BOTTLE
JONATHAN SWIFT

From the very start I threw myself into the 12-Step Recovery Program with gusto, going back to other members' houses and talking late into the night. The relief at not having to explain myself was instant. I had never experienced anything like it in my life – this fellowship of men and women who were there to share their experiences, their hopes and their strength, is a safety net like no other. There is an overwhelming sense of everyone being in the same boat and united by the wish to find the strength to stop drinking; to be a better version of themselves. Nothing is expected of you – except that you truly have the wish to stop drinking. It's very simple if you follow the program to the letter and everyone has his or her own struggle that sometimes feels insurmountable. It doesn't matter who you are or where you're from.

It was here that life felt like it had come full circle when Pete Townshend came back into my life after I met him while visiting a friend at the Priory. Throughout that first weekend of sobriety, he pointed me in the right direction and brought me the appropriate literature that would enable me to live a sober life. I noted from my diary that he threatened me with a 'good thrashing' if I went back on the drink – what more incentive did I need?

Pete was a great help and support to me once I stepped on the path to sobriety. Uncompromising about his own recovery, he soon made me realise I had to be uncompromising if I was going to stay clean. He was always at the end of the phone with a pep talk or a funny story. It was so strange for me to think this was the man, one of my musical heroes, who had picked me up as a hitchhiker all those years ago and now here we were in touch again. I had also worked on *Quadrophenia* with him; he remarked that he felt we must be on some kind of 'karmic loop' to keep meeting up as we did. He also reminded me that the 12-Step Program doesn't work for everyone, and summed it up for me, quite simply, when he said: 'One day at a time, John. God bless.'

The program became my world. I was lucky that I didn't have the commitment of an intense acting job at the time. On the one hand the structure might have been good to help keep me focused, but on the other I had no idea how quitting the booze would affect me physically and mentally. It would have been a huge risk to be live onstage with lines to deliver and characters to play, yet no idea how my body would react when suddenly deprived of a substance it had been used to for years. I did get all the obvious side effects – the sweats were terrible, my sleep was broken and fractious, my mood erratic – but almost instantly I did feel lighter in spirit too.

I started to think about myself – mainly about when the drinking had begun and why I found it impossible to simply enjoy a few drinks and then stop. With the program there is a lot of self-examination and not all of it is pleasant but it seemed to have all the answers I needed in those difficult early days. Here is an extract from some fellowship literature:

Men and women drink essentially because they like the effect produced by alcohol. The sensation is so elusive that, while they admit it is injurious, they cannot after a time differentiate the true from the false. To them, their alcoholic life seems the only normal one. They are restless, irritable and discontented, unless they can again experience the sense of ease and comfort which comes at once by taking a few drinks – drinks which they see others taking with impunity. After they have succumbed to the desire again, as so many do, and the phenomenon of craving develops, they pass through the well-known stages of a spree, emerging remorseful, with a firm resolution not to drink again. This is repeated over and over, and unless this person can experience an entire psychic change there is very little hope of recovery.

It's amazing the structure that a few rules and twelve simple steps can give to a life that is completely out of control, where you feel so consumed by addiction you fear you might drown. It gives you back the power over your own life and that's the best feeling in the world. The thing about drinking is you don't always do it to escape; sometimes it's to overcome a craving beyond your mental control. Whatever type of alcoholic you are – and there are many, many types – we all share one thing in common: we cannot start drinking without developing the phenomenon of craving. That's why total abstinence is the only answer.

It's not a race to see how quickly recovery can be completed – far from it – as some people can spend a long time on a step. It's about completing each step to the best of your ability, no matter how long it takes.

What I came to realise almost immediately was the selfishness of this disease and the way it grips all those around you in a way no other illness can. If a person is ill with cancer or MS, they have everyone's love, pity and concern. People go out of their way to ease the burden and do all they can to share the load. But not so with alcoholism: many believe we have the choice to drink or not and that we make a decision to drag others into our misery of addiction. The consequences of an alcoholic's actions ripple far and wide – it brings grief to all. Many people struggle with the definition of a real alcoholic: according to the fellowship you may start off as a moderate drinker, but at some stage you will begin to lose all control of your consumption once you start to drink heavily. Once alcohol is taken into the body of an addict it does something that makes it impossible to just have 'the one' drink – it's the first drink that does the damage.

I tried every trick in the book to convince myself I didn't have a problem: only drinking beer, or only drinking wine, not drinking spirits, not drinking alone, not drinking before 7.30pm, not drinking at lunchtime, only drinking at parties... The list was endless. It is often said that more than most people the alcoholic is master of the double life, ironically, very much the actor. To the outside world there is the 'public self', the self we allow the world to see, the one that allows us to live the lie. The inner self is a different story, though; that is a person driven by insecurity and an overwhelming sense of failure as he repeatedly breaks his promise 'never to touch another drop'. You also become haunted by 'the fear' of what you did on your last bender and what you can't remember and lurch from one hangover to the next, every new day vowing you won't drink again, that the new day is a 'fresh start'.

With the 12-Step Program way of life you have to discard the notion that one day you will be immune to alcohol and the problems it causes. The motto I always live by is 'Once an alcoholic, always an alcoholic'. For me it's as simple as that and those who relapse often do so because they think they are safe to drink again. I know I won't ever be safe and that's just the way it is for me. I am now nearly twenty years sober, and I still need to be vigilant. As they say; it's a great life if you don't weaken.

At the start almost instantly I began to draw great strength from my fellowship meetings and would go to up to two or three a day – it was very much all or nothing for me. Right from that first day, every day without a drink represented a big step forward and that feeling never goes away. On 6 April 1997 I wrote in my diary: 'Two days without a drink now.' It sounds like nothing but for me it was a great achievement.

I wouldn't say I was surrounded by support in my quest to become clean – my relationship with Rosanna was strained, and she, quite rightly, didn't believe I would stick to it. All round I had a lot to prove and it wasn't easy. Logistically it was tough as Rosanna was living with me, so I couldn't just leave her in the evenings to attend my meetings. I had to rely on Bridget coming home and taking over so I could go. It all felt like a big test. I didn't tell many people I was quitting – I didn't want the pressure of being constantly asked how it was going and having to prove myself. It was going to be hard enough, I knew. The few people I did confide in told me I was mad to try and do something so radical in the middle of my marriage breakdown. After all, that's the time most people lean on booze. However, my mother thought it was a great idea, and I'm sure deep down she hoped it would help me reconcile with Bridget and get our marriage back on track. No matter what, my mother was like a rock. Always there for me.

My dreams were so vivid; often they involved me drinking alcohol and then feeling a terrible sense of guilt. The strange thing was that in my dreams I would often be drinking white wine (which I never touched in reality when I was last actually on the booze). In the dreams I was consumed with regret and full of panic when I woke up – even in my sleep the demons were there. I would dream about beautiful, slim bottles of vodka in blue velvet-lined boxes. The bottle would be dangled right in front of me and would sparkle and look beautiful but I wouldn't drink it. Sweating and shaking I would wake from my dreams, momentarily terrified that I had once more succumbed. For a long time I would dream about almost winning an award for sobriety only for someone to wave an empty bottle in my face, taunting me about the fact I had downed the whole thing. All the dreams had the same message – how close I had come to becoming sober and how I had ultimately failed. I would go to meetings and share these experiences and I was always so relieved to hear that others also had such dreams and hauntings.

I felt myself drifting away from all my friends who socialised in pubs. At first life was hard – I remember being at a rock gig in Kew Gardens and seeing a Cointreau tent with the drinks all lined up and literally being able to taste it in my mind. Towards the end it had been one of my favourite tipples, with plenty of ice in a crystal tumbler. I had to be vigilant but it didn't stop my imagination wandering during those early days of sobriety. Today it's a different scenario – I can easily go to an off-licence and buy a bottle of wine for someone and not give it a second thought. I keep drink in the kitchen cupboard for when my daughter (who is now 29) comes to stay – they are her bottles and they live right next door to the cleaning fluids. In fact, all my recycling goes next to the alcohol and I would no more think of drinking it than I would the Flash all-purpose cleaner! It just becomes another way of life, simple as that.

I wasn't getting any pleasure out of drinking any more. I beat myself up with it for too long and the drink became the third person in my marriage. It wasn't until I started the program that I knew what a blackout actually was – it isn't passing out on the bed fully clothed and waking up the next morning. It's more like sleepwalking. You are awake and moving, talking, drinking and doing crazy things you wouldn't normally do, but you truly can't remember whole chunks of your day or night even though you are awake and participating fully. The next day your mind is a blank. That's when you ring up a friend and ask, 'What did I say and do last night?'

IN THE NICK OF TIME

IN THE NICK OF TIME

How had I sunk to this point? It was a life-long journey. As a youngster I had badgered my father for a taste of his beer. 'You won't like it,' he warned me. And I didn't. My first real indulgence in alcohol came at the age of sixteen. I had performed in an amateur production of *Calamity Jane* at the King's Hall in Herne Bay and on a trestle table at the after-show party was a bottle of sherry. One glass had already been poured so I downed it – it was sweet and made me feel a warm glow all over. I had a second glass and found my confidence increased and soon I was chatting away with the girls in the company with no hint of my usual shyness.

I drank several more glasses and then felt rather peculiar as I walked home along what had been a flat road on the way there but now seemed to have a slight slope. After crawling up the stairs I ended up throwing up into a chamber pot under my bed.

My mother heard the noise I was making and managed to calm me down. It was the first time alcohol hit my system in a big way. My bed that night seemed to be tipping up all the time and it felt like I was constantly sliding down towards the bottom of it.

The next morning I had a dreadful hangover and surely this experience should have taught me a lesson but just a few weeks later I went to a party up at Beltinge and I remembered only the sense of confidence and joviality the alcohol gave me. Before I set off, I retrieved a small, empty Lamb's Navy rum bottle from the garage and filled it with various drinks from the decanters in my father's drinks cabinet. The result was a muddy brown colour. I drank some at the beginning of the party and although it tasted like some ghastly medicine I was only interested in the good effect it would have. But it didn't – I was just sick again.

My other early encounter with drink, according to one of my diaries, was brown ale at a wrestling match. This again was a sweet drink, which was what attracted me. As I grew older I remained a light drinker, preferring hashish and LSD. My gang in Canterbury had the occasional lager and cider but we tended to look down on alcohol as an uncool, less exciting euphoric. Drink was a cunning foe and it took years for alcoholism to creep up on me. I recall drinking raki in Istanbul on the trip to India as a teen, because we didn't want to risk smoking dope in the city. On another trip to Yugoslavia I enjoyed wine, and I tasted Southern Comfort with my Battersea friends but, generally, these encounters with 'the booze' were one-offs.

Once I got to art school, I decided to leave the dope and acid behind and discovered the joys of drinking at the subsidised student union bar. In 1975, there was an advertising campaign for something called barley wine, which was a small bottle of strong ale. Each was said to have the strength of a double scotch. My father used to add a bottle of it to his pint of bitter to give it the strength that beer had when he was a younger man. Real ale – which I would discover later – wasn't around at that time (or if it was, it was hard to find). I used to drink quite a few barley wines – I didn't like the taste, but I liked the effect.

My drinking remained moderate as I began working at the Leeds Grand Theatre. The backstage bar was run by the lovely Betty Walsh, but stage manager Eddie de Pledge strictly forbade those working on the show any alcohol. Quite right too. In view of the equipment we used, it could have been highly dangerous. One inebriated lighting operator fell asleep on the memory board, erasing the computerised program that cued the lights, and wiped out the whole show. Naturally, he was relieved of his post. I made a vow to myself that I would never drink in order to boost my confidence onstage when I eventually became an actor – I'd seen what it had done to great actors such as Richard Burton, Alan Browning and the wonderful Oliver Reed.

When I moved on to Leicester I discovered the joys of alcohol mixed with amphetamines. In the Pip Simmons Theatre Group I moved up a gear with my alcoholic intake. The boys and girls were highly professional and we never drank while performing.

I arrived in London in 1977, the summer of punk, adding to my repertoire of fashion over the years, having been a mod, a hippie, and once sported the style of a glam rocker. Carlsberg Special Brew and Tennent's Super Lager had arrived and I drank gallons of them. Once again, they tasted disgusting but the effect was brilliant. I never fancied the agonies of downing twelve pints of weaker brews such as Heineken and Watneys, and I needed only four cans of Tennent's or Carlsberg to get me buzzing.

There were many phases to my drinking. I returned to the Southern Comfort, buying half a bottle and putting it in the pocket of a white linen jacket before heading off to various parties. Once there I wouldn't drink anything else, but would just take the occasional nip from my bottle. I stopped when I read somewhere that Janis Joplin drank Southern Comfort.

There was a wild drinking and social scene during the late 1970s in Maida Vale, which also took in Ladbroke Grove, Notting Hill and Portobello Road. Saturday night usually featured two or three parties that I attended with friends such as Hugh and Hetta Boyson and Mark Wingett (we met on *Quadrophenia*), Gas Wild, Marilia, Phil Brown, Brady and Jan Brown. The rules on drink driving weren't so strictly enforced then and there was a lot of that.

My drinking increased again when I worked as a waiter and behind the bar at the Embassy Club in New Bond Street. At this time, 1983, I had moved to Chelsea and I was burning the candle at both ends. As I have mentioned earlier a dear friend of mine, Karl Kholer, had gone to New York and asked me to look after his flat.

Dressed in a pair of white satin shorts and a skimpy vest I served the likes of Boy George and Marvin Gaye at the Embassy. This was where I first met my good friend, Mark Macauley. The staff were not supposed to drink alcohol behind the bar while serving customers but most of us poured a large amount of whatever we fancied in with our fruit juices.

Living my acting career by day and burning up the hours during the night finally got to me when I went home to Herne Bay just before Christmas 1983. My brother William and I foolishly consumed some Southern Comfort – despite my vow to myself not to touch it. We went for a swim in the icy-cold North Sea. I was supposed to go back to the Embassy to work over the festive season but was struck down with a dreadful fever and could barely get out of bed. Sweating profusely, I had a high temperature. My mother, Tina, nursed me back to health as she had done when I was a child. All I remember of those first two days is the light passing across the windows. Looking back, I believe I was probably suffering from alcohol withdrawal.

The Embassy gave me the sack – probably a blessing in disguise. Back in Chelsea I found a job in a far healthier environment at a restaurant in a farmers' market.

My intake stabilised with the responsibility of working at *EastEnders*. Perhaps some mornings I was a bit hungover, but then I read a rock magazine interview in which singer Rod Stewart recommended a run as a cure. He was right – although it was a bit painful at times! I'd run out of the studio gates, through Borehamwood, up a steep hill and round the local reservoir.

Bridget and I went through various phases of drinking in our marriage. We investigated the world of wine and as more money began to come in, we went on to champagne. For a while I drank Captain Morgan's spiced rum with ice and a slice of lemon or lime (to make it healthy). I gained weight through that sugary drink so I moved on to vodka, which I believed was a purer and cleaner spirit. If I stuck to that alone and ate a good meal, I didn't have hangovers. My idea of a good measure was half a tumbler with tonic and a slice of lemon.

In the mid-1990s my marriage started to crumble and I'm sure

I drank more to escape my unhappy home. I would try and write my journal before 9 o'clock in the evening because later I would be incapable of putting pen to paper. Here I hasten to add that I was a functioning alcoholic and managed to run my life quite efficiently and keep up the standards required for a young daughter in the house, despite my intake. Around this time my journey with alcohol was reaching its peak, with Bridget's suggestion that I go and try a 12-Step Recovery Program for the first time, although I was still about two years from being properly sober.

***

Giving up the cigarettes was to be the next challenge and came some years later, in 2004. It was much harder. I was on tour with *Chicago – The Musical* in Liverpool and I was reading Alan Carr's *The Easy Way to Give Up Smoking*. I'd reached the chapter with which I was to smoke my last cigarette so I decided to create a ritual – I would walk down to the Mersey, smoke the cigarette, flick the butt into the muddy waters and then photograph the clock on the Royal Liver Building to remember the hour and day on which I quit.

That same evening, just a few hours later I was on stage in *Chicago*. As I made my entrance, singing 'All I Care About is Love', I began to feel most peculiar. The words were coming out and the song was going fine but I was on automatic pilot, it almost felt like I was levitating above the stage. It was a frightening sensation: nicotine withdrawal.

As soon as I came offstage, I rushed to the office of our company manager, Steve Diamond, and in desperation asked him for a cigarette – in those days you could smoke in your dressing room. Once I'd had one I began to feel normal again. Such is the power of the addiction. Quitting, some say, is as hard as trying to give up heroin. Stopping drinking with the 12-Step Recovery Program also helped me to end my smoking habit.

But Alan Carr's book didn't help me and nor did hypnotism or good old-fashioned willpower. What finally worked was a four-week course of nicotine patches and sessions with a strict Russian nurse at my doctor's surgery. Even during the course I sneaked the occasional cigarette, but for me the one thing that tipped the balance was that she made me breathe into a tube – a bit like a breathalyser – which detected carbon monoxide. She could tell if I'd smoked in the past twenty-four hours. When she threatened to stop the patches and shut down the course that was the turning point for me and finally, on 11 April 2004, I stopped smoking for good.

None too happy about it, I told my friends that I now had a hole in my mental ozone. I missed the joy of a cigarette and a coffee first thing in the morning, and so I didn't have that morning cup for many weeks. But I will never go back to smoking, because of the pure hell of trying to give up.

CHAPTER 23

THAT'S ENOUGH OF ALL THIS PIRATE MALARKEY
JUNE BROWN

A part from the year (2001) when I was in *Chicago – The Musical* in Oxford, I've done a pantomime for each of the last 30 years. It's an extremely useful source of income, and panto is definitely in my blood. My grandfather, Johnnie Schofield junior, was a well-known panto dame of the 1940s. I myself first performed panto in Newcastle in 1985 at the Theatre Royal, alongside singer Dana, Ted Robbins and Mike Newman (I played the wicked queen's henchman in *Snow White and the Seven Dwarfs*). It was during this run that Bridget and I found out that we were going to have a baby. She had conceived during a hot, sunny holiday on Gran Canaria.

It's well known that things often go wrong in panto and when they do, the audience frequently enjoy it even more. During the run of that first *Snow White* I played a charity football match with the rest of the cast. As I went in for a tackle with one of the dwarves, I was anxious not to crush him against the concrete wall so I came to an abrupt halt. I went over on my ankle, twisting it badly, and the next night onstage the very serious wicked queen noted my pronounced limp and thought I was going a bit over the top in my performance.

I was in *Dick Whittington* at the Ashcroft in Croydon in 1993, with Cheryl Baker from Bucks Fizz and Lorraine Chase. As King Rat I had a very long, brown velvet tail. The cast had been told not to use the lift to get to the stage as they could become stuck, but in a rush to get down to the stage one day I broke the rule. My tail got caught in the door and as the lift moved off, I left it on the third floor! I had to go onstage sporting a short, brown stump. We pinned it on for the rest of the show and I felt quite foolish.

In *Aladdin* in Swansea the following year with Adam Woodyatt (Ian Beale in *EastEnders*) and comedian Joe Pasquale, at a crucial moment in the show I entered the cave as the evil Abanazar, with Adam as Aladdin. My opening line was, 'Behold, the magic lamp!' Unfortunately, there was no lamp to be seen so I couldn't say the line. We had to improvise. 'Somewhere in this cave,' I said, 'there is a lamp.'

'I can't see it anywhere, Mr Abanazar,' said Adam.

After what seemed like an eternity, a stage hand's hand appeared from the back of the stage around the rock and placed the lamp in the appropriate place. The audience roared with laughter.

Aladdin's company manager introduced me to the backstage murder game: one member of the company stalks the rest of the crew and bumps them off, one by one. Joe Pasquale was the murderer when I was sitting in the local greasy spoon one day with several colleagues. He suddenly appeared off the street and hurled a plastic hand grenade under the table. 'La-la-la,' he shouted in his distinctive squeaky voice, 'you're all dead!'

We put on an adult version of the show with a title which, I think, was my idea – *I've-'ad-him and the Magic Tramp*. This was a fund-raiser for the wife and children of one of the stage crew who had died, tragically young. Joe Pasquale – Wishy-Washy – and I swapped roles. He made his entrance as Abanazar, clutching a chainsaw and smoking a joint. 'If I say, "ha-ha, ha-ha,"' he confided to the audience, 'that means I've forgotten my fucking lines!'

As Wishy-Washy, I entered to the theme from *James Bond*, sporting goofy teeth, unflattering spectacles and a centre parting. I proceeded to shoot myself in the foot with a handgun.

Unfortunately our late-night production didn't go down well with the local council, the town of Dylan Thomas's birth was then busy celebrating the Year of Literature and Writing. But I'm still very fond of Joe and we're friends to this day. The show was a sell-out.

***

In Gravesend, Kent, I had to do a ghost gag – that's all the 'He's behind you' business. I had to rush on behind the dame and a comic, sweeping a very large cloak through the air as I went. Then I made my exit into the wings. Suddenly I heard a great roar of laughter from the audience, which shouldn't have happened at that point. It turned out my sweep of the cloak had dislodged the wig of Colin Devereux – the legendary dame Dockyard Doris. Comic Dave Lee tried to help by replacing it but got it back to front, covering the dame's face. This produced an even bigger laugh. Colin wasn't best pleased because he thought I'd done it on purpose (I hadn't). In a less heated moment, he also told me, 'Port is good for the voice, dear, and the throat,' and he had no trouble in convincing me to have the odd glass or two during the run.

As a pirate in *Robinson Crusoe* in Maidstone, I decided that I could make an impressive entrance by swinging in on a rope. Unfortunately, I had no control, knocked into the scenery and sent the whole lot crashing down.

Then there was *Robin Hood* in York, 1996, with Jack Smethurst (*Love Thy Neighbour*) and Jonathan Morris (*Bread*). At the end of the show I confronted Deborah McAndrew as Robin Hood (I was the Sheriff of Nottingham). I went to draw my sword and realised that it was still on the prop table. She and her Merry Men burst into laughter. I ran off the stage and came back with the missing sword.

In 2015 I played Captain Hook in *Peter Pan* in Wolverhampton with the Chuckle Brothers. Again, I had a face-off at the end of the show, this time with Ross Carpenter's Peter Pan. My line was, 'Pan, I don't believe it! You are supposed to be dead.' For some reason I ended up saying 'You are supposed to be alive' instead! We both cracked up, as did the cast and audience.

One of my fondest memories of panto was doing another *Peter Pan*, this time with June Brown, in Lewisham over the Millennium festive season (I was Captain Hook in that one too and she was Captain Hook's 'Ma'). The rehearsal period was something I wouldn't like to repeat. I was performing in *Oh! What a Night* at Manchester Opera House. So in the morning I'd take the first plane out of Manchester to Heathrow, the express train to Paddington and then the Bakerloo Line to Charing Cross. From there I'd finally get a mainline train to Lewisham, where work would begin at 10am. What a commute! At 3pm I would reverse my tracks to Manchester. It was a nerve-wracking experience because any delay getting back meant missing the evening performance. Luckily I never did.

As Captain Hook's ma June Brown would berate me on stage: 'That's enough of all this pirate malarkey! You're looking a bit thin, have you been eating enough?' It was a joy to work with her away from the *EastEnders* set and to show that we could be funny and light-hearted together. Sadly, our onstage partnership didn't last long. She developed pneumonia and ended up being nursed at home. That put paid to our short time as mother and son onstage.

In panto I often had to do a run of three shows in a row on a Saturday: 10am, 2.30pm and 7.30pm. It was exhausting. Once I did it with a hangover – an experience akin to walking through a sea of glue.

Live entertainment is hard – there are no concessions for any possible illness. That's why I've never understood why people sneer at panto; it's bloody hard work. You're doing two shows a day, every day, so you might be doing fourteen in a row and if you're topping the bill, flu doesn't cut it as an excuse. People often ask what happens if you get sick or have throat issues and the answer is you just have to get on with it! But there is a little trick of the trade to have up your sleeve if the throat goes in the middle of a run – it's called Sanderson's Throat Specific. Truly disgusting, it tastes like vinegar, but gargle religiously with it and you can actually feel it burning, so you know it must be doing you good!

CHAPTER 24

EXPECT NOTHING, BUT KNOW THAT GREAT THINGS LIE AHEAD FOR YOU
PAUL WILSON

During April and May 1997, I attended as many 12-step program meetings as possible. It was spring and a new beginning. My relationship with Bridget was pretty much over but gradually things improved with Rosanna. It was some time later that she turned to me and said, 'Daddy, I'm so proud of you for stopping drinking.'

The 12-Step fellowship is an extraordinary group that welcomes people from every walk of life, no matter what part of society you come from, your religion or your creed, race or colour: you are welcomed if you have a drink problem. The one thing you do need is a belief in a Higher Power. There are meetings available all over the world. When I toured the UK, I went to meetings in every major city, because it is very important to keep them up, long after you have stopped the drinking.

One of the key things I learned on joining was that it was the first drink that did the damage. Apart from the meetings and the

Big Book, the 'Just for Today' card was a strong part of my early recovery:

Just for today I will try to live through this day only, and not tackle all my problems at once. I can do something for twelve hours that would appall me if I felt that I had to keep it up for a lifetime.

Just for today I will be happy. Most folks are as happy as they make up their minds to be.

Just for today I will adjust myself to what is, and not try to adjust everything to my own desires. I will take my luck as it comes, and fit myself to it.

Just for today I will try to strengthen my mind. I will study. I will learn something useful. I will not be a mental loafer. I will read something that requires effort, thought and concentration.

Just for today I will exercise my soul in three ways: I will do somebody a good turn and not get found out; if anybody knows of it, it will not count. I will do at least two things I don't want to do just for exercise. I will not show anyone that my feelings are hurt; they may be hurt, but today I will not show it.

Just for today I will be agreeable. I will look as well as I can, dress becomingly, keep my voice low, be courteous, criticise not one bit. I won't find fault with anything, nor try to improve or regulate anybody but myself.

Just for today I will have a programme. I may not follow it exactly, but I will have it. I will save myself from two pests: hurry and indecision.

Just for today I will have a quiet half hour all by myself and relax. During this half hour, sometime, I will try to get a better perspective of my life.

Just for today I will be unafraid. Especially I will not be afraid to enjoy what is beautiful and to believe that as I give to the world, so the world will give to me.

At the time of writing I have been sober for 19 years..

Within weeks of sobering up, I auditioned and got the part of Vinny 'the camel' (because of his camel-hair coat) in a 1970s musical called *Oh! What a Night*. It would mean working in Blackpool – home to 25 per cent of all Lancashire pubs. The show was directed by Kim Gavin and my co-stars were Kid Creole (of …and the Coconuts fame) and Will Mellor. We performed at the Winter Gardens for the entire summer season. I was slightly worried about being away for so long having been sober for such a short time, but as it turned out, I was sober for the entire five months. As luck would have it, August Darnell (aka Kid Creole) was teetotal and didn't smoke, although he sure did love the ladies. We became great friends and took days out to the Lake District. His children befriended Rosanna when she visited and terrorised the backstage area.

After local estate agent Colette told me Blackpool could be rough after dark, with axes and Stanley knives the weapons of choice for the local yobbery, I stayed in Lytham St Annes. I became good friends with most of the cast, including Jonathan Avery, Steve Varnom and Gary Lloyd.

The show was a big success and for the first time in my career, I had to do two minutes of stand-up comedy as part of my character's role. It was a frightening experience and I have great admiration for comics. In the true tradition of the form, my repertoire began to grow as people such as producer Stuart Littlewood gave me more material. Now I understood the addiction to the buzz of making people laugh and if I got the gag wrong, it was like falling into a black hole.

I was supposed to say in my American accent to a lady in the audience, 'That's a real nice dress you're wearing, it reminds me of the shower curtain in my momma's bathroom.' One night I said, picturing a bathroom in my head, 'Your dress reminds me of a toilet seat...' Nobody laughed and I moved on swiftly.

I was given an award by the production team for falling over the most. The sole on my patent leather shoes had worn down when I ran up the stone steps to my dressing room after every show. I played a game with myself that I had to reach the top before the band finished playing the finale. My shoes became very slippery and, making an entrance one day, I fell right on my bum. Once when singing 'New York, New York' I had to jump up onto two cane chairs. One was placed out of line and I found myself, mid-song, falling backwards onto the stage. I lay on my back, gazing up at the lighting bars, while the band played on. The audience roared with laughter, thinking it was part of the act, my two co-stars dragged me to my feet and luckily, I was unharmed. We managed to finish the number in style.

All in all, it was a great season and we had free access to the Pleasure Beach and all the rides. If I got bored, I would take myself off to the *Pepsi Max Big One*, at that time boasting the steepest drop of any rollercoaster in Europe. One time a little old lady got onto the ride under the impression she was on a gentle train trip around the Pleasure Beach. Little did she realise that we were going to climb hundreds of feet into the sky and then drop rapidly! It was not for the faint-hearted – even some youngsters were too afraid to go on it. The poor old thing had to have her hands prised off the rail at the end of the ride.

My mother came to visit – taking a taxi for the full 300-mile journey from Herne Bay up north. She wasn't rich, but she didn't drink or gamble so she could afford it. She adored the Lake District and we took trips up there.

***

One sad day was 31 August 1997. I awoke to a phone call from Bridget, telling me that Dodi Fayed, boyfriend of Diana, Princess of Wales, had died in a car crash in a tunnel in Paris. Rosanna put the TV on in our flat and then told me the devastating news that Diana herself had also died. We couldn't believe it and for the rest of the day, the news didn't seem to sink in. I wrote in my diary: 'I feel so sorry for her two sons, Harry and William … The weather today reflects the sombre mood of the nation: grey, wet and overcast. Out on the streets of Lytham, no one was smiling. I saw a man with his head in his hands. At the Pizza Express the conversation was low and muted. We are all in a state of shock, living in a bad dream.'

***

I would do more with *Oh! What a Night* – the show went on to great success in 1998 at Manchester Opera House and also played down south for a summer season at the Hammersmith Apollo. After the run, Kid Creole and a couple of friends and I headed to Barbados, where we holidayed in a house on the beach.

I came back to the inescapable reality of my personal life in the immediate aftermath of the long Blackpool summer season of 1997, when I returned to Townend House in Kingston. I'd been sleeping on the floor in the front room. Now I had finished the show I couldn't go on staying in the former marital home, comfortable as it was by the glow of the log fire.

I still had a good relationship with Bridget's parents, Lambert and Ivy. Lambert kindly rented me a flat they owned at Hockney Mill in Worcester Park, Surrey. It was comfortable, clean and ideal for me to once again get used to living a single life. I really didn't want to move from Kingston though, and I felt as though I was in exile from which I hoped to return one day.

The saddest thing about leaving our home was that I no longer got to say goodnight to Rosanna but she would come to see me on the weekends and we had great fun. We would go on to celebrate the Millennium New Year together at Hockney Mill. It wasn't until later in 2001 that I moved to the Borough of Richmond.

I also got to spend holidays with Rosanna and together we have travelled abroad on many occasions over the past 30 years. We flew to New York when she was about ten to stay with my oldest friend, Paul Bennett, his wife Consi and their three sons, Jacob, Joel and Samuel, and Ruth their daughter. We had a fabulous holiday on Long Island, sailing on Paul's boat and exploring Manhattan.

Another time we returned to New York via Chicago, which was a free flight because of my involvement in *Chicago – The Musical* – I helped publicise Virgin Airlines' new route to the city. We travelled on the top deck of the plane, which was very special. Once again we visited Paul and his family.

We went to Tunisia for a week, where we stayed in a beach resort on the Mediterranean coast. We visited a Roman coliseum and saw the Sahara for the first time. In a bazaar in Tunis one of the shop owners offered me 35 camels for Rosanna! To this day I'm still not sure whether or not it was a Tunisian joke. Sadly, the resorts of Tunisia are now out of bounds, while there is such a threat from the terrorists following the 2015 massacres on the beaches. The local people must be suffering from the lack of business as tourists stay away – I feel so sorry for them.

It rained nearly every day when we stayed in Vilars, Switzerland, but it was still an enjoyable trip.

Last, but not least, I took Rosanna to Mexico, staying in a resort south of Cancun. We watched the sun rise over the Caribbean and marvelled at the Mayan ruins of Chichen-Itza. One of the most extraordinary things about the Mayan temple was standing in a certain position away from it and clapping my hands loudly. The sound of an eagle then emanates from the top of the temple. And when the sun hits the steps that rise up to the top of the temple on one particular day in the year, the shape of a snake forms on the steps. How sad it was that the Spanish destroyed so much of what was once a very advanced culture.

Rosanna and I share a similar zany sense of humour and we always find plenty of things to laugh about when we go away together. She's the perfect travelling companion. She took herself off to India with her former boyfriend Dominic, following in her dad's footsteps, as I had with mine. As I write this, I think it's about time we took another trip – this time with Lily, my granddaughter.

***

On 14 February 2000 I appeared on *Noel's House Party*. Other guests included the lovely Annabel Croft, Diane Louise Jordan, Leslie Grantham, Samantha Janus and Bradley Walsh. Annabel and I did some detective work to avoid being gunged instead of the brides and grooms on the special Valentine's Day edition of the live show. We had to guess which of three couples were genuine. I even phoned Reception to find out if a bride and groom had entered the building! We guessed right and avoided the dreaded gunge.

That summer I began to be extremely busy. First of all I played a coal miner in a pilot for HTV called *A Child in the Forest*. Melanie Hill was my wife and Karis Copp played my daughter. It was based on Winifred Foley's book. A joyous time in the Forest of Dean and I got to hack away with a pickaxe at a coalface, deep down in a mine. Then producer John Yorke at *EastEnders* had set up a half-hour programme, *The Nick Cotton Project*. They called this a 'soap bubble' – an episode away from the Square featuring a particular character, and it was later retitled *The Return of Nick Cotton*.

Frankie Fitzgerald had been cast as Nick's son Ashley. Before filming began we met in the West End of London to get to know one another. We took a boat out on the Serpentine in Hyde Park. The entire episode was to be filmed in Birmingham, standing in for north London. It would also mean a return for Chris Hancock, the actor who had played Nick Cotton's dad Charlie during the early days of *EastEnders*. He was to play Nick's father as a ghost. I wrote about that time in my diary:

SUNDAY, 20 AUGUST 2000

I had an easy journey on the train to Birmingham. I'm in room 412 of the Copthorne Hotel. I met Frankie and his mum Wendy at reception. Chris Hancock joined us for dinner – I haven't seen him for quite a few years. We went over our ghost scene. I must say I feel quite honoured to be part of this production.

MONDAY, 21 AUGUST 2000

Up at 7 again. I looked through my lines again and had a swim in the hotel pool. Our first day of filming. Frankie Fitzgerald and I did our first scene, did a few car shots and finished late. The lighting for Charlie's ghost scene was first class. Didn't get back to the hotel until 10. Another long day. Getting on well with the director, Chris Bernard. We see eye to eye and he has a good sense of humour. Met Tara Ellis this evening at the bar. She is playing Zoe, Nick Cotton's former girlfriend (Ashley's mum). All 118 sailors died in the Russian submarine *Kursk*. Tragic. Snow and tornadoes hit some of the UK today.

TUESDAY, 22 AUGUST 2000

It's 11pm. I've been learning lines with Tara, Frankie and on my own. Only two scenes to go and I'll have them all under my belt. Another good day's work. I lost the thread at one point, but got back on track after a short break. It was my heaviest day for dialogue. Tara Ellis was full of spark and we even got an extra scene done. It was a hot, sunny day in the garden of the house at 18 Elm Bank, Mosely. Spoke to Rosanna on the phone today. She sounded well but said that B [Bridget] was unwell.

WEDNESDAY, 23 AUGUST 2000

Another good day at 'Zoe's house'. Hot weather outside and hot drama inside. Crushing little Colin's fingers in a door. In the bathroom with a chainsaw coming through the door. Fighting Zoe. Climbing down a drainpipe and leaping over a fence. Tara Ellis went home this evening and I swam in the pool with Frankie and Wendy. Two coincidences happened recently: I came up to my room at 9.40pm in the evening on Monday and I was going to call B and Ro. The phone was ringing as I opened the door and it was them! The other thing was I was talking about somebody owning a spaniel during lunch at the location and a spaniel appeared and sat next to me. Only two more scenes to learn now. Spoke to Mother; she sounded well.

THURSDAY, 24 AUGUST 2000

A nasty little so-and-so called Emma Jones from the *Sun* ran a piece in the 'Bizarre' column saying I was in rehab in the Priory clinic at Roehampton. The entire piece was a lie. I was furious and as Auntie Von [Yvonne] said, I should sue the paper for slander and defamation of character. That may be too expensive, though. Managed to laugh at the ridiculousness of it all on set. Shot the scenes of Nick selling *The Big Issue* in Moseley. A student walked past and said, 'Ah! Nick Cotton in Moseley, eh?' Did the stunt shots on the bonnet of the Ford Fiesta and at the end of the day we filmed the last scene of the episode up on Barr Beacon, high above the twinkling lights of Birmingham.

FRIDAY, 25 AUGUST 2000

Swam first thing and went over my lines. Merlyn (one of the runners) took me to the new unit base for filming and Christopher Hancock and I finished off Charlie's ghost scene. Chris Bernard was very pleased and I managed to bring on the tears again. The squat location is very grim – it's an old maternity hospital that once caught fire. I had a two-hour break in the middle of the day. Ro gave me a hard time about having to work in the evening on her birthday. She later phoned and said she was sorry, bless her! The BBC are going to demand an apology from the *Sun* and report them to the Press Complaints Commission. Shot the last scenes in the squat today. Only one more day to go. It has been hard work and great fun.

SATURDAY, 26 AUGUST 2000

At 8 o'clock this evening Ian Barber, the first assistant, called out, 'It's a wrap on *The Nick Cotton Project!*' We were in Winson Green prison. Almost 60 pages of dialogue later and I've finished filming. It's been a week to remember and always cherish. The director, Chris Bernard, said that my performances made him laugh and cry. We got on so well. I accidentally sprayed Eddie 'the extinguisher' in the face today. The rain stopped whenever we needed to film outside. 'Thanks, God!' Heard tales of the prison inmates, Charles Bronson and Fred West. Heard that Reg Kray is to be freed today. Had a last chat with [producer] Beverley Dartnall today at the hotel. She reminded me that a rasta man had called out, 'Eezy, Nick!' on the street in Moseley.

SUNDAY, 27 AUGUST 2000

Outside the prison today Beverley presented me with a thank-you present, a very expensive book called *Film Noir*. Some fine photos from some classic films. It has been an incredible three weeks for me: Switzerland with Rosanna, filming *A Child in the Forest* and *The Nick Cotton Project*. I thank God for my good fortune.

As a footnote, I'd like to add that I did indeed have to work on the evening of my daughter's birthday – 29 August – at BBC Elstree. I was with Frankie Fitzgerald, filming one of *EastEnders*' 'Everybody's talking about…' trailers. We had to stand in the doorway with the rain pouring down. We got very wet and a black cat called Chico was supposed to run through the rain and nestle at our feet – it was a bit like trying to get a fish to go shopping at Waitrose! The poor wet creature dug its claws into my legs and ended up on my shoulders.

***

The following year, 2001, I shot scenes in which Nick cuts the brakes on Mark Fowler's motorbike. Ashley Cotton steals the bike. Crashes and dies. We filmed the crash in April. I found it quite sad seeing Frankie lying amid the broken glass by the motorbike. June Brown was as fine as usual as she cradled him in her arms (Frankie's real mum, Wendy, had to look away). It was sad for me as an actor to see that they had decided to kill off yet another member of the Cotton family. Frankie was a very receptive actor to work with and had even practised some of Nick Cotton's habits and gestures – like father, like son!

In another scene we had to film Nick standing beside Ashley's coffin. For once I showed that he does have a soul and a conscience beneath the tough exterior; he was truly remorseful for what happened to Ashley and his monologue over the coffin really got to me. I shed real tears. As a father, you obviously find things like that more affecting because you imagine it being your own child.

Despite all my usual reservations, I think this return was probably the most fruitful for me – it got great reviews, people were thrilled to see Dot and her beloved Nick reunited, Nick was at his most dastardly, Ashley died and Nick had crossed the line and killed his own son. It couldn't get much worse for him, but for me things were looking up. I was on the show for one of my longest contracts – a godsend as, financially, I was in trouble. I was paying two mortgages and Rosanna's private school fees, things were still quite unsettled with Bridget, so having the structure of the soap schedule was a welcome distraction.

For me this was a time of great change. I embarked on an affair with a beautiful actress called Emma Clifford, whom I met during *Oh! What a Night* at Hammersmith Apollo. I remember watching the eclipse of the sun with her in Richmond Park. A couple of years later she played Roxie Hart to my Billy Flynn in my second tour of *Chicago*. I introduced her to my agent, Roger Carey, and, as I thought she would, she went on to do very well.

I also moved from my home in Worcester Park, which I had rented from Lambert and Ivy, to a new property in the Borough of Richmond, with my own garden for the first time – I was delighted. It has often been said that the closest you can get to God is in a garden.

From an early age I was fascinated by plants and we had a large garden at our home, Little Hinton, in Hurst, Berkshire. My father used to grow runner beans and that fascinated me. Mother had a great love of roses and I remember the exotic scent of her flowers from an early age, when I was no taller than the bushes themselves.

I was given a gardening set when I was seven, consisting of a trowel, a small fork and some packets of seeds. I tried to grow carrots, which wasn't a great success. Over the years I got better at it and whenever I get the chance, I plant vegetable crops of all kinds.

While tending my plants I often think of Kenneth Williams as gardener Arthur Fallowfield in *Beyond Our Ken*, a radio show in the early 1960s. He would begin by answering any question on horticulture with, 'Well, I think the answer lies in the soil…' As I've got older to me this has sounded less like a catchphrase and more like a wise Zen Buddhist mantra. Some people hate gardening – I often say jokingly that my brother is allergic to it – but I find it very therapeutic. You can head out into the garden with a big worry hanging over you and after a few hours of intensive digging, cutting back and planting, solve the problem in your mind.

Today I take care of what I call the 'four gardens': that's my patio, my girlfriend Diana's terrace, my brother's front garden in Kent and Lambert and Ivy's front and back garden in Hayward's Heath. In another lifetime I think I would have made a good landscape gardener.

CHAPTER 25

THE ONLY WAY TO ENJOY ANYTHING IN THIS LIFE IS TO EARN IT FIRST
GINGER ROGERS

Sometimes one action you take in life can cause a totally unexpected event later on. Back in the 1970s, as I have mentioned earlier, I changed my name to John Clarkson Stewart Altman because of a clash in Equity (I'd taken the name from director Robert Altman, whom I greatly admired). I once spotted him outside BAFTA as I walked along Piccadilly and I felt the urge to approach and tell him how much I'd love to work with him. But I wasn't in an outgoing mood and so I was too shy to do so. Then a few years later I finally got to meet him when I came into contact with Stephen, his son, whom I knew through Tom Walls, who had worked on *Birth of The Beatles* many years before. The Altmans were in the UK shooting *Gosford Park* (2001) at Shepperton Studios. At their apartment in Kensington I was introduced to Robert and this time I seized the opportunity and gave him my showreel.

Stephen asked if there was anything for me in *Gosford Park* but unfortunately there wasn't. I did visit the set that Stephen had designed, though. He and the art and props department had done a wonderful job of recreating the downstairs servants' quarters of an old English country house. As I walked on the set, Robert Altman himself stood up to greet me.

'Ah, welcome, John,' he drawled. 'So you're going to be slumming it with us today?'

He had a gentle sense of humour. Just a few years later sadly he passed away and so I never got the chance to work with him.

***

As an actor, every decent role is a challenge, but for me *Chicago – The Musical* was a career-defining moment in so many ways. Although looming through people's TV screens as a much-recognised villain does offer maximum recognition, there is nothing like live theatre. Joining the cast of *Chicago* in the summer of 2001 really did allow me to divest myself of Nasty Nick and throw myself into something completely different.

Over the years I had sung many times on stage, in pantomimes and as Bill Sykes in a production of *Oliver!* at the De Montfort Hall, Leicester. During my entrance, singing 'My Name', I had been given an untrained pitbull who was Bullseye, Bill's dog. I walked down the centre aisle into the tavern with the dog on a lead and tied him to a table. Being a tough little critter, he dragged the table across the stage, upstaging my grand entrance. The next night he upstaged me again when he cocked his leg, on the table leg!

In 1992, I appeared in *Little Tramp* in Basingstoke, a musical about the life of Charlie Chaplin. Three years later I was heard on BBC Radio 2's production of *Carousel* as Jigger Craigin, playing alongside Mandy Patinkin (later of *Homeland* fame) and West End star Janie Dee. It was performed and recorded at the Golders Green Hippodrome with an audience that included Anita Dobson and her husband, Brian May of Queen. I'd separately kept a career going with music and singing and later in 2001, I would take part in a concert at the Hammersmith Apollo with Tom Jones and other stars.

***

In February 2001, my agent Roger Carey sent me to audition for the part of Billy Flynn in *Chicago – The Musical*'s first UK national tour. I prepared 'All I Care About is Love', Billy's first number, with my music teacher, Penni Harvey-Piper, at her home in Wimbledon Village. A wonderful woman, she was one of the best teachers I could hope to study with. She has coached many big West End stars over the years. The song was Billy's opening number, in the Busby Berkeley style, with him surrounded by a group of girls and an array of ostrich feathers. I spent a week or so on that song, meticulously learning and putting my own stamp on it.

The audition was in Marylebone Lane with the West End show's MD. It went well and I was asked to do a recall at the Adelphi Theatre – I had time to perfect the song with Penni.

The night before the recall, I went out for a dinner dressed in a tuxedo – Billy Flynn's costume. The next day I wore that and a black Homburg hat and I carried a black cane that had belonged to my grandfather, Johnnie Schofield junior. The recall was a huge success. I sang for director Scott Faris, executive producer Max Finbow, Walter Bobbie, the director of the original New York production, and Gary Chryst, the choreographer.

I wasn't primarily known in the business as a singer, but Penni had certainly brought me up to the standard they required, so I won the part of Billy Flynn. My diary tells me that Roger Carey phoned me with the news on 3 March – the day after my birthday. I added in my entry: 'The only way to enjoy anything in this life is to earn it first.' It was a quote from Ginger Rogers and I had worked very hard to get that part.

Then suddenly it dawned on me, crikey, I've got to do it now! It was a complex piece, but I knew that they would give us the rehearsal time we needed – the American team wouldn't allow it any other way (the production team always oversaw each international version).

***

I never found that the process of auditioning got any easier – being faced initially by a small panel of people on the first round and then the further you go, the bigger the panel gets until sometimes there can be nearly twenty people in the room watching you and jotting notes down. You do get hardened to the process in the end – you have to, or you would never get up on the stage again and audition for anything else. The key is not to take the rejection personally.

I was once up for the part of the innkeeper in *Les Misérables* and one of the recalls was at producer Cameron Mackintosh's house. The audition process took over three months. While I was waiting to hear about the next call, I went on holiday and ended up performing the songs standing in the Indian Ocean off the coast of Lamu, Kenya, singing to the seagulls so that I would stay word-perfect for when they called me back again. My old friend Mark Macaulay had invited me there. I did actually get called back for a final audition at the theatre with Cameron in attendance. This time they asked me to sing only one song, although I had rehearsed three. A few days later I heard that I hadn't got the job. I'd spent many weeks and quite a lot of money preparing for this role but to no avail. Such is show business! Once again!

***

We didn't start rehearsals for *Chicago* until mid-August 2001 at the Jerwood Space on Union Street, near Waterloo. Having taken plenty of time to prepare my other songs with Penni, I arrived feeling on top of it all. I performed with Jane Fowler as Roxie Hart and Amra-Faye Wright was to play Velma. Martin Callaghan was Amos and

Marjorie Keys was Matron 'Mama' Morton. Morgan Crowley played Mary Sunshine.

Rehearsals went very well. I also got on very well with the director, Scott Faris, and then the company moved to the Manchester Opera House on 10 September. It was the best theatre work I've ever done – it was a great team and a fab young chorus line but nothing prepared us for the day after we arrived.

Around 2pm the following day I was at the stage door. I thought what I saw on the black-and-white television there was a scene from an old movie. In my dressing room, I turned on my television and realised that two hijacked planes had been flown into the World Trade Center in New York City. Both towers were destroyed, another plane hit the Pentagon in Washington and the last one crashed in Pennsylvania. I have never been so shocked. Totally numbed, I felt sick: thousands of people had died in the worst terrorist attack in history.

Then, as the day unfolded, the sheer horror of it all descended. We all sat in my dressing room, watched it on my TV, and words failed us. We debated long and hard about whether we should carry on rehearsing or cancel out of respect, but we all decided that the show must go on.

We all saw first-hand how the experience affected our American team, so far from home. There was a dialect coach in the company who had a relative working in one of the towers. That morning in New York was a beautiful one with clear blue skies and because her relative wanted to soak up some extra sun, instead of taking his coffee to his desk in one of the towers, he sat on a bench in Battery Park – that coffee saved his life or else he would have been at his desk and almost certainly dead by now.

That night I wrote in my diary:

What do these evil, insane people want? How can any good

come from such a wicked deed? Everyone in the cast was shocked, especially Gary, our choreographer, who has a place in New York. I shall pray for the victims and wounded. Spoke to B, Ro, my mother and brother today. This has been a dark day for the whole world.

We opened the show on 14 September 2011 to 2,000 people at the Opera House in Manchester. Gary said we should be 'fearless and free'. This would be the beginning of a twelve-month tour, which then rolled into a second year.

Having just come out of a long run as Nick, I was fully in work mode and used to long days and nights; I couldn't wait to throw myself into it. It was one of my happiest working experiences and the cast were fantastic. There was a young chorus line who were loads of fun and I felt very proud to be associated with something so slick.

Billy Flynn was one of my all-time favourite characters. As honest as an attorney can be, he could bend and manipulate the truth and put words into people's mouths when he wanted to, but unlike Nick Cotton, he was a more sympathetic and charming character to play and the costume was definitely a step up in terms of sartorial elegance. I couldn't have been more delighted to shrug off Nick's leather jacket and chains and slip on a tuxedo. The first Manchester review said:

A surprise success is Altman, who thankfully keeps his Nick Cotton *EastEnders* persona well at bay – and he can sing a bit too. The individual performances are captivating and the musical numbers are performed with great passion and energy.

***

I decided to give a big thank-you to my mother for everything she'd ever done for me over the years. One of those things had been, in 1967, buying me a ticket to see the last ever Cream concert at the Royal Albert Hall. An old diary entry from that time said: 'I can't believe that my mother has arranged all this for me. It's so amazing. I will repay her ten-fold one day.' That opportunity came when I was engaged for a celebrity cruise on the *QE2* in the summer of 2003. I took her along as my companion.

The voyage took us from Southampton via Gibraltar and then around the Mediterranean. She was absolutely delighted with the whole trip, which took in Lisbon, Barcelona and Majorca along the way. We had luxurious cabins with a steward attached and dined every night at the Queen's Grill with Wendy Richard and her husband John. Also onboard at that time were Esther Rantzen and her husband Desmond Wilcox, Stuart Hall and Jimmy Savile. What a mixture! This was long before the shocking revelations about the latter two, but even then I found Savile a bit strange. He kept himself to himself and would often be found jogging around the decks on his own in his shiny shellsuits. One morning I came across him at the concierge's desk. He seemed to deflect interaction by saying something inappropriate, or trying what he thought was an amusing quip.

'Good morning, Jimmy,' I said.

'Good morning to you too, sir,' he said. 'I'm just about to pay my child maintenance.' I remember thinking, 'What a weirdo. Who would pay maintenance via a desk on the *QE2*?'

As for Stuart Hall, he was absolutely charming to my mother and we got on very well with him and his wife Hazel. He had a great sense of humour and he and I used to improvise being gangster characters as if we were in *The Godfather*. It's very strange to think that we can have absolutely no idea of someone's inner thoughts when presented with such a charming exterior.

IN THE NICK OF TIME

That cruise remains a great memory. My mother adored it and was the perfect travelling companion as she didn't live in my pocket – she was very happy to go off and do her own thing and would often go to bed at 10pm and leave me to it. I met a beautiful girl – she was the harpist on board. I had actually seen her the minute we boarded the ship. She was called Lisa Tannobaum, she was from New York, and I was enchanted by the way she played the instrument to welcome us all. I have always thought there is something very sensual about playing the harp, very delicate – I was extremely impressed by her. A few days later I saw her sitting in a chair on deck in jeans and flip flops, still looking amazing, and we got chatting and ended up seeing each other for a while after the cruise ended. I remember getting a shock when I went to see her quarters, though: our cabins were plush and comfortable with plenty of room whereas hers was the size of a tiny cupboard, way down in the bottom of the ship with no porthole.

As a footnote to this journey, I would also like to mention other holidays including the wonderful week I spent with my mother in Banff in the Canadian Rockies in February 1999. She had always wanted to go to Canada and I remember a husky ride across a frozen lake. I also took her to a Virgin resort in Barbados for ten days in May 2002 and we explored the island together. As I write this my mother, bless her, has turned ninety-six and she still talks about these trips with great fondness. Before we went away together, she had only been outside England once – to Austria.

Something else I wish to thank my mother for: I have already mentioned how well she cooked and it is to her that I owe my ability to produce the perfect boiled egg. Here are her tips: if you keep your eggs in the fridge, place them next to the pan that heats the water because if you put an egg straight from the fridge into boiling water, it will crack. If this does happen, quickly pour salt over the egg to seal it. Ideally, you would place a room temperature egg in boiling water for four minutes. When you take it out, pour cold water over it and tap the top with a spoon to stop it cooking. You will then have the perfect boiled egg: hard, white exterior and partially cooked yolk with a runny centre. Place in an egg cup and cut up toasted soldiers.

Let's complete the cooking section of this book with a guide to the perfect roast potato. Use good-quality roasting potatoes. Cut each medium-sized potato into four and boil until a slight film appears around the saucepan. Place the potatoes on a lightly oiled baking tray and gently brush sunflower oil onto each quarter. Keep the tray in the oven separately from the joint at 200°C (for a fan-assisted oven). Once the potatoes have become crisp and golden on one side – after about 45 minutes – take them out of the oven, gently turn them over and brush with sunflower oil. Cook for another 40–45 minutes to be ready with the rest of the meal and by then you should have the perfect roast potato: crisp and golden on the outside, soft and fluffy on the inside.

As with the boiled egg, it's so easy to ruin them. You can't just chuck potatoes in the oven. You need to concentrate. I still remember my father's words of wisdom regarding all cooking – 'Keep the gas down low.' Sound advice – you'll avoid burning pans and saucepans boiling over.

***

By the time I finished *Chicago* – in Nottingham in 2003 – I had appeared in 525 performances. It was the best piece of work I ever performed in theatre. I became great friends with Jane, Amra, Martin and Morgan – not forgetting Steve Diamond, our wonderful company manager. We travelled the length and breadth of the UK – from Bournemouth to Norwich via Cardiff.

In Aberdeen we heard that the Queen was doing a walkabout in a nearby park. It was grizzly, drizzly old Scottish morning but we turned out to see Her Majesty as she made her way around the far side of the crowd. A gentleman appeared out of nowhere, dressed in a raincoat and clutching an umbrella. I did a double take and realised it was the Duke of Edinburgh making his way around our area. Prince Philip could never resist a witty quip and he was true to form as he approached us.

'You don't sound like the locals,' he said. 'What are you lot doing up here?'

When we told him he said he'd seen and enjoyed the show in the West End and in a nod to the skimpy stage gear compared to our civilian outfits added, 'You certainly didn't have this many clothes on last time I saw you.' It was a privilege to meet him; he is an entertaining soul and I should add to this that I'm definitely a royalist and not a republican.

During my last show, as I performed 'All I Care About is Love' shrouded by the ostrich feathers held up by the girls, they decided to pinch my bum. Perhaps they had been dying to get hold of what had, two years earlier, been awarded Rear of the Year alongside Claire Sweeney, although I think it was more likely that they were trying to put me off at a moment when the audience couldn't see what they were up to. I was taken aback, but managed to get through the number without laughing.

This was a musical that I never grew tired of – it was so beautifully written and presented. But we all have to move on in this crazy business and my next stop was playing Glenn Miller in the spring of 2004 in a show called *American Patrol* at the Mayflower, Southampton. Looking at me, you might not think that I would be an obvious Miller lookalike, but with US uniform and trademark glasses, the resemblance was quite close.

The show was devised and written by the late John Latus. Special guests were Michael Knowles (*It Ain't Half Hot Mum*) and DJ Mike Read as the chat-show host. It was a snapshot of Miller's final six months. We got some pretty bad reviews but, personally, I thought it was very entertaining and would have sold well on tour –Miller remains very popular to this day.

In researching my part I discovered that he once performed an open-air concert in Bushy Park – not far from Teddington, near where I live – long before The Stones had their show in Hyde Park! Prior to D-Day, the Americans had set up a huge camp in Bushy Park, Surrey, mistakenly, because they meant to go to Bushey, Hertfordshire, but they decided to stay put when they realised their mistake. As to the bandleader's death, there are many theories, but no one has ever discovered the true facts. The most believable story is that his plane was hit in 1944 crossing the Channel by some bombs offloaded high above from a British plane coming back from an operation in Germany.

Later that same year, 2004, I was the dentist in Jersey Opera House's production of *Little Shop of Horrors*. I played alongside Tracy Shaw (*Coronation Street*) as Audrey. What a joyous way to spend the summer! Rosanna and my mother both flew over to visit, and I learned to surf on the westernmost beach on the island.

That summer I also flew to Argentina to shoot *Celebrity Fear Factor* in Buenos Aires with Andrew Castle, Sophie Anderton, Annabel Croft and John Alford. I fell for Annabel in a big way, although I didn't say anything to her – alas, she was very happily married with children. It was an exciting, non-stop week of thrills and spills. The highlight for me was a wing-walk along a biplane thousands of feet above Argentina.

I had to climb out of the open cockpit with what looked like a length of washing line as a safety rope, walk along the wing – holding the struts firmly – and hit a button at the tip of the wing to release some smoke. I was given about half an hour's warning of the stunt! As I made my way along the wing I glanced down at the countryside far below me and thought I had to be mad. Hold on tight!

At the end of the week, Annabel, Sophie and I did a quick tour of Buenos Aires, including Casa Rosada (the Pink House) and the tomb of Evita Peron.

***

I entered 2006 in panto in Crewe with Bobby Crush. But times were tough: I had no girlfriend and work was scarce until the summer and a Ray Cooney farce. I toured in *Funny Money*, directed by Ian Dickens and Giles Watling, and starred alongside Chris Ellison from *The Bill*, Vicki Michelle (*'Allo, 'Allo!*), Peter Blake (*Dear John*), *Emmerdale*'s Sally Ann Matthews, David Callister and Terry O'Sullivan.

The rehearsal period was diabolically short and we were on very thin ice at the preview in Horsham. It was good to be working with my old friend Chris, and Vicki became a new friend and was a great team member who always seemed to know the best digs to stay in, from town to town.

In Plymouth, I took the Cremyll ferry across to Mount Edgcumbe one sunny day. I helped a pretty young blonde girl get her pushchair on and off the ferry with her two daughters; I was quite dazzled by her. I went for a swim in the sea just off Edgcumbe and when I emerged from the water I noticed that she and the two girls were picnicking on the grass at the edge of the park so I walked over, we began chatting and I invited her to see the show. Her name was Haylie Oliver and her two girls were Sunny and Daisy.

Haylie watched the production and we had a great night out on Plymouth Hoe and got on extremely well. We promised to meet again, although I was leaving town in a couple of days for Cheltenham. We next met in Exeter which, after a passionate time together, we renamed Sexeter. And so began a long and passionate relationship, my first in a long time. Being more mature, I had felt that I preferred to be on my own rather than going out with someone for the sake of it. I'd been quite happy being a bachelor boy for a year or more but despite an age gap of some twenty years, Haylie and I had something special and we were together for more than four years.

She would join me on tour whenever she could and supported me when, on 5 October 2008, I did a big fundraiser for Kingston's Rose Theatre with a host of stars that included June Brown, Barbara Windsor, Steve McFadden, Jeff Stewart and many more. We had a lovely holiday with the girls in Calpe, Spain, including climbing up the great rock in the bay. Haylie and I became engaged, but sadly it turned out this was towards the end of our affair.

On one of my visits to Plymouth I met up again with the Reverend Mike Brotherton, a ship's chaplain. He had become well known to TV viewers through the BBC1 series *Shipmates* and over the years we have become great friends. He and his mother, BB, are two of the kindest people you could ever wish to meet. He organised a day for me with the Royal Navy on board HMS *Westminster*. I took part in a wargame at sea, one of the navy's regular 'Thursday Wars', and it was not just exciting but also a privilege and honour to be there. Planes swooped overhead and high-powered boats simulated attacks from over the water with navy crew dressed as terrorists. Others played victims of a simulated bomb blast and we had to rescue them amid clouds of smoke.

Lunch was eaten on the run during the operation. We dined on minced meat and peas in a paper bag using a plastic spoon. When you're in the middle of a battle there is no time to sit down with expensive cutlery and fancy plates.

Mike Brotherton is also renowned for the parties he holds at his farmhouse on the beautiful Angle Peninsula Coast in Wales. He's since retired and joined the Royal National Lifeboat Institution (RNLI), a charity I've supported for years.

***

Haylie and I quite often went out for a run together. One cold, damp day in 2006 we were running from Land's End to Marazion as part of my training for the London Marathon. A few days later we celebrated the birthday of an old friend, hotel manager Tim Burnham, with a party. I began to feel quite unwell and so I returned to the hotel room Haylie and I were sharing. In the morning I woke up on a pillow that was drenched in sweat.

I felt worse as the week wore on. Back in London the doctor tried me on two different types of antibiotic, neither of which helped what he thought was a flu virus. By the Thursday night I was shivering and shaking, my face was ashen, my eyes had dark rings around them and I was still sweating profusely. I felt as if I'd been hit by a bus and then gone two rounds with Mike Tyson. Everything was a huge effort.

I returned to the doctor for the third time but he wasn't there so I saw a locum who took one look and told me to go to hospital. Somehow I managed to drive myself to Kingston Hospital, despite the way I was feeling. Exhaustive tests at length resulted in the shock news that I had pneumonia. I couldn't understand it – I was fit as a fiddle, I didn't smoke or drink and it wasn't as if I was sleeping rough. The only thing I could think of was the 13-mile damp run that had caused it.

I was restored to health through the expert attention of Dr John Chinegwundoh. A true gentleman, he was charming and had a great aura of warmth and kindness about him. He told me that my years as a smoker had weakened my lungs and the passageways to them. I might have stopped, but the damage had been done. Haylie was upset as she couldn't make it to London to see me, but she had the girls to look after. My second bout of pneumonia came a few years later but at least I was able to recognise the condition from the shivering, sweating and shaking symptoms.

***

Towards the end of 2006, just before going to Canterbury to perform in *Jack and the Beanstalk* with Amanda Barrie (*Coronation Street*), I was invited to take part in a 'goodies and baddies' charity episode of *The Weakest Link*. I prepared myself for the famously confrontational Anne Robinson by composing a few putdowns of my own. The show was recorded at Pinewood Studios, a place I adore for its atmosphere and its incredible history. I shot my first film there and more recently, a feature called *Photoshoot*, about a paparazzo, with Debbie Arnold.

Before recording *The Weakest Link* I had an hour to spare so I took myself off to see what was being made. I saw the set of *The Wolfman*, where Anthony Hopkins had been filming, and decided to take a look at the James Bond Stage, where apparently they were then filming *Harry Potter and the Deathly Hallows*. As I walked along the side of the stage, I spotted Daniel Radcliffe. I waved to him and he waved back from his side of a fence. We'd never met but he knew who I was, and of course I recognised him too. I was curious to know, having seen Daniel, what the set looked like inside the James Bond Stage. Security seemed very tight and I decided to walk up some steps at the far end of the stage. When I opened the door who should be sitting there but Alfie Oldman, the son of my old friends Gary Oldman and Lesley Manville. I hadn't seen him for a few years but he recognised me. He was now a runner and doing Security for *Potter*.

'Come with me, John,' he said. 'I'll show you around.'

We stepped into the Forbidden Forest, a phenomenal set to behold. The trees seemed to disappear into infinity high above our heads and the forest floor was so real. We toured parts of Hogwarts, I had a brief chat with Daniel and they gave me tea and cakes. My time was soon up and I returned to *The Weakest Link*. What a treat it had been!

Anne didn't give me a hard time on the show so I had no use for my prepared rejoinders in the end, although she did rather archly comment, 'Who *does* your hair, John?' I crisply replied, 'Mel of Teddington.' This wasn't an exclusive boutique, but rather a very attractive woman called Mel who lived locally. I reached the final three but was outvoted by two members of *The Bill*, who had worked together for a long time.

***

It wasn't always easy for Haylie and I to meet because she had the girls and I was often on tour. In addition, she lived in Plymouth while I was in London. But I thoroughly enjoyed the days we spent together on the coast, going to Dartmoor, spending time on Cornish beaches and I had become attached to the two girls. I missed them all terribly when we broke up, just before I headed off to perform in a tour of *PopStar! The Musical* in the spring of 2010. I spent much of that tour suffering with a broken heart. It was a few years before we saw each other. We've since become good friends again, and the great sadness and pain of that parting has faded away. Over the years I have kept in contact with Haylie's grandmother, Gwen, who lives in Marazion, Cornwall. She is a wise and kindly lady.

PopStar! toured in 2010 and I played alongside Sam Kane, Sarah Jane Buckley (*Hollyoaks*), Blue's Antony Costa, Ciaran Janson and Rob McVeigh. I thought of Haylie when I sang the ballad 'Right Here Waiting for You' by Richard Marx every night. There were times when I felt quite emotional as I performed it. I also sang Bryan Adams' hard rock number 'Summer of '69' and that would put me back on course. Sam was very kind to me during the tour and listened to my tales of woe.

I won't name names, but the producers failed miserably to publicise the show properly and it was poorly attended, even though our cast could have appealed to all the family. So it was a sad occasion when the entire production folded and sank into the sea just off Bridlington, three-quarters of the way through the tour.

CHAPTER 26

**ARSON IS NOT REALLY A CRIME. THERE ARE MANY BUILDINGS
THAT DESERVE TO BE BURNED DOWN**
H. G. WELLS

Many of my returns to *EastEnders*, particularly the very last one, were down to June Brown. She always looked out for others, she's generous like that. After the death of Ashley, Dot cast Nick out and truly meant it this time. She adored Ashley and saw him as everything Nick had never been – her grandson was her chance to get things right and Nick took that away from her in the most brutal fashion. It would have to be a very meaty storyline to bring him back and get Dot's resolve to weaken. The viewers always knew with Dot and Nick that it would never be over unless one of them was dead, but he had gone too far this time. I took quite a long break from the show, but it felt very much like unfinished business after such a brilliant storyline.

Enter Dotty: she was introduced in December 2008, as the big show-stopping 'Christmas Day moment' that the soaps like to have every year. She was the result of a one-night stand between Nick and an alcoholic woman called Sandy. While serving time in prison, he received a letter from Sandy telling him that she had given birth to their daughter. Once he was released in April 2008, Nick was given custody of Dotty (actress Molly Conlin who, I must say, was a joy to work with – a consummate young professional who always knew her lines and was good fun, too). He told the child that her mother had died in a tragic car crash and then took her back to meet long-suffering Dot. But 'Dotty' and Nick are cut from the same cloth – early on they decide to go after Dot's money. Dotty was key to getting Nick back over the threshold; only the promise of another grandchild would have meant Dot was willing to open her door to the errant son who had caused her so much heartache. They trick Dot into believing that she has dementia and plan to poison her with medication while making it look like an accidental overdose, taken by someone losing her mind.

But Dotty comes to love Dot and so switches the plan and crushes up the medication and puts it in Nick's beer instead. This drives Nick to drag Dottie to the café, where he holds everyone hostage. The place explodes and burns down. Nick does a runner.

I was first contacted about going back in the summer of 2008. Dot and Nick's relationship has always been wonderfully dysfunctional – she lives in the eternal hope that he has changed, and their relationship was all the more intense as there was no father figure around. I thought Charlie's demise was a somewhat gratuitous one – he was a great actor and a fantastic character.

CHAPTER 27

IT IS NEVER TOO LATE TO BE WHAT YOU MIGHT HAVE BEEN
GEORGE ELIOT

Deep down, I was a bit sad to learn that I was to be killed off after playing my character for 30 years, someone I helped to create and made a household name. Really it's the ultimate cutting adrift and there was always a part of me that wondered if they simply couldn't think of anything else to do with Nick. To be honest I didn't see it coming – I had been out of the show a while and when the phone call came through I just assumed it was to offer me another bad-boy storyline they wanted to introduce to push up the ratings.

I met up with Dominic Treadwell-Collins and Alex (head of the script department) and I was told that they wanted to kill Nick off in an elaborate storyline involving his son, Charlie, the attempted murder of Roxy Mitchell and a fake death. To me it sounded like a classic Nick storyline. They went through what they wanted and it required a good few months' work, which was the upside, I guess.

I thought I would have time to think it over but it soon became clear that Nick Cotton would be killed off whether or not I agreed. If I said no, it would simply happen off-screen. As June Brown wryly observed to me at the time: 'You may as well do it. If you don't, they will kill you off anyway so you might as well earn a few bob.' As ever, she had hit the nail on the head – he was my character and I needed to see him through to the end.

Upon my arrival at BBC TV Elstree in 2014 I was not best pleased to be allocated a so-called 'dressing room' that was actually one of the worst portakabins, usually reserved for extras or people who were only doing a day's filming. There was no running water, no shower and not even a toilet. I immediately rang my agent, who got in touch with Carolyn Weinstein, the executive secretary, and they eventually found me a decent dressing room, which was absolutely fine. I didn't expect champagne and roses whenever I came back and I didn't like to act the superstar but a few home comforts never went amiss. Especially after being involved in the programme for almost thirty years.

This wasn't the first time that a return lacked a certain warmth. On a previous occasion, many years ago, I turned up at Reception and checked in. The runner took me to the tea bar with all the extras. By chance I knew most of them so I thought, 'I'll let this one go and see what happens.' About twenty minutes later another runner came dashing up in a mad panic: 'John, John – you're supposed to be on set, you should have been in Make-up and Costume…'

'Oh, really?' I said casually. 'Well, I suppose we should go then.'

So began another term at St Julia's.

***

Signing on the dotted line to play Nick meant that many, many doors shut on me and they have never opened again. It did make me bitter and I struggled a lot. My greatest love has always been film – both as a child and then as a jobbing actor – and it never happened in a big way for me after Nick. People make assumptions about your capability but there is also a huge snobbery when it comes to some people's attitudes towards actors who have been on soaps – there is an automatic decision about capability and intellect that simply isn't true or fair.

From the outside being on a soap and being famous appears to be a charmed life but it was hard – and still is – especially when you have to deal with the people who shout abuse and say stupid things, it definitely makes the hard times harder. Some people just behave in a way that makes no sense to me: why would anyone scream and shout at someone in the street just because they are on TV? That said, most of the time the fans are great, lovely even. I remember one particular occasion when I was at the height of Nick's fame and doing PAs in nightclubs. There was one particular gig where I lost my grandfather's precious signet ring. It was a gold ring with a bloodstone in it and my Aunty Mamie gave it to me. I was shaking hands with the fans who were lining up to get pictures and autographs and the ring must have slipped off my finger. It was only as I was travelling home in the car up the M4 after the event that I realised it was missing.

In a panic I phoned the club and they got the cleaners to check everywhere, even going through the rubbish bags. It turns out a girl had grabbed hold of my hand to shake it; she had been pushed out of the way in the scrum and pulled away, taking the ring with her by accident. She was waving her hands to try and get to me but couldn't be heard over all the noise and the bouncers wouldn't let her move back to me. I put a notice in the local paper asking for any information and she came forward with it, didn't want a reward or anything from me, just a straightforward decent girl doing the right thing. However I sent her a reward and some photos in gratitude.

If I had my time again, would I say no to Nick? I don't know, is the genuine answer. When they decided to kill him off, what did I think? My genuine first thought was, 'Crikey, there goes my pension fund!' To be honest, I never thought they would do it; I didn't see why they would need to as he came and went and didn't bring any long-term harm or stress to the producers or storywriters. He was the perfect character to have up your sleeve in case of emergency and if you needed to give the show a jolt or grab some headlines.I thought he would go on forever. Being evil isn't dependent on youth, as the 2015 Hatton Garden robbery, with its gang of OAPs, proved.

The way he died was quite neat really – 30 years after his first appearance and in the very chair that had been occupied by his first victim, Reg Cox.

What really became apparent to me during this time was how politically correct the soap had become, and perhaps how there really wasn't a place left for the very un-PC Nick. There was a strand in this final storyline where he instructs Dot to throw out Fat Boy, in case the young man works out that Nick is still alive and hiding upstairs. There was a line Nick had to say to Dot, full of his usual vitriol and racist intent: 'Well, we're alright now that the Paki has gone.' It's not how I would ever speak, but it was 100 per cent Nick Cotton. In turn Dot's response was perfectly in keeping with her Christian values: 'Don't you dare speak like that to me, that's disgusting talk. May God strike you down!'

As we were rehearsing the scene, suddenly the filming stopped and we were told: 'Not sure we can go with this.' Now, my argument was like it or not, this is how people like Nick speak; this is what you are likely to hear in any major city. That aside, it's coming from the mouth of Nick – a racist, murdering, semi-psychopathic lunatic. Phone calls were made; we waited. June was smoking. Word came back that we might not be allowed to use this, so we were told we had to film two versions – one with 'Paki' and one where Nick calls Fat Boy an 'illegal immigrant'. When it was aired they went with the latter – a sign of the times perhaps, or just a sign of the BBC being politically correct.

***

I was not exactly thrilled to miss out on Best Villain at the 2015 Soap Awards – I really felt that it would have been the right way to send off Nick after 30 years. I truly believe his awfulness set the bar for soap baddies and has provided the show with some of its most memorable scenes and storylines. He had the highest murder count (four) in the show, never mind the drugs, attempted murders, putting Mary on the game – you name it, he did it.

I was pleased so much of the last day's filming involved June Brown and me, as I felt it should have been at the end – just Nick and his devoted Ma. June and I went through our usual ritual of spending time together beforehand and making adjustments to the script, tweaking lines and inserting our own special 'Nick and Dot' dialogue. They were precious times and I learned so much – I will deeply miss working with her.

On 16 January 2015 I filmed my final scenes with June in the burnt-out house. Some of the scenes with Nick as a corpse went out in the live episode so I suppose you could say I was 'dead-and-alive'. The art department and the props team had done an extraordinary job of creating a house that looked as if it had been on fire. It was strange to walk through the scene of desolation, the burnt walls and charred woodwork without also having the acrid smell of a recent fire or being covered with soot whenever you touched anything.

Between scenes I waited with June in Dot Cotton's kitchen. At one point the executive producer, Dominic Treadwell-Collins, appeared out of nowhere. I turned around and a group of more than thirty people had gathered in the studio to say goodbye. Dominic made a speech, thanking me for my work and for creating a legend that would always be remembered in the history of soap operas. He presented me with a beautiful bouquet of flowers and silver cufflinks inscribed 'Nick Cotton 1985–2015'. They had been chosen by the executive secretary Carolyn Weinstein.

I made a brief speech, thanking everyone for my gift and saying that for me it had been an incredible 30 years.

When the director, John Greening, called 'Cut!' on the final scene there was a round of applause from the crew, and the floor manager, Julie, came up to me and said, 'I was determined never to be emotional filming scenes on *EastEnders*, but today, you and June did make me cry for the first time.' When I watched it back I was concentrating on the technical aspects but when I saw it for the second time, I too became quite emotional.

***

People often ask if I watch the soap now and the answer is off and on really, it all depends on the storyline. As I have said, there are over 55 different characters in the show now as opposed to the 20 or so when I started – back then it could pull in audiences of 23 million. I did watch the show when I was in it – I believe you can learn a lot as an actor by doing that, even though it is not always easy. My family were very proud of me and my dad, Cecil Clarkson Stewart, wasn't a great soap fan but he tuned in every week as an act of support. He told me how pleased he was with my success, and it was great for me to show him that I could make a living out of the whole 'acting thing', as he had been very wary of me not taking a 'proper job'. There was one occasion when I had been invited to open a seafront garden in Herne Bay, Kent, and it made the front page of the local paper:

EastEnders Star Opens Seafront Garden

He framed that headline and put it in his office.

I also found out that as part of his daily shopping routine he would take signed pictures of me to the girls in the local supermarket. It meant a great deal to me to know that he took such pride in what I'd achieved, even if it wasn't what he had in mind for me as a career.

CHAPTER 28

A LIFE ON THE OCEAN WAVE . . .
YOU NEVER GET TIME TO SHAVE . . .
PARODY OF EPES SARGENT'S 1838 SONG

The last thing I ever thought I'd enjoy was cruising the Seven Seas on an ocean liner. I first got a taste for it when I took a trip around the Mediterranean with my mother on the *QE2* back in 2003 and later on *Explorer of the Seas*, a brand-new US cruise ship that I boarded with Rosanna from Miami. The trip was organised by my good friend Roger Burnett. We sailed out in an exciting thunderstorm and took in the Bahamas, Puerto Rico, Haiti and the British Virgin Islands, going south. In the Virgin Islands we hired a sailing boat for a day. It was owned by a young British couple who had sold everything they had in the UK and now made a living chartering their vessel for tourists, particularly the cruise ship passengers. I was pleased to find a 12-step program meeting on board the *Explorer* and a kids' club for Rosanna. One morning, sitting on the deck, Rosanna and I composed a silly rhyme after we'd had a comical argument, calling each other 'an idiot' after we'd narrowly missed being decorated by a passing seagull.

IDIOTS
You're an idiot
You're an idiot too
Together we're one big idiot
Looking at the ocean blue
Idiots are great
They're stupid, thick and dull
Look out here comes some poo
From a great big bad seagull!

In 2004 Rosanna and I ran the Leeds 10 kilometre charity run. We enjoy running together whenever we have time. She spurs me on.

I was more than delighted when I was later invited to work on the P&O ship *Ventura*, sailing to the Norwegian fjords, where I saw some spectacular sights and met the all-girl rock band JOANovARC. I gave talks illustrated by photos from my life, sang a rock song to complete the evening and chatted with the guests onboard.

Some months later I did another tour on the same ship, where I met an elderly lady called Pat Sylvester. She told me that she was a great fan of Status Quo – the last person I would have expected. Some months later I had a spare ticket for a tribute to the band at The Dorchester hotel on Park Lane and she was thrilled to bits when I invited her. The Quo got up and played, and star-struck Pat danced at the front of the stage and also got to meet her heroes – I think she had more energy than me at that gig!

In October 2011 I sailed with the P&O ship *Ventura* again out of Southampton for the Caribbean (we called in at Madeira on the way). The further south we went, the better the weather was, with the air becoming noticeably warmer. At 3 o'clock one morning an alarm call sounded, all the ship's deck lights were turned on and the tannoy announced someone had gone overboard. A young man, who had been observed by Security acting rather strangely over the previous few days, had leapt from the fifth deck – some fifty feet or more – into the pitch-black waters of the South Atlantic Ocean. A man two decks above saw him jump and immediately hurled a lifebelt after him. It held a tracking device that could be followed by the ship, which slowed to a virtual halt. A rescue boat was launched from the side of the ship – like a lifeboat from the mainland – it was catapulted into the sea.

I stood on my balcony, looking up and down, and soon realised the entire ship had been woken up. Other passengers came onto their own balconies and we all found it very upsetting. Slowly the ship turned around to follow the rescue craft and, miraculously, thanks to the tracker, they found the young man still alive. Imagine searching the seas in the middle of the night for one person – even given the tracker nearby it was incredible that they found him and brought him back within an hour. The man was taken to the ship's hospital and we continued on our way to Antigua. Nothing much more was said about the event, but it was reported in the *Daily Mail* and on the Internet. I never knew what eventually happened to him but I trust that he fully recovered.

The rest of the cruise was by comparison uneventful. I flew back from Barbados.

It's a sad thing but I discovered while cruising that people do actually 'check in to check out', so to speak. They purposefully book a cruise with the intention of jumping overboard at some point during the voyage. If you jump off the back of one of those ships in the middle of the night generally you wouldn't stand a chance and your disappearance would only be discovered when your room was checked the next day. Cruise ships are so tall that the effect of impact after jumping from one of the upper decks can be severe in itself.

One of the magical things about cruising is the ever-changing view. You may well think that a ship full of 3,000 people is going to be horrendous when it comes to mealtimes or trying to find some space on the sun deck but once everyone is on board and spread out it can be hard to imagine there are so many people in one place. There was never a queue for dinner and checking in was itself a joy, compared to fighting your way through Heathrow or Gatwick airports. You drive to the terminal at Southampton, unload your luggage, the car is taken away and your luggage whisked away too. It magically reappears outside your cabin door. Checking in itself takes no time at all.

After my first cruising experience I drove back to London up the M3 and couldn't understand why I felt so relaxed and unstressed. It was then that I realised I didn't have jet lag, having moved across the face of the planet at a more natural pace.

I took my fourth cruise on the P&O ship *Azura* with my new girlfriend, Diana Marchment, in 2013. We once again left Southampton, stopping off in northern Spain, Portugal, Gibraltar and Morocco, and I gave a talk about my life. Both of us had romantic notions about Casablanca, but visiting it turned out to be a rather dangerous, dirty and unpleasant experience. We docked next to a cement factory and its dust settled all over the ship. As we walked into the town we watched in horror as a local lowlife snatched a chain from around the neck of a fellow passenger.

Diana and I also cruised on a smaller P&O ship, the *Adonia*. Once again I was working – nice work if you can get it! I had a week's cruise for two hours' chat. This particular trip followed the route of RMS *Titanic*. We stopped at Liverpool, sailed across to Belfast, Dublin and then travelled to Cork. In Limerick we learned all about flying boats, which, just before World War II, were the quickest way to travel to the US. They were a mode of transport reserved for politicians, film stars and the top brass in the military.

South of Limerick we hit a terrible storm between the Irish Sea and the Atlantic, with waves reaching between thirty and forty feet. We took quite a battering! Diana stayed in her cabin and everything in the ship shut down, from the lifts to the restaurants. I made my way to the top of the ship, where there was a bar and a viewing platform and there I sat, rocking-and-rolling with the ship until it heaved so violently that I was thrown from my chair. Back in the cabin, Diana was trying to stop everything flying about the room.

It was the second-biggest storm I had experienced after one in the South Atlantic. I never got seasick, almost certainly thanks to my father's side of the family, which had a strong sea-faring element. My grandfather, William Stewart, was captain of the *Mackay Bennett*, a cable ship that was one of the first to reach the site of the *Titanic* when it went down. He was then living in Halifax, Nova Scotia. I have photographs of him at that time; also of a priest on board the *Mackay Bennett*, blessing the bodies wrapped in canvas that had been retrieved from the icy waters at the site of the sinking. Another photo shows my grandmother Frances standing outside their house next to a deckchair salvaged from the stricken ship. I wished the family had held onto it when I read that one was sold at auction in 2015 for £100,000.

***

I had remained single for a while after my passionate affair with Haylie, but an attack by a deer in Bushy Park in the summer of 2011 changed all that. It wasn't the first time that I had experienced aggression from deer in the Royal Parks. Some twenty years or so earlier I was driving my Mazda in Richmond Park. I glanced to my right and saw a herd of wild deer stampeding down a hillside, pursued by a dog. Traffic ahead of me had stopped and when I came to a halt, I left a gap for the deer to pass through. Unfortunately, a section of the herd leapt over my car and in five seconds or less of mayhem they dented the roof, the bonnet, took out a window and one of the headlights. One of the deer only just missed the back of my head with its hoof. I was in a state of shock; there was glass all over the back seat and everything was covered in deer hair.

A truck driver across the road leant out of his cab window and said, 'Cor blimey, mate! I feel really sorry for ya.' After virtually destroying my car the herd, seemingly unhurt and unaffected by the episode, stopped in the grass on the other side of the road and began grazing as if nothing had happened.

I took the car to my local repair centre but I think the Mazda was cursed because the oil seals went soon after that so I got a refund and bought a Renault instead. More than anything else, though, I thanked God I was OK. Despite what you might think from films such as *Bambi*, one whack from a deer's hoof could take out anyone. There have been dogs and even humans killed in the parks by deer and you need to be careful at certain times of year, particularly when the females give birth in the spring and during the rutting season in the autumn.

My second encounter with a deer came as a result of the Bushy Park 5K run on 4 June 2011. On my way to take part, I got chatting to a very attractive lady who was out for a walk – Diana Morley, an actress also known as Diana Marchment – who was with her golden cocker spaniel, Mr Monty. We arranged to meet again after the run. It was hard work! I managed to knock 23 seconds off my best time and at the end I threw up after all the exertion.

Once I had recovered I looked for Diana and was disappointed that she was nowhere to be seen. As I left the park I found her again, this time at the roadside and in a state of shock: she had been attacked by a deer and was suffering from cuts and bruises. I took her for a coffee to console her after showing her my apartment. We talked over the attack and thought maybe the colour of Monty's coat and his size made him look like a young deer. But that wasn't the first problem Diana had encountered with deer in the park and it wouldn't be the last.

Diana and I exchanged numbers and agreed to meet the following week. Together with Mr Monty we drove to an area I call 'Secret

Surrey' for our first date, and after lunch at the Parrot pub we climbed Leith Hill, a beauty spot just over 900 feet above sea level – there were just two other people at the top. We got caught in a downpour and had a kiss and a cuddle under a pine tree. Our next date would be a picnic the following Saturday.

As I write, we've been together now for over four and a half years. We've travelled to Tobago, climbed Mount Snowdon, cheered guitarist Joe Bonamassa at the Apollo in Hammersmith and we share a love of top-quality films. We live just five minutes apart, which has been very convenient.

***

Shortly after I started seeing Diana, I took on a job I'd previously turned down three times: *Celebrity Coach Trip*. My partner for the show was Derek Martin (Charlie Slater in *EastEnders*) and we flew to the Savoia Excelsior hotel in Trieste, Italy. We were confined to our rooms on the first night in July 2011 so that we didn't know who else would be on the programme with us. At 6am we started work, being interviewed on the quayside, and we still had no idea who else would be there. On board the coach we met Brendon, our camp coach coordinator, a great host and guide for the week. The other contestants were former royal footman Paul Burrell, ex-principal of Lucy Clayton School Jean Broke-Smith, former MP Edwina Currie and her husband, John Jones, comedy duo Tommy Cannon and Bobby Ball and Nikki Grahame and Aisleyne Horgan-Wallace from *Big Brother*. Our first destination was Ljubljana in Slovenia and they were paying us so little that I was determined to stay on board for as long as possible.

We stopped off at a different point each day and were given a new challenge to perform, from cooking fish over a campfire to making pasta in Bologna (where we also took a trip through the ancient Roman sewers) and out in the Slovenian countryside we went shooting over a waterfall in a kayak – a hair-raising experience. It was odd to be filmed from breakfast to dinner and at all times when we were on the coach. At one point Derek Martin pretended to be Hitler, amusing several others and me, but he was asked to tone it down by the producers. Good old Derek. Ever the comedian.

We visited many interesting and beautiful locations, including Maribor, Zadar and Rimini (where we took part in a sandcastle-building competition). At the end of the trip, Derek and I were voted the winners by the rest of the participants. I was so pleased, especially for Derek. He's a good, kind man.

The trip wasn't always easy. It was a full-on challenge, all day, every day. Voting people off was hard when you had grown quite fond of them, but that was the game so we had to play it, and I was thrilled to come out on top.

EPILOGUE

**GO CONFIDENTLY IN THE DIRECTION OF YOUR DREAMS.
LIVE THE LIFE YOU'VE IMAGINED.**
HENRY DAVID THOREAU

I'm writing this in May 2016 as I celebrate 40 years in the business. I consider myself very lucky to have survived this long – I know full well how tough it can be. I've had a lot of luck along the way and as you will have gathered from this book, some great adventures too. The whole Nick Cotton saga was a double-edged sword. It closed some doors to me as an actor but also opened many more, such as when I was offered the part of Billy Flynn in *Chicago*. At the age of sixty-four I have no thoughts of retirement – I don't think we do in this business. I will happily continue to work in the worlds of TV, film and theatre until I'm content to just take it easy and lounge in a chair in an English country garden or on a tropical beach.

There is, however, one cause I need to mention that is very close to my heart. Founded on 20 July 1998 by Virginia McKenna, Bill Travers and their eldest son, Will, the Born Free Foundation is a charity that works to save and protect threatened wildlife all over the world. I was very affected by the story of the lion Cecil in Zimbabwe, who was murdered in 2015 – there's no need to kill elephants, or indeed rhinos or any other wildlife for sport. There aren't strong enough words to express the way I feel about the ignorant lowlifes who organise holidays for people to hunt down creatures that could very soon become extinct.

I fell for Virginia on the silver screen when I was a little boy. It has been a joy to get to know her and to work with her and her son, Will, to help raise funds for their truly worthwhile cause.

I also hope that peace will one day come to the Middle East; in Syria, Iraq, Yemen and Afghanistan. Not forgetting Libya, and also the persecution of the Palestinian people.

***

It has been an amazing thing to look back over my life for this book, but it has been a hard experience too. I don't believe anyone is able to look back in detail at the choices they have made or the things they have done and not feel a twinge of regret, or wonder 'what if?' I have also felt quite emotional at times.

EastEnders gave me a great deal and the best thing of all was my daughter. If I hadn't been introduced to Bridget by Nejdet Salih (Ali Osman), then there would have been no marriage and no Rosanna. Despite how toxic the union with Bridget became, my daughter remains the very best thing I ever did and I couldn't be prouder of the woman she has become. She achieved a Classical Literature and Civilisation BA Hons, a Classics MA and a Graduate Diploma of Law. She is now a very successful businesswoman in Luxembourg and a wonderful mother. I am also on very good terms with Bridget and her husband, Paul O'Halloran. Rosanna in turn has given me the ultimate gift – my granddaughter, Lily. These days my happiest times are spent with her and I must admit there have been moments when I have longed to do it all over again, and to have more children myself. I have as an actor experienced a lot more of Rosanna growing up than some other dads out there. My daughter and I are closer than ever now and I feel so happy to be a big part of Lily's life.

***

In 2015 I received the Washington, DC Independent Film Festival Best Actor award for my part as Dr Tom, the psychiatrist in *My Lonely Me* (2015), directed by Joe Scott. I also appeared in Radio 4's production of Ray Bradbury's *The Martian Chronicles*, alongside Derek Jacobi and Hayley Atwell; it was directed by Andrew Sewell, who made a great job of it. The desolation and dryness of Mars was somehow realised through the radio – it was very atmospheric, and won an award in New York for best radio drama.

As for professional dreams, there are still many I have: a movie in Hollywood, a West End show, there is nothing like the buzz of live theatre. I love singing with my favourite band, JOANOvARC, and there's nothing I'd like more than a hit record. Over the years I have quietly devoted myself to my music, my voice and learning my instruments – it's a huge part of my life and something that brings me great joy.

Since giving up the alcohol I have become much more spiritual and in the 12-Step Program you have to nurture a 'Higher Power', something greater than you. Every morning and night I pray and give thanks to God for getting me through another day. I pray for the health and wellbeing of others and meditate to concentrate the mind and keep me steady. I have gathered gems from across a wealth of religions, Christianity (I am a fairly regular churchgoer), Buddhism and Hinduism, etc., rather than being dominated by any one element. I like to think that we carry on after death in a purer and different form; and become part of heaven as God intended. I truly believe that the very essence of us, the spirit that we cannot touch, goes on.

I remember spending my youth smoking dope and lying back

under the stars and thinking: 'What's at the end of the universe?' No one can answer that question, be he a scientist or a spiritual leader. I've come to the conclusion that's just something our minds cannot conceive. My final thoughts are that we should love and care for one another and enjoy each day we have as a gift. Every day I remain grateful that I have spent my life doing a job I always wanted to do and I have met and learned a great deal from great actors and actresses along the way.

But mostly, I am grateful that I wake up each day sober, healthy and eager to embrace whatever is around the next corner. To quote 'Desiderata' once again: 'It is still a beautiful world. Be cheerful. Strive to be happy.'